DISRUPTION
REVOLUTION

Also by David Passiak

Red Bull to Buddha:
Innovation and the Search for Wisdom

DISRUPTION
REVOLUTION

INNOVATION, ENTREPRENEURSHIP, AND
THE NEW RULES OF LEADERSHIP

DAVID PASSIAK

Social Meditate Press
Brooklyn, NY

Logo design: David Mindel
Cover Layout: Miko Graphics

Printed in the United States of America

First Printing, 2013

ISBN 978-0-9898233-1-9

Social Meditate Press
197 Nassau Ave 3R
Brooklyn, NY 11222
www.SocialMeditate.com

This book is dedicated to anyone with the courage to fail, the audacity to question what is possible, and the perseverance to push through and do the work

Contents

Preface

This is the most comprehensive and in-depth collection of perspectives on disruptive innovation compiled into one volume. Most of the 20+ contributors are household names in their fields. Each interview is intended to represent a particular perspective on innovation. There are no duplicate questions either. My goal is for the book to read like an evolving conversation.

As a former academic, I approached the book as if I were interviewing people in front of a class. What do my students need to know? What is the heart and soul of innovation? What trends will define the next 5-10+ years of everything we do?

I self-published because once the book was finished a traditional publisher could take an additional 12-18 months bringing it to market—that is a lifetime in the scope of innovation. From start to finish—first interview to publishing—took just five months. A book on innovation also deserves to be published in an innovative way.

This is the kind of book to underline, mark-up, write in the margins, and engage deeply. It's also the kind of book to read between meetings or on the train on your Kindle or iPad. I believe that if you buy a book, then you should not pay full price for a digital copy. That is why the eBook is offered as pay-what-you-want at DisruptRev.com or SocialMeditate.com

Innovation is about discovering new connections and solving new problems. By placing the most innovative people in the world in conversation, lightbulbs start to go off and new ideas form for readers. I hope this is a catalyst for lots of "a-ha" moments and that you will have the courage to follow through and share them with the world.

Welcome to the Disruption Revolution!

Acknowledgments

Normally this would be the place to provide an extensive list of people, but that would be redundant—I am most thankful for all of the 20+ contributors that were gracious enough to offer their time.

Everyone seems to ask me, "How did you get all of those incredible people to do an interview?" The truth is, I simply asked them. I had about a 90% response rate for interview requests. I picked people whose success is really a byproduct of being incredibly excited about how innovation can change the world. They did the interviews because they believed in the project. Thanks again, I'm deeply honored.

Thanks also to David Mindel for the wonderful logo design, my literary agent and good friend Matthew Guma for encouraging me to embark on this incredible project, and my writing partner and editor Theo Horesh, who is doing a similar project on climate change. And last, thanks to my parents for encouraging me to follow my dreams.

WHAT IS THE DISRUPTION REVOLUTION?

Introduction by David Passiak

The rapid pace of innovation can feel overwhelming and incomprehensible at times: a never-ending stream of links, trends, and buzzwords; new technologies, platforms, and companies; like this, share that, follow me, etc. Our society and culture is based on linear thinking, and so our natural inclination is to brace ourselves and wait for things to settle down. But that won't happen. The rate of change will only continue to increase exponentially faster. And social media was just the beginning...the real revolution will occur when the social sharing ecosystem evolves and disrupts how we buy, sell, deliver, share, give, and access products and services. Everything is changing.

We are at the beginning of a fundamental, irreversible shift in human history. As Seth Godin says, there is no going back to normal. This is the "new normal." The days of making a good living being told what to do are over. Jobs are not coming back. In fact, drones, robots, 3D printing, and software automation solutions will only make it more cost-effective to replace workers with machines than outsourcing to China or India. The rules of leadership have also changed. Nobody is unaffected. The good news is that in an era of lowest common denominators—cheap labor, cheap products, and cheap access—there are extraordinary opportunities for people with the courage to be remarkable.

Disruption Revolution refers to how innovators, entrepreneurs, and investors all rallied around the term *disruption*, creating a revolution of innovation that was accelerated by the economic crash of 2008-9 because constraint in resources drives innovation. As companies were forced to cut costs and find new ways of generating revenue, CEOs and pragmatic business leaders invested in innovations that previously might have been considered too "experimental" or disruptive to their core business. Meanwhile, public trust in companies fell dramatically, which reinforced the need to adopt social media platforms like Facebook, Twitter, and YouTube. Innovations such as cloud computing made it easy for anyone with a laptop and a credit card to found a company, while the loss of employment and limited job prospects forced everyone to think like entrepreneurs—renting spare rooms on AirBnB, selling goods in marketplaces like eBay or Etsy, crowd-funding projects on Kickstarter or IndieGoGo, etc.

Disruption has now become a type of aspiration and rallying call—we're disrupting that market!—for startups that might not even have customers or users. Strictly speaking, many self-proclaimed disruptors aren't disrupting anything yet. But in embracing the term as a mantra of their core identity, they reinforce that (1) there is a "new normal" way of doing things now and (2) being "disruptive" is somehow better. This also drives the creation of revolutionary new business models around sharing and collaboration that arguably will redefine capitalism in contrast to the unsustainable "borrow and spend" practices that caused the recent economic crash. The desire for change is moving from early adopters into the mainstream—what in innovation terms is called "crossing the chasm"—setting in motion irreversible shifts in society and culture that coincide with a billion people on Facebook, millions of smartphones and tablets, and ubiquitous access to the Internet.

There is a tendency among leadership within larger companies to try and force innovations into conventional patterns of operating—for example, to transform social media into a marketing and communications channel, or to segment innovation into a silo-like product development. These approaches fail to comprehend that the ground is moving. Innovation is not simply a matter of adapting to market forces, or integrating a hodgepodge of tools into your workflow. It requires revolutionary approaches to how an organization operates and runs that must be systematically implemented from the top down, with full C-level executive support and a clear vision.

Technology becomes the most powerful when we cease to view it as "technology" and it just becomes part of our daily life. For example, if I use the Xbox, laptop, mobile phone, tablet and Google Glass to access my favorite websites, Twitter, Facebook, Instagram, YouTube, Pinterest etc., then I expect a consistent brand identity, messaging and user experience on all devices and platforms. It's all just "stuff I do" as a normal part of my day.

Companies think of this in terms of "communications across multiple channels" with different resources allocated for various departments (customer service, marketing, public relations, sales, etc.). This is really hard to manage internally at a larger organization where messaging and brand identity are carefully controlled. However, consumer expectations have changed, and their loyalty (and dollars) will go to companies that engage them at the right time, right place, and with the right personalized message.

Lifestyle now matters more than conventional demographics, as online communities form around likeminded interests that transcend age, race, ethnicity, gender, and national geographic boundaries. Delivering shared experiences across devices and platforms, with real-world touch points, becomes the future of marketing. One area of lifestyle marketing that I expect to grow dramatically is electronic dance music or EDM: futuristic music made on innovative digital instruments, uniting people at festivals or via headphones with beats instead of lyrics, sprawling across social platforms and all Internet-connected devices, tapping into what Brian Solis refers to as true digital convergence.

The Disruption Revolution is also creating a new type of hero and shaping the aspirations of an entire generation, perhaps best exemplified by Facebook's Mark Zuckerberg and the movie that mythologized him, *The Social Network*. The master narrative of college-to-career is being replaced by the story of gigs and temporary jobs, buried in student loan debt living at home, forced to forge a different path defined on your own terms: becoming an entrepreneur. This generation exhibits shifts in behavior characterized by collaboration and sharing, preferring access to goods and experiences instead of ownership, sustainability instead of consumption less is more. It is as if the collaborative sharing tools of social media and mobile/tablet devices act like training wheels to reorganize society in a way that is more democratic, egalitarian, and meritocratic.

Yet disruptive innovations are, by definition, disruptive to our preconceived notions of how the world could or should be. As Henry Ford once said, "If I had asked people what they wanted, they would have said a faster horse." Today's science fiction will become tomorrow's mass market consumer products, as technology gets exponentially cheaper, faster, better and smaller year over year. This book is designed to prepare you for the challenges and opportunities that lie ahead. Welcome to the Disruption Revolution.

HOW DISRUPTIVE INNOVATION REVOLUTIONIZES SOCIETY AND CULTURE

I have worked in social media and tech startups since 2004, and previously studied how trends in disruptive innovation throughout history tend to coincide with fundamental shifts in religion, culture, and worldviews, or what are more popularly referred to as "Great Awakenings." My Ph.D. research at Princeton focused primarily on the Civil Rights and Sixties counterculture movements, looking at how innovations like radio, television, movies, music, and underground magazines empowered new ways to communicate perspectives on race, ethnicity, gender, and equal rights. My M.A. thesis at Arizona State University was on the revivalist movements known as the Great Awakenings in the 1700s and 1800s. These were accelerated by innovations in printing pamphlets, signs, and grassroots organization, and helped establish an ethos of individualism that would inspire the Revolutionary War and the abolition of slavery.

Nearly twenty years of professional and research experience informs what I consider a general theory of how disruptive innovation revolutionizes society and culture. We like to think that ideas change the world, but in many ways innovation is the underlying mechanism of human history. Innovations systematize and shape expectations for what we can and cannot do in our daily lives, creating new ways of being in the world that empower people to re-imagine what life could or should be like. The newfound sense of freedom and openness made possible by the adoption of innovations combines with the excitement and enthusiasm of using tools to form new communities of likeminded individuals. This provides the ideal precondition for revolutionary new ideas to spread by word-of-mouth that can culminate in religious, political, and cultural awakenings.

Simply put, early adopters of ideas tend to be early adopters of innovation, and vice versa. They are often motivated by making the world better and are less concerned with money or power. As innovations and ideas begin to gain traction, more pragmatic leaders recognize the economic and/or political benefits of scaling them to challenge incumbent industries and reigning institutions. This often leads to financing investments in infrastructure and promotions, which in turn allows innovations to "cross the chasm" into mass adoption and disrupt preexisting ways of doing things. As innovations scale towards mass adoption and ideas spread by word-of-mouth, benefits outweigh the risks to shift behavior. Friends tell their friends, then they tell their friends, and so on, until a tipping point occurs when people demand change from incumbents or replace them entirely.

It is this combination of new ideas and shared expectations of a better way of life made possible by innovation that leads to revolutionary changes in society. For example, if I can write and express my thoughts freely, then I expect a church or government to acknowledge my individual freedoms and represent my interests. If I can go online and voice my opinion, then I expect my favorite brands and leaders to listen and engage in a public dialogue with me. If I can form communities based around interests with people anywhere in the world, then categories of race, religion, ethnicity, gender, and nationality become less important. If I can use a 3D printer or buy things directly from the crowd, then I don't really need companies or retailers. If I can start my own company with just a credit card and a laptop, or learn any skill for free on the Internet, then I expect to forever be in control of my own destiny.

In other words, the "a-ha" moments of awakening do not occur in a vacuum—innovation gives ideas context and provides a vehicle to scale, evolve, and disrupt. Transitions are messy and hard. In general, the larger the size of the incumbent, the more difficult it is to adapt. Those who have the most to lose and are the most risk averse also are often people who least understand innovation. Because of the high rate of failure involved in testing breakthrough innovations, most management in larger organizations have incentives NOT to innovate in order to protect their jobs. Their inclination is to work harder at what they are already doing, rather than learn the necessary skills and strategies to innovate and adapt to new market forces.

THE DISRUPTION REVOLUTION – FROM ECONOMIC CRASH TO ENTREPRENEURIAL OPPORTUNITY

I began to notice a trend around the term disruption in the wake of the economic crash of 2008-9. At the time I was working as a Senior Director at M80, a WPP agency where I oversaw social media for Volkswagen, including launch of their Facebook, YouTube, Twitter and first company blog. First we braced ourselves for cutbacks as companies slashed budgets and jobs, but soon we found ourselves invited to the table for discussions about strategy by CEOs and heads of larger agencies. Spending hundreds of millions of dollars on TV, print, radio, banner and display ads didn't seem like such a good idea anymore. Suddenly, they needed to be accountable for better Return on Investment (ROI), budgets were being carefully scrutinized, and all attention shifted towards the misfits and outcasts of the social media world. Before we were fighting for scraps of discretionary marketing budgets, and now we had keys to the kingdom. The rules of the game had changed.

Drawing upon a decade of research on how revolutions of disruptive innovation grow and evolve over time, I became convinced that what was now being called "social media" would catalyze one of the most abrupt, fundamental shifts in human history. The term *social media* grouped together all forms of two-way communications and essentially validated the basic idea that the voice and opinion of the customer was important. There soon became "social media" everything—platforms, experts, organizations, conferences—though the shift wasn't so much media becoming "social" as it was a democratization of broadcasting by giving everyone a voice.

Standardizing a common language or vocabulary is a critical milestone in "crossing the chasm" because it unifies a hodgepodge of ideas and innovations into one cohesive movement with a shared sense of purpose. I knew from my studies that real changes tend to happen after new ways of communicating and sharing ideas reach mass adoption, shaping expectations for larger institutional changes (economic, political, cultural, religious, etc.).

Social media provided pragmatic leaders with solutions in the context of the economic crash, but it also opened up Pandora's Box in terms of accelerating the adoption of innovations that would ultimately disrupt and revolutionize everything—what Jeremiah Owyang refers to as the democratization of business in his new model of the Collaborative Economy. Social media was much more than just "social" or "media." In fact, it was driving an entirely new ecosystem and laying the foundation for what in Thomas Kuhn's language would be a "paradigm shift" i.e. the Disruption Revolution.

I perceived two different narratives around the economy: (1) the story about how Wall Street greed combined with excessive consumer spending and bad debt created an unsustainable and broken system that collapsed on itself; and (2) the Disruption Revolution of really smart engineers, technologists, and strategists backed by Silicon Valley investors capitalizing on opportunities to plug holes, fill vacuums, and further disrupt business as usual by leveraging the social sharing ecosystem to change the way that we buy, sell, deliver, share, give, and access products and services. Eventually, I decided to write books on each narrative, which tell a kind of before-and-after story about why the economy crashed, and how to innovate our way to a better future.

In my first book, *Red Bull to Buddha: Innovation and the Search for Wisdom,* I opened with the basic observation that you can't sustain a national economy on credit, bad debt, and over-spending. The deeper lesson from the economic crash was that the desire to live beyond our means caused our own suffering. This is essentially the essence of Buddhism, which I have practiced for almost 20 years, and a core teaching at the heart of the world's religious traditions. From my perspective, the starting point was a conversation about values.

The rise of modern media and advertising turned wants into perceived needs—*I need more cars, clothes, homes, to be "normal"*—and created a culture of instant gratification that led us to act against our own best interests. Traditions that historically embodied the accumulated wisdom of our ancestors had failed because our leaders no longer engaged in public dialogue or served as role models that inspired us to greatness. Part of the challenge was to find balance between disruptive innovation and traditional conceptions of wisdom and community, starting a deeper process of recovery that would allow society to collaborate and move forward.

In *Disruption Revolution,* I started with the basic assumption that the best way to approach innovation was to focus on specific use cases in roles, responsibilities, and industries. There was not just one story of the Disruption Revolution, but instead a plurality of overlapping and interrelated stories to tell.

The same way that a marketer or product strategist identifies persona types and does customer development, I interviewed experts that represented particular perspectives on innovation. I became like a cultural anthropologist, allowing the real revolutionaries to tell their own stories. As such, this book reads more like an evolving narrative than a compilation of interviews.

ORGANIZATION AND APPROACH

Disruption Revolution is a book by and for innovators and early adopters. It consists of five thematic sections of 20+ interviews intended to provide the most comprehensive collection of perspectives on innovation compiled into one volume. The key to success in this new era of exponential change is to facilitate connections and create solutions that transcend traditional operational roles and industry boundaries. Our goal is to empower you to see the forest through the trees, and how the trees are part of a larger ecosystem:

First, you need to understand the big picture trends in innovation. We open by covering Experience Design and the next evolution of social business with Brian Solis; 3D printing and innovations in manufacturing with Chris Anderson; entrepreneurship around the world and the uniqueness of Silicon Valley with Sarah Lacy; how Google Glass, sensors, wearable technology, cloud computing and mobile/tablets are converging in an Age of Context with Robert Scoble; and finally how companies, startups, and everyone else are working together to create a Collaborative Economy with Jeremiah Owyang.

Second, we go deep into the heart of entrepreneurship and leadership. Seth Godin tells us why we all need to be remarkable and do more than just try to survive; Erik Qualman teaches us the new rules of digital leadership like how to fail forward, fail fast, and fail better; Harvard Business School professor Noam Wasserman walks us through the difficult dilemmas faced in founding a company; James Altucher shows how a healthy mind, emotions, body, and spirit is the foundation for success in a world turned upside down; and Jerry Colonna walks us through some of the deeper psychological challenges of persevering on the journey of entrepreneurship.

Third, innovations need to scale in order to have a big impact. Shail Khiyara of Spigit illustrates how collaborative tools and software can help engage employees and customers to contribute ideas; Innosight's Scott Anthony tells us about how innovation can be systematized to create what he refers to as a growth factory; Alex Osterwalder teaches us the importance of business model innovation in an era when we compete in arenas, not industries; Paul Wittenberg explains how to take a customer-centric approach to increase deal flow and sell innovation; and Dr. Natalie Petouhoff demonstrates how to create ROI models around qualitative subjects like engagement, customer experience, and acknowledgment.

Fourth, we all need to communicate and engage our audiences. Steve Rubel opens the section by explaining the imperative for all companies to create quality content; Faris Yakob shows us what innovation within a larger agency is like and describes the future of advertising; Terry Young gives us a tour of his newsroom-style agency sparks & honey and their pioneering approach of wave branding; Mark Hughes of C3 Metrics tells us the magic of buzzmarketing and the value of attribution in media buying; and SocialFlow's Frank Speiser explains how big data can actually help brands to sound more human on platforms like Facebook and Twitter.

Finally, whether you are a CEO or looking for your first job, there are basic strategies and best practices that we can all apply to our daily lives. Leading career consultant Joshua Waldman shows us how social media has changed the way we network and find jobs; corporate misfit and host of Blogcast-FM Srinivas Rao explains how to build and maintain a personal brand; and Vincent Horn of Buddhist Geeks elaborates on the benefits of mindful approaches to technology.

Each interview adds an incremental layer of detail to the story of the Disruption Revolution. Innovation requires a new way of being in the world. It cannot be compartmentalized into a few things that companies do, or be just one isolated part of your current job. The fundamental assumptions about everything you do are being disrupted by innovations that could make your current role or company obsolete. This book is designed to help you anticipate the unknown, take advantage of opportunities, and forge your own path.

Embrace change. Be courageous and brave. And remember, we are all in this together!

PART I

WHY DISRUPTION IS THE NEW NORM

THE FUTURE OF BUSINESS

Brian Solis

Brian Solis is the closest thing that the social media and technology startup industry has to a rock star—relentlessly speaking, author of several bestselling books, founder of Pivot, one of the industry's most innovative conferences, advisor to hundreds of companies and global brands, and partner at Altimeter Group, a leading firm focused on disruptive innovation. Highlights include:

- Why Experience Design is the next evolution of social
- The connected consumer and true digital convergence
- Why branding is more important now than ever
- How constraint drives innovation, and why we should always be in perpetual startup mode

This entire interview focuses on the big picture. It starts with how social media disrupted business, and then moves to the next iteration of the social web that Brian refers to as true digital convergence. Brian reminds us that there are always constraints on resources. True innovation requires creativity and is a way of life.

DP: I remember meeting you with a group of bloggers back in 2006 before social media was considered a formative field. You were one of the first people that I thought really "got it" in terms of understanding the revolutionary potential of these emerging communications platforms to change everything.

Was there an "a-ha" moment when you realized social media was going to be so big?

BS: I've been working on this officially since 1997, when I created a new department within the marketing organization aimed at message boards, communities, and influencers. They were essentially the precedent of bloggers writing about trends, but using websites to create online magazines. I believed that this was the future of engagement, marketing, and services, and so I started a company in 1999 called FutureWorks dedicated to that practice i.e. the works of the future, sort of a lab but also an agency. I ran that company until 2011.

In those iterations, there were web 1.0, web 2.0 social media, etc. I always believed that the next thing was on the horizon, so I constantly reaffirmed my belief that it was OK to be in this perpetual startup mode. I always called that company a startup—whatever year we were in, it was a 7-year-old startup, a 10-year-old startup—because we were constantly experimenting and practicing new philosophies.

Even today, I still wouldn't necessarily say that we are at that next big thing. Social media was one of those specs, those iterations—albeit, one of the bigger ones—but the next thing on the horizon is true digital convergence. That is what I've been focusing on with my last two books and my latest work with Altimeter Group.

DP: Do you think we'll still use the term social media in 5 or 10 years or is it the new norm now that we are moving to this era of digital convergence that you are talking about in your past two books?

BS: That's a really good question. I used to be a staunch defender of the term because it was much more than a classification. To me it was a representation of a shift in philosophy. Meaning that you're not just creating, pushing and distributing media; you are sort of facilitating and democratizing it. That comes with a tremendous shift in the culture.

Five years from now, I could see us still using the term social media, though not as a classification but as a movement. For example, social media is sort of delivering this undercover boss movement to a lot of organizations, if you will, by allowing people to better see and reflect on the activities that are taking place outside the C-suite. It also humanizes the organization from the inside out so that it forces people to have conversations that they might not have otherwise had. That would be the context in which I see it being used.

But from a technology standpoint we would have been deeply ingrained in this shift from social to digital convergence.

DP: I know in recent years there's been a lot of focus on disruption, particularly among entrepreneurs and investors. Do you think this has changed the way people approach creating startups? For example, is there more emphasis on a quick exit and repeatable patters vs. trying to think really big and build the next Google?

BS: Well, it's almost a trick question. Disruptive technology and disruption is an effect. It means that it is already disrupting something. Entrepreneurs say that they are disrupting something as a form of aspiration, which is to some extent desensitizing or diluting the term and its importance. There are people who are becoming the next AirBnB for dog kennels. And then there are people focusing on true innovation. We see this in some of the most traditional industries going into biotech and green. If you look at Elon Musk, he disrupts anything that he touches. So I think it's also a matter of your vision of creativity.

The word means innovation and that's the word I think we need to consider more than disruption. At some point innovation could shift into disruption, but with disruption—this goes back to early economic theory, for example, creative destruction—something comes along and completely upsets the business model that exists only to be disrupted again with the next innovation. So it is a matter of focus, it's a matter of state of mind. If you set out to disrupt something then you better disrupt it, but if you are saying you are going to disrupt it or that you are working on a disruptive technology, then you are fooling yourself and the people that are investing or trusting in you.

DP: That makes a lot of sense. I know that you work with a lot of advertisers and global brands. With social media, consumers are essentially involved in co-creating brands. What is the value of a brand and how do you help to define it if you have limited control over its creation?

BS: I don't believe you have limited control. I believe you have more control than you ever had before. I just think it is a matter of understanding what the word control means in this situation. Before, commanding control was "I speak, you listen" but the joke I used to tell everybody was that social media didn't invent conversations or opinions. They have always been around. It's just that now they are concentrated, searchable and indexable.

This becomes the future of branding in the sense that it is not just that they are co-created, but that they are concerted into a searchable collective. What I mean by that is if I go to Google and punch in key words, then you can't control that moment of truth of what comes back. So what happens in a world where I ask somebody their thoughts, whether it is in a network or an app or I just review community exchanges? That's a world that has completely been ignored up until now, and it is a world that's been here since the Internet began, going back to the bulletin board system.

My point is that positive conditioning reinforces the types of conversations and exchanges that you want to have. Otherwise, you are just reacting to technology and you are reacting to impressions and experiences. The future of co-creation starts with the owner of the brand, meaning that I am defining what this brand means in today's economy and what it means for you tomorrow from an aspirational standpoint.

It means that I have to put in a concentrated effort to define what it could be not just from an image standpoint, but from an emotional standpoint— what are you going to feel and what are you going to share?—because the future of co-creation has to do with shared experiences, not your ability to publish a thought but the experience that you have and share. Technology becomes an enabler to facilitate the positive conditioning of the experience you want people to have. That is why I talk about the future of branding as experience architecture. You define and strengthen it in every way and in every place possible.

DP: In your latest book, you are championing a new movement that aligns user experience with innovation and leadership. How does providing experiences create real business value?

BS: If you ask Apple what business they are in, they will tell you they are in the experience business. If you ask Colgate what business they are in they will tell you they are in the confidence business. If you ask Virgin what business they are in, they will tell you they are in the high roller jet set business.

It's a matter of giving your customer something to align with, not something to transact with. You look at one of the brilliant aspects of the Apple Store and now the Tesla Store, it is not about products, right? It is about experience. The experience is sort of embodied in the product, but it is also embodied in interactions with the company. It's a holistic thing. That is the value of experience.

You will pay a premium for an experience. Some studies show as high as 15% more for a similar product if you believe you are going to get a better experience with it. So the value becomes something bigger than just the widget. That changes the entire model for business—how you support and interact with customers, how you attract and keep them. And that to me is something a little bit more substantive, meaningful over time.

Think about the future of brands as a collective of shared experiences—there is this disconnect between what you think your brand is and the experience of your brand that people are sharing with one another. So your first step is to figure out how do you close that gap. Second is how do you meet it so you're not reacting to it—essentially creating value through experience where UX [user-experience] almost becomes like a philosophy or a way of life, a way of business, not just a series of designs for products or screens.

DP: So experiences are essentially qualitative and yet without analysis there can't be any really relevant insights. How do you use technology and data to optimize experiences and create feedback loops, and where does the human interaction element fit into that?

BS: That's what I talk about in terms of the human algorithm: it's that intersection of data science and social science. I think one of the biggest ways to solve this is the balance of quant and qual, where you take the idea of a focus group—intentions, aspirations, etc.— and you solve them with data and a/b testing. The research starts with a hypothesis and then ends with a series of educated questions.

Even outside of this promise of what is possible, you don't know what you don't know and you don't research what you can't envision. This is why I think the future really comes down to digital anthropology. It's just better understanding of behavior so that you can meet the needs and expectations of your target audiences before they actually show up as a data point, if that makes sense. That is where the human interaction element fits in, because otherwise you are trying to force people into a box.

DP: I really like this especially—I was a former scholar of religion and culture before I got into social media.

BS: Wow!

DP: I used to study the disruptive impact of the 60s impact and civil rights movements, so I looked a lot at grassroots protest and their use of new and emerging media—things like pamphlets and magazines and how they tried to culture jam and get pictures syndicated throughout the world to facilitate real meaningful changes.

I'm curious, in your latest book you referenced Joseph Campbell's concept of the hero's journey. What does it mean to go on a journey together with your consumers and basically evolve as a company focused on great customer experiences?

BS: That's a great question. Being a scholar and having studied religion and culture, you and I both know that the hero's journey has deep roots in alternative religious aspects. I didn't want to tackle that in the book (laughter). Most people actually believe—and I found this fascinating—that the hero's journey aligns with popular culture (Star Wars and The Matrix) more than with actual religion. Academia really understands its true roots and I thought I would take a gamble to see if I could introduce it in a way that leaders could take at face value rather than try to unravel it.

In that regard, there are two journeys in the book. The first is this idea of digital ethnography and in all fairness you can't unravel this. The hero's journey shows you that someone really smart aligned mythology in religion to these certain paths that these characters seem to follow. The point was that it took research and it took someone really smart to draw the lines and draw a map. And you can do the same thing for your customer journey today. You can understand where they're going, what is the context of what they're trying to do, and what happens in each one of those stages.

The idea was just to align the digital ethnography to paint your own hero's journey for your customer. Then, I wanted to inspire you to go along the journey with him or her to reduce the friction and create an ecosystem that was really special to be around before, during and after the transaction.

The second reference is the idea that it is not just about the customer and the journey you need to help and transform. It is also this idea the person within the organization who has to really think about its promise and opportunity is going to meet his or her own path of resistance. You too are going to have to be your own hero in the hero's journey and that's why I talk about the psychology of change at the end of the book. In sales, they sometimes refer to this type of person as an internal champion for the customer—the person that becomes the customer advocate within an organization.

You are going on this journey together—you and the customer—each with your own areas of resistance, so you need to know what you should expect to encounter so you can be empowered instead of delusional. You're going to tackle something that is challenging but is also great, and what you're about to take on is truly a hero's journey: something that is bigger than you, something that's bigger than the customer, because it is co-created. This is at the true heart of relationships and engagement, so you're essentially chang-ing business, the philosophy of business, in the process.

DP: We've heard the term Gen X and Gen Y. In your new book you give us the term Gen C or the connected consumer. So what is the connected con-sumer and how are they different from traditional consumers?

BS: This is a big, big conversation. The easy answer is this—when we talk about Gen Y, Gen X and Gen Z, or Boomers and Millennials, we really tend to go down the demographic spiral. That limits our view of what is possible.

For example, you and I are both analog. We had to learn how to use digital in every iteration that has been thrown at us and they had to learn analog, which is crazy. And when you start to study behavior, you start to realize that older demographics, once they start using an iPad, a smartphone, or if they start getting a Facebook or Pinterest account, actually start to exhibit a lot of similar behaviors to Millennials. It's fascinating. While it is not as extreme, there are similarities. This really introduces psychographics.

Talking about Gen C was my way of saying, "Stop looking at demographics and look at behavior. Generation C is a collective of connected consumerism that just acts, thinks and influences differently than our traditional customer. It is a way to get people to see things differently, not by age but by their behavior.

DP: Without awareness there can be no consideration. How does advertising factor into the whole equation and how do you think advertising has evolved since everything has become so social?

BS: Traditional advertising still works. Don't get me wrong. There's a reason why the Super Bowl is amazing in terms of what a good creative spot will actually do. The way I look at the difference between the Super Bowl and everyday advertising is that they're actually trying to make it a shared experience. They want you to feel it; they want you to talk about it. That to me is the premise of how advertising can be more meaningful. It is not just a creative idea: it comes back to good old-fashioned storytelling, if you will.

The evolution of advertising takes the storytelling format and gets it into the stream in a way that's much more meaningful. This is why you see native advertising starting to take off, things like social networks, and different blogs starting to plug in in-stream advertising in the form of posts or sponsored posts. But they are all rooted in this idea of a journey. So it's a story, a clickable journey that makes it a little bit more meaningful. I can't just send you to a website because that will ruin the opportunity to capitalize on curiosity or an emotional connection we might have. I think awareness is a big deal but it's just different. It's much more thoughtful. We are already starting to see this happen today.

DP: Is what we're saying here related to how the importance of the brand is really, really critical right now?

BS: Yes, it's more important than ever before. For example, I have a relationship with MTV. You and I probably used to watch music videos and that was what MTV meant to us. And then somewhere in our young adult life, it started to become a TV channel—things like *The Real World*. It would be videos and then programming, but today MTV is something completely different to the Millennial and to Gen C.

If you look at the relationship they have with MTV and even the relationships they have with artists, it's no longer the idea of an artist taking on a meaning where I'm going to put posters on my wall because that artist sig-nifies who I am and the artist becomes the avatar for that person. Instead, it's this notion that the artist becomes part of who you are. You have a di-rect connection and can have meaningful exchanges across social platforms, which are integrated into your own network of relationships. It's almost like a piece of your DNA, not your total DNA.

So the idea of a brand has to have an emotional connection that people will feel like you are part of them. This is why customer studies show that things like values, vision, and human empathy are becoming much more important triggers in terms of a brand relationship rather than sexiness or typical paid endorsements, and this is why—going back to your original question about social media—I believe that social media is going to have the true impact because the idea of becoming social means that you are by default becoming human.

The brand is more important than ever before because it's going to make you re-think what you vision is, what your mission statement is, what your promise is. And then how do you bring that to life in everything you do in-side and outside the company.

DP: You've advised over a thousand startups. As we were talking before you have essentially treated your own work as an evolving ongoing start-up looking at the next big thing. How do you think startup culture has changed? How do you implement essentially a startup culture within an organization?

BS: Startups back in Web 1.0 were really different. Technology was really new, it was really trying to find an early sense of mass appeal and just even the idea of a technology startup would get a lot of really creative funding. You really didn't have to do much to get the attention of the world. In fact, you didn't even have to do much to monetize.

Today, there's still a sense of that legacy where your idea is great because it is your idea but I think the best businesses, the best startups, the best entre-preneurs are realizing that there is a mission to what they are trying to do and trying to solve for. There is a sense of purpose behind the startup and this constant growth hacking. Trying to solve for a problem using traditional means to do so only means that you have traditional outcomes.

So what if you had to solve for something in a new way? I think the reality would be that you would find a new way. That to me is the source of the most successful startups and the most successful entrepreneurs. They are not satisfied because they are trying to disrupt something. They are not satisfied because they have series A or B funding and a valuation of a billion dollars. They are relentless in their pursuit of actually having an impact and measuring its impact in terms of permeation into a market.

That, to me is the true meaning of startup entrepreneurialism and growth hacking—the relationship between cause and effect and that—believe it or not—even as hot as startup technology is and startups in general are, and how important entrepreneurialism is to the American economy or even just the economy in general, it is still a rare trait amongst entrepreneurs: that true desire and passion to build something so meaningful that you never lose that core fire in everything that you're trying to do because it becomes the impetus for how you make decisions moving forward.

Hopefully that made sense, because that for me is the spirit of entrepreneurialism in startups that gets missed out on in the allure of money, the lifestyle and publicity.

DP: Related to this idea of constraint, how does constraint relate to innovation?

BS: There are so many catalysts for innovation, but I believe that constraint is the greatest. It's also the one I mostly align with. I have never had resources. Even today, I don't have the richest resources that allow me to do all the things that I have to do. Even with my latest book and all that I'm trying to do in my professional and personal life, I still have to find creative solutions to do it.

I'm constantly innovating. Innovation, to me, is a way of life and it is not something that I see in a lot of entrepreneurs that I talk to. They are trying to build all-star advisory boards, trying to get celebrities to invest so they can align with names. They are trying to really hustle but I don't know that they're trying to innovate as much as they are trying to push. Swimming upstream isn't the same thing as innovating.

Brian Solis *is principal at Altimeter Group, a research firm focused on disruptive technology. A digital analyst, sociologist, and futurist, Solis has studied and influenced the effects of emerging technology on business, marketing, and culture. Solis is also globally recognized as one of the most prominent thought leaders and published authors in new media.*

His latest book, What's the Future of Business (WTF), *explores the landscape of connected consumerism and how business and customer relationships unfold and flourish in four distinct moments of truth. His previous book,* The End of Business as Usual, *explores the emergence of Generation-C, a new generation of customers and employees and how businesses must adapt to reach them. Prior to* End of Business, *Solis released* Engage, *which is regarded as the industry reference guide for businesses to market, sell and service in the social web.*

THE NEXT INDUSTRIAL REVOLUTION

Chris Anderson

Chris Anderson's editorial vision at *Wired Magazine* and his first book *The Long Tail* had a formative impact on how I view the world. As a Ph.D. in physics, bestselling author, award-winning editor, and now CEO and co-founder of 3D Robotics, his eclectic and diverse background has also been a huge inspiration. Highlights of the interview include:

- The next industrial revolution and the Maker Movement
- How 3D printing is like the new personal computer
- Why he picked a 21-year-old from Tijuana as a co-founder
- The implications of open innovation to the future of business

We initially scheduled the interview to talk about the Maker Movement, but the conversation quickly gets super geeky and interesting as we speculate about the implications of emerging trends in innovation to the future of business. This is such an enjoyable and engaging read—you just wish it never ends.

---

*DP: When I look at your three books—*The Long Tail, Free, *and* Makers*—there appears to be a natural progression, as if each lays the foundation for the next.*

First, there is this flattening of the world and creation of these little niche markets for everything in the Long Tail. Next, there is this incredible amount of innovation on the Web, which leads to an explosion of tools and apps that are free for distribution, marketing, sales, and so on. Finally, all of this innovation in software is now being applied to how we make goods, driving an industrial revolution that in many ways better serves the niche markets of the Long Tail, bringing everything full circle.

Can you tell us a little bit about your three books in a larger context?

CA: The first book, *The Long Tail*, was recognizing what abundance would do to choice. Abundance is the one thing digital does. By the way, there's nothing in my books that wasn't anticipated by Nicolas Fontaine and others. It's all kind of obvious. It's creation. He had to work through all the implications but didn't have these examples. One transformative thing about digital is the ability to make copies at no cost. It's the zero-zero marginal cost of reproduction that changes everything.

We call that abundance. Let's just say that the transformative aspect of digital is that it is driven by intentionally replicating abundance. The first book, *The Long Tail*, is about the effect of abundance on choice. The second book is about the effect of abundance on price. The third is the evolution or projection of digital onto the real world, which is effective. And that's it. I can't say that I neatly fashioned it like this in 2004. But in retrospect, that's the way it looks.

DP: I heard you describe the Maker Revolution as a combination of the Industrial Revolution plus the Digital Revolution. Can you tell us a little bit about what that means? Could you walk us through the giant steps of these different revolutions as you see them occurring?

CA: At risk of gross reductionism, if you'll forgive me, the Industrial Revolution replaced muscle power with machine power. The Information Revolution replaced brainpower with computing power. This new industrial revolution, the third one, just combines the two.

DP: Let's go through the three revolutions. Most Americans associate 1776 with the American Revolution, but the Industrial Revolution really started at the same time. We tend to think of the Industrial Revolution primarily in terms of manufacturing, but it really had a larger impact on the entire growth of civilization, which you have done a great job of elucidating. Can you tell us a little bit about how that impacted the way we systematize everything?

CA: The Industrial Revolution, like any true revolution, takes centuries to really play out. You could argue we are still in it right now. So picking any start date is a little arbitrary.

1776 was the commercialization of the spinning jenny. It wasn't exactly the invention of the spinning jenny. The much more important machine, the water frame, was actually a more industrial version of the spinning jenny, but many historians feel it was the first Industrial Revolution machine. It was used in cottage industries. It emancipated women by allowing them to become entrepreneurs. It allowed people to make more clothes than they could wear, and increased human productivity. Basically, it allowed people to spin multiple more threads than you could on a spinning wheel.

This multiplicative effect is really what the Industrial Revolution does. It allows one person to make many people's worth of labor output. That was one machine. That one machine, if anything, created a cottage industry. It didn't create the factory. That was the next development: the water frame, the steam engine, and so on.

The reason the Industrial Revolution doubled life spans in the United States and exploded the population was that it increased quality of life dramatically. It had very little to do with the clothes that people were wearing and more to do with the reformation of society around the means of production. Unlike the farm, which was naturally distributed—you had to go to the land—these human industrial machines were driven by modes of force and sources of power.

These sources of power started with the horse, went to the water wheel, and then eventually became steam and ultimately electricity. Those first big modes of force, big engines, were water wheels and steam engines, and you had to go to them. You couldn't bring them to you. As a result, we concentrated around these machines and built modern industrial cities.

When you concentrate people, you actually have to accommodate crowds. That meant sewage systems and clean water, health care and education, and better housing became a priority. Nothing changed the human condition more than clean water and sewage systems. You could argue that although the catalyst of modernity was the factory and these mass production techniques, the real game changer was the sewage systems and the water supplies that came with them: the toilet and water purification.

Although there were cities before this, there were a lot more cities after these machines because they grew up around these machines basically to house the labor force that was drawn to these powerful economic tools. What you ended up seeing was a very quick maturation of modern infrastructure. Suddenly you just had so many people leaving the farms and crowding into one place. You had to do something. And that something initially was dark satanic mills and crowded conditions, but very quickly became better living, education, and quality of life for these new city dwellers.

DP: Let's jump ahead to the Digital Revolution. A lot of people start to look at the changes occurring in the 1950s and 1960s with the first computers. You've written that the big innovation was really when the computer came on the desktop and with the rise of printing.

Why was that technology particularly disruptive in the laying the foundation for the big changes that we are now starting to see in the real world with the Maker Movement?

CA: It's interesting to look at the three industrial revolutions, if you will, and look at the differences in terms of who's using it. The first one concentrated power putting the tools of production in the hands of a few. These are the so-called capitalists, the factory owners, or industrialists. This led to Marxism and all sorts of objections to such concentration of power.

Whether their prescription was right or wrong, their diagnosis was correct. Even though the farms were often owned by big landowners—there was also kind of a serfdom, and by and large, farming tended to be distributed technology—farmers tended to own their own tools of production. The factory was just the opposite. You worked for the man. There were social consequences of that as well as political ones.

The next two revolutions were largely antidotes to that. The invention of the mainframe computer was important, but not nearly as important as the invention of the personal computer. Why is that? The personal computer was the worst computer you could buy in 1987, not the best. So why did the worst computer turn out to be more important than the best computer? The answer is that it was the only computer you as a regular person could buy. It was not the technology, but rather the user, that turned out to be transformative.

The real lesson from the Second Industrial Revolution, the Computer Revolution, was a social revolution. It was putting powerful tools in the hands of regular people and allowing for people's creativity, energy, entrepreneurship, and complex ideas, just massively expanding the pool of innovation by not limiting who had access to the necessary tools. That was a social revolution, and it played out again with the Web—it's the extension of the same thing.

All of these things involved the power not of the technology, but of democratization. I'm sure your book, and everyone you've talked to, makes clear that the real lessons of the last 20 years have been social lessons about new innovation models that are open and inclusive, including both the credentialed and the non-credentialed, the domestic and international, and involving border and culture crossing. Those are all social lessons.

The Maker Movement and the Third Industrial Revolution involved not the invention of digital manufacturing technology because that happened 30 years ago. But the first couple decades of that were just like the mainframe, expensive tools in the hands of big companies. Once we democratized by adding the word desktop to these tools, then suddenly you could tap into the Web's innovation model. That became a game changer. It's happened over the last 5 years, so it is just starting. I'm part of it. My book, *Makers*, is about that. I think we are just now seeing the beginnings of what a democratized manufacturing economy really looks like.

DP: I've heard you tell this great story. Your grandfather was an inventor who had invented the automatic sprinkler system, and there were all sorts of required skill sets and levels of expertise that you would have needed at the time to manufacture and distribute something like that. Jump ahead and you're essentially able to order things directly from a factory in China using your credit card or PayPal.

Can you tell us a little bit about going from your grandfather's time to now? What are the barriers to entry that have been removed, and how does this relate to the democratization of manufacturing?

CA: The automatic sprinkler system was a 20th century invention. My grandfather was a rare victor of the 20th century invention model, but it required crossing two huge barriers. One was going from the idea to the prototype. That required machine skills and incredible expertise in the machine shop. You needed to be an engineer, which he happened to be. The second was to go from prototype to production. This required a factory, which he did not have. But he was able to patent and then license his invention.

To have one of those was hard, but to have two of those was almost impossible. Very, very few ideas made it to market because either you didn't have the skills to prototype it or—and this happened all the time—you couldn't get a patent. Or if you did have a patent, no one would license it. Or if they did license it, the invention was never put into production. Or if they did put it into production, they didn't do it well. As a result, almost all ideas died on the vine. The barriers to entry were too high.

Today, both of those have fallen to truly low levels. I'll give an example. As a thought experiment, I said, "What would Grandpa do if he invented the automatic sprinkler system today?" Now you can buy the fruits of that thought experiment called Open Sprinkler. It was created by a bunch of guys. I'm not sure any of us actually have a sprinkler system in our garden. It was just so obviously easy to do and needed to exist. We just did it for fun. Today you can buy it. It's cheap and good, better than most commercial alternatives. We did it for fun on a couple of weekends.

The first barrier, going from idea to prototype, was solved by Arduino and Raspberry Pi, all these super easy prototyping tools, 3D printers. It was ridiculously easy. The second, going from prototype to production, was global manufacturing. The guy who ended up doing it, Ray, just ended up using a contracted manufacturer on the web. He had studios making some things, probably all Chinese factories, but it doesn't matter. He just uploaded the designs and put in his credit card. Now you can buy it.

DP: As 3D printing scales into an industry that allows ordinary people to easily create useful and attractive products, what do you think the implications are for businesses that are built on design and brand identity? A related question would be as prices of 3D printing keep coming down do you think localized manufacturing could potentially disrupt or ultimately compete with the factories currently outsourcing things to China?

CA: I would answer the question with a single analogy. How did the Web, and bloggers in particular, affect the media?

In answering that question, you can project that to manufacturing. You give everyone the tools to publish, and you give everyone the tools to distribute. There's a new aesthetic, if you will. It's not a single aesthetic, just an alternative, an opening of space, a new class of producer, and new business models including none at all. It was also competition, but the media could use it. Some did well with competition and survived, while it hurt others.

YouTube didn't kill Hollywood. But by the same token, Hollywood didn't kill YouTube. The two co-exist. I don't know how it's going to play out exactly. Physical goods, because they do have marginal cost of production, are slightly different from digital goods, but the social forces are still the same. Whatever the Web did to media, I think you can imagine, the Maker Movement will do to manufacturing.

DP: Do you think down the road we might have 3D shops on every corner? If there comes a point where we can access everything we need on demand, do you think that could potentially change our living habits or even decentralize the importance of cities?

CA: I wouldn't go that far. Today, there are copy centers. There are printers on every desktop, and copy centers, not on every corner, but there are a lot of Kinkos around. If you're reading the printed *New York Times*, you're probably not printing it out yourself. If you're reading a book, you're probably not printing it out yourself. Personal printing didn't really change the manufacturing of printed media. It could have. We do have those tools. It just turns out, the physical form didn't want to be changed that much. We switched through the Web to the digital form, which didn't require any manufacturing at all.

By the same token, I wouldn't expect that China would be hollowed out and replaced with corner micro-manufacturing centers. I think it is very easy to imagine that just as your computer has multifunction capability— a printer, a scanner, and a fax machine—you could add a 3D printer function to your multifunction center, and you could print plastic as well as paper.

I still don't necessarily think you're going to stop going to Wal-Mart. There are real advantages to mass production, for example, cost and quality. There are also things 3D printers can't do and maybe will never be able to do involving material science and texture. It's hard enough to have 3 or 4 different ink cartridges. Imagine how many chemical cartridges you'd need to print something as simple as textured rubberized vinyl. Maybe someday we'll have matter compilers, and they'll begin binding matter on the atomic level, self-assembling into stuff, but I don't know how we get there.

DP: I'm curious about your recent company. As the editor of Wired *and a best-selling author, you could have started a company with almost anyone. You ultimately picked Jordy Munoz, a 19-year-old from Tijuana, as your co-founder.*

CA: I have to confess, by the time we started the company he was 21. But the point is taken.

DP: I've heard you say that he would have been bypassed by traditional hiring systems that filter by background, education, past job experience, etc. Could you tell us the story? I think it speaks volumes for the future of leadership and entrepreneurship, and it has huge implications for how we view education as well.

CA: The story of Jordy is not unique to me. It's just what happens on the Web. I think at least the Web I live in is the ultimate meritocracy. The best people rise to the top. And by the time they come to your attention, based on their merits, what they've accomplished and can do, their energy or intelligence, you don't even care where they came from. Nobody asks their favorite blogger for a resume. It just doesn't matter.

Likewise, in the Maker Movement, in our Web innovation community, it's a do-ocracy. The people who do win the respect and the attention of others in the community, and they become leaders. Nobody ever asks, "How old are you? What country do you live in? What degrees do you have or not have? Do you have a selling record? What's your work experience?" Nobody cares. It's immaterial. They can either do it or they can't.

Jordy's the perfect example. When we started our community, or when I started the community at GeekDad.com, I knew nothing. That's why I started the community using my philosophy of making my ignorance public. I was hoping by being ignorant in public, two magical things would happen. First, people would answer my dumb questions, and second, it would liberate people into asking their own dumb questions, and that collectively we would figure things out. That's exactly what happened.

Jordy was just the guy answering the questions. He was clearly ahead of us in terms of his thinking and, more to the point, his doing: making YouTube videos and posting code. It was a no-brainer. He was just the go-to guy. When it was time to start the company, he was the go-to guy. By the time I asked him how old he was, where he lived, and what degrees he had or didn't have, we were already partners. It was immaterial at that stage.

When you look at the top contributors in our community, some of them are complete winners of the old model. They work for Google, IBM, Apple, or Microsoft. They have computer science degrees or PhDs and incredible work histories. Others are exactly the opposite. They work for a Japanese bank or a Brazilian advertising company, or they're students. They are both equally valued. Now it's true of course that the PhDs in computer science have certain coding skills that guys who work at a Brazilian ad agency don't have, but it's because they do different things.

They have different roles in this community, in this collective, in project teams, and they are equally well respected. They are peers. One of them would have succeeded in the 20th century. The other would have failed in the 20th century. But in the 21st century model—I'm being kind of grandiose in centurion phraseology—but in this model, those talent filters are simply based on earned respect. The guy with the PhD works for IBM. We don't respect him because he has a PhD. We respect him because of what he did. Likewise, we don't respect the guy who works at the Brazilian ad agency because he works at a Brazilian ad agency. We respect him because of what he did.

It's about as color blind, education blind, and nationality blind as you can get. English language skills might be a slight discriminator. Jordy's English skills were not great, but it didn't really hold him back. I don't want to be too Panglossian about this, but this is about as meritocratic of a culture as I've ever experienced. Open source has been at it for 20 years. This doesn't seem to be a flash in the pan. At least in these innovation communities, we seem to have removed a lot of the barriers, prejudices, and stereotypes that have kept smart people out of productive environments because there are talent shelters along the path, and innovation communities still have it.

DP: As your business has grown and evolved, it's brought into being a community organized around interest that's also your customer base. They provide feedback, help with bug testing, and there's an incredible sense of synergy and collaboration that drives growth of the business.

Given your background writing about trends in media, technology and business, what potential is there for companies to build other communities around interest, product development, or stories the customers tell? What do you think are the implications of what you're doing in terms of being a disruptive business model?

CA: We're at the far right end of a broad open innovation trend. We're really hardcore. We're open source, which means we have specific licenses. We started a community and then built a company. We are tied to our community in the best way. Not all companies either have that dependency or want that vulnerability to a community. That's fine. There are multiple models.

Broadly open innovation is the trend that all companies are thinking about right now and that some companies are pursuing. It broadly involves breaking down walls between your employees and your customer, between your employees and potential contributors who are not employees, and walls between secrecy and openness. It is also accommodating non-zero sum markets, where you're allowing other people to benefit from your intellectual property at small cost to you but large benefit to the community at large. These are all relatively radical things.

When I tell people that most of my contributors don't work for me and are not locked up by contract, that we release all of our intellectual property under license terms that allow Chinese cloners to copy and make the things we sell at lower prices, and that we don't patent, they are horrified. They just can't believe it. Why would anyone do that?

That model breaks all the rules. And it certainly isn't for everyone, but it works for us. I'm not dogmatic about this. I'm not saying I think it's the only way. I do it because it works. It's not a religion for me. It is just pragmatism.

Turns out, when we give away stuff, we get back more in return. Long may it last!

DP: You founded GeekDad. You have five kids. I've heard you talk about how you're always trying to engage your kids in geeky activities.

CA: Emphasis on trying.

DP: (Laughs) I find it particularly interesting that you referred to the personal 3D printer as the new personal computer. I remember having an Apple IIGS growing up, and it had a radical effect on the rest of my life. Can you just tell me a little bit about how the 3D printer is the new personal computer? What are the broader implications of this type of technology in terms of inspiring education?

CA: I, like you, was the first generation who had home computers. Our parents brought us home computers. They weren't sure what it was for probably, and it was a home computer, not a personal computer. There was one. There was a sense that it was broadly important to a child's education that maybe you could program it. It wasn't quite clear. Maybe we could play video games on it. The point is that it changed your life. And it changed mine.

If you bring a 3D printer into a home with children, what you're telling them is that anything they can imagine, they can make real. It's not just the 3D printer. It's also software, which is super easy and fun on the iPad. If your kids are playing MindCrack, they're doing CAD. They just don't know it. They're doing 3D science on a 2D interface. They think it's a game. But they're doing sophisticated design.

If they can push a button and print it out and hold it, the moment that happens—and I've now seen it happen 5 times with 5 kids—and something they drew and designed on the screen is printed out and they can hold it in their hands, paint it, and put it on their shelf, that has an effect. Now, whether that effect is so profound they are going to become industrial designers when they grow up or whether it is just going to be locked away for future reference, they now know that making stuff is not hard. It is just something they can do.

Whether it is something they want to do, have any skills at, or think is fun depends on their personality. That lesson, the lesson about computing you got from your Apple IIGS, is that computing is something I can do. What you did with it was up to you, but now our kids are growing up understanding that industrial design is something they can do. It's not called industrial design. They may not call it design at all. But ultimately, that's what it is.

They're doing stuff that would have required so much for us to do. Just imagine! Big companies, mold making, injection molding presses, 4 years of training using CAD software, and God knows how much permission, paperwork and drives to factories. It used to be something that was impossible. My kids went from mildly intrigued to annoyed that our 3D printer is not as good as their friend's 3D printer.

"Why don't we have two colors? Why can't we print as fast as that other guy?" They went from mildly interested to blasé. That's kind of how change happens. Technology only becomes powerful when we don't call it technology anymore, when it becomes taken for granted. I'm less interested in the technology than what people do with it.

My kids are just printing out designs from Thingiverse today, which is mildly interesting. It's when they learn a lesson from that, which is that I can make something, then that is when we get a revolution. That's when we get what we saw with the PC and what we saw with the Web, an explosion of innovation. And it starts with something as simple as "I can do this." And that's all the 3D printer does. It says, "You can do this. It's easy." That process is a button. What you do with that button, now that's interesting. Forget how it works.

DP: I would connect the Maker Movement not just to advances in manufacturing with 3D printing, but also to the resurgence of interest in things like handcrafted goods, artisanal foods, small batch breweries, and organic groceries. Etsy is a great example of a thriving marketplace for makers of all types of created goods. How might the Maker Movement, what you've been writing about, and your vision for your kids be connected to the rise of a more creative economy?

CA: I don't know whether it's a more creative economy or whether it's a more discriminating economy. Look at the long tail. Yes, the long tail was enabled because anybody could be a creator, and what this new class of creators made was different from what the mass producers of the previous generation made. But the reality is most of us still consume what we produce.

I think you're right to identify a broad trend. I just think the trend is toward being a more discriminating consumer. Being a more discriminating consumer means understanding what you want better and being better informed about products. It starts with coffee and beans, wine, couture fashion, and chocolate.

Where do you live? In New York?

DP: Yes, I'm in Brooklyn, New York.

CA: You're in New York, so whatever the latest artisanal foodstuff is in New York that people are becoming hyper-informed about, that just comes with affluence. People who become more affluent become more discriminating. That's kind of natural. The discrimination that came with affluence was limited to products that existed. It tended to be quite high-priced ones like wine and fashion, you know couture, but as the long tail extended that to media and other things, you could be discriminating in your choice of websites, communities, or channels.

Today, you have micro-sliced incredibly granular media and are incredibly discriminating in our media taste. That's because it's out there. This includes our music taste and our film taste. Now, with the Etsys, the Kickstarters, and the Corkys etc. there's an explosion of choice of fiscal things. If you're into bicycles, you can now be a really discriminating bicycle consumer. I thought that a $5000 bicycle was expensive, but now I'm seeing $30,000 bicycles out there because of the nuance available, for example, the carbon fiber layout technique. People who care about this stuff really care about this stuff. That's now possible.

You don't need to go to big dealers out there to be able to get what you want. You're now seeing the extension of the long tail. You see these consumers turned into producers creating unique niche items for discriminating customers. That's the story of the blog and the seller—the same social sets. What's nice about it is that because it is on the Web you can find it easily, and it's pretty affordable. I think it speaks to something republican in our culture and maybe in our species just waiting for a marketplace to emerge that could both create that choice and then fulfill it.

Chris Anderson is the CEO of 3D Robotics and founder of DIY Drones. From 2001 through 2012 he was the Editor in Chief of Wired Magazine. *Before* Wired *he was with* The Economist *for seven years in London, Hong Kong and New York in various positions, ranging from Technology Editor to US Business Editor. He is the author of the New York Times bestselling books* The Long Tail *and* Free *as well as the new* Makers: The New Industrial Revolution.

Awards include: Editor of the Year by Ad Age (2005). Named to the "Time 100," the newsmagazine's list of the 100 most influential people in the world (2007). Loeb Award for Business Book of the Year (2007). Wired *was named Magazine of the Decade by AdWeek for his tenure (2009). Time Magazine's Tech 40–The Most Influential Minds In Technolgy (2013).*

He lives in Berkeley, California with his wife and five children.

ENTREPRENEURSHIP AROUND THE WORLD

Sarah Lacy

I place Sarah Lacy on top of the podium for the gold medal of best tech reporter in the world. What I love about Sarah is that she pushes the boundaries of conventional journalism, and follows a story where it leads, even if that includes spending 40-weeks bootstrapping her way around the world to write her last book, *Brilliant, Crazy, Cocky: How the Top 1% of Entrepreneurs Profit from Global Chaos.* Our conversation explores:

- Silicon Valley vs. entrepreneurship around the world
- What American entrepreneurs can learn from China
- The flow of capital, talent, and technology into regional and international markets
- Sarah's vision for *PandoDaily* and the future of tech journalism and media brands

As editor-in-chief and founder of *PandoDaily*, former reporter of *TechCrunch* and *Business Insider*, and a bestselling author, Sarah is an ideal person to help understand how the Disruption Revolution is impacting the entire world. This interview is a poignant reminder that the best entrepreneurs solve problems in their own backyard, and their closeness and familiarity with local markets often makes them better qualified than anyone else.

DP: I really love the story behind the name PandoDaily—*the idea of a colony of Pando trees in Utah with an interconnected root system that makes them the oldest living organism in the world. Regardless of what goes on above ground the root system supports and lives on.*

Can you tell us a bit more about why this is a great metaphor for Silicon Valley and the technology startup ecosystem?

SL: I think if you look at the history of Silicon Valley, it started out being a place where we were physically manufacturing transistors and semiconductors through a pretty painstaking manual process. There were rows and rows of women who were actually putting these transistors together. Then it became mass assembly. Some of the big problems in Silicon Valley several decades ago were factory workers abusing amphetamines so they could work all hours assembling these transistors.

That really bears no resemblance to the modern Silicon Valley—what companies do now, what they pay people to do, what your average startup worker's life is like, etc. It is not that Silicon Valley is particularly good at one part of technology, and that is why it is all here: it is the root system underneath. The connections to people in the hottest companies today can all be traced back to those early semiconductor days that seemingly have so little to do with incubating what goes on above ground, so to speak.

That is what makes Silicon Valley so unique and so different from any other place on the planet: this infrastructure of angel investors, accountants, lawyers, and mentors; people who serve on boards and can be an interim CEO; and all these little things that need to come together to help create these companies cycle, after cycle, after cycle. It's not the expertise. It's not the tech chops. It's that systemization of creating companies.

That is really what we try to write about at *PandoDaily.* We try to write about the trees above ground, if you will, the companies that are hot right now and the people behind the scenes who are continually driving this. Because, just like with the Pando trees, they could all be burned to the ground and more trees would come up. That's the position the Valley is in now, which is very different than other startup ecosystems.

You see different fits and starts in other areas of the world, but it's different. For example, it looked like Seattle would become a dominant one because they had Microsoft, and then Amazon, but what's really come since? There was a period of time where different states like Texas were doing really well because you had AMD, Dell, and a couple of these big companies, but what's really come next?

DP: I'd like to connect that to some of the themes that came out of your last book Brilliant, Crazy, Cocky: How the Top 1% of Entrepreneurs Profit from Global Chaos. *The opening story is about this Brazilian entrepreneur, Marco Gomes. He grew up in the favelas, or ghettos of Brazilian cities. He had a father who had a cocaine habit. He goes on to found an Internet company using some of the skills he learned initially in his uncle's business building computers from different smuggled parts. We learn later that he raised VC money and built an incredible ad platform that was acquired for $750 million.*

That story ends with a statement that I think connects to your first book and what you do now at PandoDaily: *"Simply because of when he was born, where he was born doesn't matter." Can tell us a little bit about how Web 2.0 technologies, mobile phones and other recent innovations have empowered entrepreneurship around the world and why it is such an interesting time for global entrepreneurship?*

SL: I would say two things to that. First, I think there is a part of what's going on in terms of global entrepreneurship that is very real, and very powerful, and that is really why I wanted to write my second book. But there is also a part of the story with global entrepreneurship that people think is true, but actually is not.

Let's take the latter part first. Lots of people think now—because the world is flat, the Web, mobile and everything else—that the next Facebook or the next Twitter can come out of anywhere. I don't actually think that is true. I think it can, but I think it is highly unlikely. If you are going to do something that you want to be a mainstream, consumer Internet business, then it is just so much easier to do it in Silicon Valley because of all the things you're going to need to do that. You need to hire an army of engineers to scale it. You are going to need lots of capital.

All the companies in the category of being the next Google, Facebook, Twitter, etc, raised hundreds of millions of dollars of capital, and the reason they were able to be so large is because that was their business model. They weren't focused on revenue from the get-go. For example, if Facebook had taken Eduardo Saverin's advice and monetized its early traffic by throwing up banner ads everywhere, it never would have become the company that it is today.

You need huge access to capital and people with all of these other skills who have done it before. Someone like Sheryl Sandberg, or, even lower in the chain, who knows how to manage a team of 500 salespeople in whatever the category is. In Silicon Valley, there are all these off-the-shelf executives who have done exactly the same thing before. Even in New York, which has a super thriving startup ecosystem, companies have a hard time scaling past 50 employees, or going from 50 to 500. You can hire 50 really good engineers, but after that it starts getting really hard. So I think this sense that the next Google, Facebook or Twitter can come from anywhere really isn't true. I think that the deck is stacked against you to such a degree that if that is your goal as an entrepreneur, then you should really be in Silicon Valley to maximize what you can control.

However, I do think what's exciting about global entrepreneurship is that there are so many opportunities that are more exciting than just building the next Google, Facebook or Twitter, and most of those are found in emerging markets. I think people gloss over the demographics and we don't think about how staggering they are because we have heard them so many times now, but roughly half of the world's population is surging into the middle class and modernity for the first time. Half of that number, so a quarter of the world's population, is under the age of 25.

That's an amazing disruptive force in the world that is either going to be a disruptive force in a bad way or a disruptive force in a good way. For example, I write about the role that the State Department has been playing in trying to encourage cyber-entrepreneurship in countries like Indonesia. If you look at where there is a lot of fundamentalism or terrorism or, in Colombia, certainly where organizations like the FARC were getting a lot of their soldiers, it is young people who don't have jobs or money. They are disenfranchised and don't have a voice. You look at Nigerian hackers and scammers, they come out of a country where there is 10 percent economic growth every year, and yet something like 30 or 40 percent of the country is chronically unemployed. This is why people turn to crime.

Now, certainly there are people who would be criminals or radical under any circumstance, but a lot of these are people who need a job and need something to do. Outsourcing and government jobs are not going to do it. The only way you can create enough jobs for the world's population is hybrid entrepreneurship.

On the flipside, there are so many opportunities. These countries are all creating challenges and problems that innovation can solve. They are also challenges and problems the West never faced because the West did not modernize this quickly and the West did not have megacities at the rate that these places do. Marco is a little bit unique in that he's doing an ad network. Most of the entrepreneurs that I write about in the book are doing things like this other Brazilian company I wrote about, BS Construtora, which found a way to make prefabricated houses in less than twenty-four hours; or this fascinating company out of India that found a way to very simply extend mobile phone footprints into rural Indian villages at a rate where poor villages could afford mobile service.

These are things that a Western entrepreneur isn't going to do, but they are really applicable to a large part of the world. So whenever I go to these countries and I hear about an entrepreneur who is trying to do the next Google, Facebook or Twitter, and they say, "Oh, but I can hire cheaper talent here," nobody cares. That is not how that game is played. It is not played on cheaper talent. It is played on the best talent money can buy, and it is not only not in those countries. It is not even in other parts of the US or the West. It is only really in Silicon Valley. So don't play that game.

Play the game of solving the endemic problem that your country is facing, because most emerging markets have that problem, and use technology and innovation to do that—that, to me, is the really exciting global opportunity.

DP: You have covered the startup ecosystem in Silicon Valley and the emerging world, and there has been this back-and-forth idea that Silicon Valley is replicable in terms of VC funding, incubator programs, and recruiting talent. I'm curious, how much of innovation do you think is driven by entrepreneurs responding to local or regional needs?

Or, to build upon or elaborate on what you just said: to what extent should people be trying to develop different Silicon Valleys around the world? How do you help encourage a culture of entrepreneurship through investment, mentorship, and other programs, targeting the types of opportunities you've described which are responding to more immediate needs and aren't necessarily in the tech field?

SL: I think Silicon Valley was a totally unique phenomenon that had to do with the moment in time. It tied in with the wars that were going on at the time; it tied in with military spending; it tied into the space race; it tied into the transistor being invented. It tied into the fact that William Shockley's mother grew up in Palo Alto, so he happened to come back here. Fred Terman worked at Stanford; Stanford happened to be doing cheap leases for land, so companies could get space.

There were so many serendipitous things that went into the creation of Silicon Valley. It's just like any startup. There is timing, and there is luck, and there is serendipity. You can have all the greatest products in the world, but if you don't have those things, it doesn't become a big company. I just don't see another wave like that starting that is that consuming. There is also not that big of a greenfield opportunity because Silicon Valley exists, and so the people who want to build the next Google, Facebook or Twitter would come here to do it. So I don't think a Silicon Valley will really be recreated.

Now, that doesn't mean that there is not an importance of building a startup ecosystem. I think they are tremendously important. I think that being an entrepreneur is one of the loneliest and hardest things you can do, and so you need people around you who are also going through that, but also people who can help jump onboard your journey as well. I think that we have seen a lot of great startup ecosystems formed around the world—trying to hold them to a standard of Silicon Valley is just a losing proposition.

I think the places that do it well are the ones that almost have that idea in their DNA. They are not trying to be Silicon Valley. They are not calling themselves "Silicon Something." If you look at when New York really started to excel, it was almost when they dropped the name Silicon Alley. You play your own strengths, because you are not going to win at Silicon Valley's game. You have got to win at your own game.

You have seen this in LA in terms of a lot of celebrity tie-ins, a lot of commerce content companies that involve storytelling and brands. Those are things LA does very well. I think you have seen this in New York around Tumblr or Foursquare, or even a lot of the e-commerce companies coming out of New York. The most lucrative area with the biggest exits has been ad tech, and that is because advertising is centered in New York and it's simply a market that understands advertising better.

So, I think geographies need to play to whatever their demonstrated strengths are. Why does this company need to be formed where you are? I think that is really how you create a good ecosystem. There is always a lot of handwringing about, "We can't do this because we don't have enough venture capital." I think the money is a second-order thing that flows to where a great community of entrepreneurs and ideas are. You don't start with the money; you start with bootstrapping, and scrappiness, and maybe some local angels. If you do interesting things, there is so much capital in the world that the capital will come to you.

DP: One of the things that I found very interesting in your book was the regional difference in how people use the Web. For example, in Indonesia the social Web was first, and then email only really started to gain traction because most sites required email for login. In China, most users are under thirty, many of them are playing games, and they are on social sites accessed in Internet cafes, so being on the Internet has a real-world communal component as well.

Particularly with respect to China, most Chinese Internet companies win by innovating not around the product, but around process and monetization, which is an area where Silicon Valley entrepreneurs typically tend to be weak. Having covered both the emerging world and Silicon Valley, what do you think Internet entrepreneurs in the West can learn from Internet entrepreneurs around the world? What are they doing better?

SL: I think a lot of them think about monetization earlier on, because they don't have billions of dollars of venture capital sitting in their backyard. I'm never one of these people who likes to jump up and down and say, "Well how are you going to monetize this?" in the early stages of a company, because I think that simply is not how it's done here, and I think it is a stupid argument.

The flipside of that is: it works if you are building the next Google, Facebook or Twitter, because you can just figure it out later and there is some value to it. But that value, all too often, is just massive amounts of eyeballs that are looking at display advertising. As we've seen with a lot of the troubles even with Facebook being a public company, it is just kind of a bad business. The only company that has really done a truly innovative ad product is Google, and the fact that no one has done it since then is kind of sad.

Everyone talks about innovative ads or monetization in the early days of their companies, but no one really does it. I think even mobile and virtual payments were not pioneered here. It was really ripped off of Asia, and most Asian companies are still doing it better than we are. I just think the Chinese are much more creative in how you come up with business models. It is not that we won't keep creating big companies that can tap into huge amounts of display advertising, because we can, but there is a limit to it. We are getting to the point now where every startup has to have a billion users in order to do that. We're going to get really lowest common denominator, homogenized products.

At some point, we need more LinkedIns of the world. You need more high-value, consumer platforms where 100 million, 200 million users makes you a massive, massive company, because then you can have a pretty good company when there are only 30 million people who really get value out of your service. Somehow we have to make that value per user a lot better. I think that is where creative monetization comes in, and I think that's what other countries have, by and large, done better.

Now, making something off of fewer users is certainly not the China playbook, but I think their creativity and constraints drive innovation because there is certainly not as much venture capital as there is in Silicon Valley. You look at something like Tencent, which was able to make a profitable company that basically came out of instant messaging (IM). AOL, Yahoo!, Microsoft, all of these great companies never found a way to monetize IM. All too often, the creative people in Silicon Valley are the ones doing the product with an almost an allergic sense of not wanting to touch revenue, and I think that has to change.

DP: In your book, you reference Vivek Wadhwa's work, whose recent book Immigrant Exodus *talks about how immigrants are basically coming to the US for education, but due to visa restrictions and other reasons, they're often returning to their native companies in what's being referred to as a brain drain.*

I also find it interesting that you describe this new class of aspiring entrepreneurs from the West that are leaving to pursue opportunities in the emerging world. They're basically skipping Wall Street and conventional careers that they might have here. How do you think the flow of money and talent is changing entrepreneurship globally?

SL: I definitely think everyone acknowledges—I shouldn't say everyone, because actually there is opposition, but everyone I know in Silicon Valley acknowledges—that there are major issues with immigration. The idea that someone comes here for school, we train them to be phenomenal engineers, there are companies desperate for phenomenal engineers, and then we force them to go back home, doesn't make any sense for anyone. PayPal, eBay, Google, etc.—look at how many great companies are started by either children of immigrants or immigrants. Unless you are very xenophobic or have some sort of baggage, that seems like a no-brainer.

In terms of people leaving and going to other countries, I think the biggest risk-takers are a lot of the ones self-selecting into that. As big as the opportunities are, it is still really hard to be in a different culture, particularly in some of these markets. In China, there are a lot of very real things that you have to navigate, and being Chinese is a massive advantage. Even if you speak good Chinese, being a white person trying to build something and navigate through China, you are just at a massive disadvantage.

Now, some people like Vivek Wadwha would argue that early Indians, being in Silicon Valley, were at the same disadvantage, and a lot of them prospered. So I don't think it is undoable, but it is certainly hard. I think that some of the more renegade, maverick, risk-taking, even-more-misfit-than-your-typical-entrepreneur entrepreneurs are the ones who are going to go elsewhere. I think that the most mainstream talent that those places will get coming from the US is a lot of their own countrymen who can't stay here.

In terms of money, there are really interesting flows and counter-flows of money going on. One of the reasons I decided to write my book was because I think a lot of my job is to follow the money. There was an undisputable trend over time I've been in Silicon Valley where, when I first moved here, other than Israel as a possible exception, no VCs would invest in other countries. Now almost every single one of them do.

I think you have a lot of the "smart money" in Silicon Valley increasingly around the world, and it speaks to the opportunity because it is actually really hard to invest in these markets. For example, it is way easier to invest in a kid coming out of Stanford. You speak the same language, you can keep an eye on them, and you know that you can help them because he or she is doing something very relevant to what you have done in the past. When you think through all the risks, plus the time differences and culture differences, you have to really believe in the opportunity to start devoting funds around the world.

I think what's fascinating, though, is their money is increasingly coming from emerging markets. There is a huge trend with international LPs funding US venture firms. So you have this odd situation where all of this money is being made in emerging markets, and there are all of these opportunities to re-invest back into emerging markets, but the money is essentially coming to Silicon Valley first and then going back out.

I think that sort of flies in the face of all the people who say there is no value in VCs. At least international LPs seem to think there is value. So the money piece is very interesting, and it will be interesting to see how that plays out over time—if there is a point where international LPs start feeling like they can skip that step because there are good enough investors and money managers in those countries to start investing more directly, and if local entrepreneurs are able to tap into the money that really exists in all these countries, etc. But for now the money wants to go to Silicon Valley first.

DP: Do you think there is a certain cachet for people in the emerging world to become an investor in a Silicon Valley company?

SL: Oh, for sure.

DP: I'm curious how the Steve Jobs and Mark Zuckerbergs serve as role models to people in the emerging world.

SL: I definitely think the brand and cachet of Silicon Valley goes a really long way. Entrepreneurs in other countries want to have Silicon Valley investors, so a Silicon Valley investor is probably always going to get a better deal flow if they parachute into a country, even if they are not a very good one.

I think that when it comes to limited partners, endowments, big pension funds, family offices and sovereign wealth funds, all those groups, it is kind of like the "No one got fired for buying IBM" thing. It is easy for them to say a Silicon Valley venture fund that has x returns is a safe place to put their money vs. really taking a risk with that money just because you want to bolster entrepreneurship in their native country. A lot of portfolio managers are looking to do the safe thing within a fairly risky asset class.

But I think in terms of role models, this is one thing that is really interesting, and this is one way that the Internet and new media has played a huge role in entrepreneurship around the world. People feel like they know these people. Marco is a great example, who you mentioned earlier that I wrote about in my book. This is someone who read *TechCrunch* every day, even though he grew up in a favela in Brazil.

On paper, he has very little in common with any Silicon Valley entrepreneur, or, at least how he grew up, he shouldn't. In any other era, he would have known nothing about these people. He may have used Facebook eventually, or could go see a Hollywood movie, but he wouldn't have known who Mark Zuckerberg was, any details about his life, or how he built the company, any more than he would know details about someone who made a movie he went to see on a weekend. So I think the fashion and story around entrepreneurship, and how big and global that has gotten, has really made all of these people role models for the entire world. The role models are not necessarily local entrepreneurs—they are entrepreneurs from Silicon Valley.

We see this all the time with the *PandoMonthly* interviews. Tens of thousands of people all over the world watch them from start to finish. They relate to those stories because there is something about creating a company that really is the same, whether you are a kid in the middle of India or Ben Horowitz trying to keep Loudcloud from going down in flames. There is this timeless human struggle aspect to building a company: things like surrounding yourself with people smarter than you; or trusting your gut because if you get led astray, then you are never going to know if you had the right answer. There are all these big truisms to entrepreneurship that are relevant to everybody. I think that has been a really defining thing.

Sometimes I've described what we want to do at *Pando* in terms of what *Rolling Stone* did for the music generation. Music became this major global thing that tied everyone together into one pop-culture creative consumption class, and I think Web entrepreneurship has been a little bit the same. I think there is a whole generation of people around the world who define themselves based on that, and feel like that is the bucket they fit in. Almost anything that goes on in the world can be told through the lens of entrepreneurship and technology, the same way it could have through music for that early *Rolling Stone*/MTV generation.

DP: You have this concept of an outside entrepreneur: these people who grew up outside of wealthy families and conventional ways of doing business, different immigrants and risk takers. The entrepreneurs of the emerging world certainly fit into that category in the same way as the Silicon Valley twenty-something college dropout in a hoodie and flip-flops.

I think of that and then I think of looking back on your earlier writing. You had a 2006 story on Kevin Rose, how this kid made $60 million in 18 months, that was followed up by your first book, Once You're Lucky, Twice You're Good. *I think in many ways both of those pieces of writing helped to create a master narrative around what you might call the geek genius.*

You've covered these outside entrepreneurs and geek genius founders throughout your career. What makes them so fascinating to you as a writer and a journalist, and, as an entrepreneur, would you place yourself into the same kind of category?

SL: That's an interesting question. I'll start with the first part because I think it is easier to answer. I think what is so fascinating about them is really just the impact they can have on so many lives in a really short period of time. In an age of mega-corporations, it is really hard for people to do that.

It is kind of similar to how I was describing why there couldn't be another Silicon Valley. I'm obsessed with the history of Silicon Valley, and in particular Robert Noyce, who was one of the founders of Fairchild and then one of the founders of Intel. There were so many weird happenstances and coincidences that led to Robert Noyce coming to Silicon Valley to begin with, and having the skill sets of transistor technology and physics that he did.

These pivotal moves were so core to a lot of the creation of Silicon Valley. You can really trace all of Silicon Valley, which is thousands and thousands of companies, billions of dollars, and huge numbers of jobs, back to a handful of guys who had this huge outside impact on all of this being created here. That sort of almost mind-boggling narrative is the same thing that you see with companies today.

It's not quite as big because they are not creating a whole ecosystem, but what would have happened if Larry and Sergey had sold Google early on and Google weren't in the world the way that it is today? Think of what they are doing with fiber, Google Glass, and Android—the force that Android has been, being another big smartphone alternative, and the role Android is playing connecting people to the Internet all over the world. Think about the world with this Google vacuum, and that was started by two people.

Think about the same thing with Facebook. It connects a billion people to each other. Did we ever think a single form of media would connect a billion people? Think if Mark Zuckerberg had just decided not to do it. I think if you love to tell stories, there is just so much drama and poetry, and this happenstance of circumstances, and what-if, this-could-have-so-easily-not-happened element that always underlines every great startup story. I just don't know why anyone wants to write about anything else.

It's the same thing that we love about John Hughes movies, if you are my age and grew up with *Sixteen Candles* and stuff like that. There are a tiny percentage of people who are the cheerleader and prom queen, and everyone else roots for the other. That has been a lot of the story in Silicon Valley.

I would never be so arrogant as to put myself into a category with most of the great entrepreneurs that I covered over my career, but I have definitely been inspired by them. There were moments in my career where I was a misfit, and where I didn't fit in. When I worked for *Business Week* and I worked in old media, I was far too radical, and when I worked at *TechCrunch*, I was far too old school in terms of media.

The luxury of being able to build something that is sort of the Goldilocks moment of your career, where it is a place that you fit into perfectly because you are building it, and you are putting together this company of your dreams—what if you could shape anything, any place you'd ever worked, to be different, how would you do it differently? Building something solely off your gut. That is such an evocation of who you are as a professional and who you are as a human being, and being unafraid to do that, and unafraid to trust yourself. I've been very inspired by the great entrepreneurs because that is what I have tried to do with *PandoDaily*.

In the early days, when a lot of the media empires we take for granted today were being built, the publisher and the editor were really the same person. Then we had a whole wave where you just had these different custodians of a lot of these great media empires, and everyone thought it was very important that the publisher and the editor be separated in order to protect the editorial integrity of the organization.

That made sense for that time, but I think we are in a time now where many people, and hopefully *PandoDaily* included, need to create the next major hundred-year-long media brands. For that to happen, the editor-in-chief needs to also be the publisher, or the CEO, depending on what title you want to give it, because I think the only person who can truly protect the editorial integrity of an organization is the CEO.

I think the CEO has to be so bought into the editorial integrity that they don't sell the company for a paltry amount of money, or they don't take shortcuts or do some revenue strategy that undermines it. I think in that sense, media has a lot to learn from the product CEO, which was the big thing that was ushered in by a lot of the Web 2.0 generation: not hiring the grown-up salesperson to run your company.

In that sense, there is a sort of a lineage, you could say, or a way that I've been inspired by those people. For the media world, I'm a product CEO. I'm a reporter, and reporters are the rock stars of our company, the same way that engineers are the rock stars of a company that is led by an engineer. A lot of what I do is try to create a dream job for a really great reporter, the same way engineer CEOs try to come up with: what would be a nirvana for a great engineer to work at? In my own way, I'm certainly not a coder, or programmer, or a genius, but I think that there are a lot of analogs to the way I'm building this company and the way I've seen a lot of successful people build companies.

....

Sarah Lacy *is the founder and editor-in-chief of* PandoDaily. *She is an award winning journalist and author of two critically acclaimed books,* "Once You're Lucky, Twice You're Good: The Rebirth of Silicon Valley and the Rise of Web 2.0" *(Gotham Books, May 2008) and* "Brilliant, Crazy, Cocky: How the Top 1% of Entrepreneurs Profit from Global Chaos" *(Wiley, February 2011). She has been covering technology news for over 15 years, most recently as a senior editor for* TechCrunch.

....

THE AGE OF CONTEXT

Robert Scoble

Robert Scoble is the undisputed king of early adopters. Interviewing thousands of entrepreneurs over the years, constantly searching for the next big thing, and so generous with his time—a true inspiration. His book *Naked Conversations* (2005) anticipated the revolutionary impact of blogging and helped solidify much of my thinking about social media. We sat down to talk about his latest book *Age of Context*:

- How Google Glass might be with a developed apps ecosystem
- The convergence of sensors, robots, wearable technology, and cloud technology that is happening now
- Self-driving cars and hyper-personalized devices
- What might be described as a geek's heaven in the future

The conversation focuses on the implications of these innovations when they eventually reach mass adoption. There is nobody closer to the future than Robert, and it is incredibly exciting to get a window into what lies ahead for us all. The interview gets progressively geeky, culminating in a wonderful image of how life might be in 30 years.

DP: You have interviewed thousands of entrepreneurs and founders over the years—probably more than anyone else. Why are you so passionate about the latest innovations in technology?

RS: It began when I unboxed an Apple II in junior high or maybe even before that. I grew up in Cupertino and my Dad was an engineer. He always brought new things home. We had one of the first Apple IIs in the school and I got a tour of Apple when it was one building. I always loved new things because of that. It is not just new computers—it's new music, new cars, new cameras, new everything. And it just built from there—I was just into what's coming next.

DP: Your latest book project, Age of Context *with Shel Israel covers the convergence of mobile, social media, big data, location-based servers and sensors. How do you picture these five technology forces coming together?*

RS: I started seeing a pattern where the number of sensors is going up exponentially—things like Nike Fuel Band and Fitbit Bed. Cell phones have sensor data in the last 18 months. Then there are all these sensors around, whether it's in a thermostat or things like cube sensors that are measuring your air quality. So we just noticed the number of sensors going up exponentially. Add on the number of computers and database innovation going up exponentially along with the size of databases. Then add that on to the exponential growth of social media; Twitter has a billion tweets every 36 hours right now, and in 18 months I bet that is every 18 hours.

So all of this innovation is on its own Moore's Law, meaning the technology keeps getting exponentially faster, better, and cheaper. Next, add on location data going up exponentially with things like FourSquare or Facebook check-ins or Google Maps. Add those five things together and I started seeing a few fundamental shifts in consumer behavior.

First, very personalized products. When you put on my Google Glass, it doesn't serve you very well unless you switch it to being yours. We are seeing the beginning of a new assistive kind of product. Google Now is probably the strongest example of this trend but there's a lot more coming out that try to assist and help you. For example, when you ask for sushi it will know what kind of sushi you're talking about and then place an order for you based on personal preferences.

Next, you are going to have very sharp details on everything about your business. What that means is that someone like Travis Kalanick, the CEO of Uber, can see every piece of inventory, every worker, every customer, etc. It also means that companies will be capable of knowing their customers in much deeper detail.

Right now, if you walk into a Ritz they sort of know you a little bit, but not really. I've been to the local Half Moon Bay Ritz more than 250 times and do they have a database on me? No. Right now, social media experts don't even know who I am and they give me clueless answers. Those are the best of the best; they actually spend money on customer service systems. This is all going to start changing in the Age of Context.

DP: I know in 2005, people thought you and Shel were a little crazy when you wrote Naked Conversations *because you predicted that blogging and social tools would usher in an Age of Conversation. Now, social media is sort of becoming like oxygen in the sense that it's everywhere.*

Is the Age of Context going to be just as ubiquitous and is it going to disrupt or impact our lives just as fast in the years to come?

RS: I think every product is going to be affected by one or all of these five trends. And I think every business will have to know their customer in deeper detail otherwise their competitors are going to run away with the game. Is it as deep as social media?

Social media was a pretty deep and profound shift for human behavior. I'm not sure it comes up to that level, but it will get close. For example, if Google Glass is popular, then we are going to have something on our face that watches our eyes, knows where we are looking and responds to our voice. That is a pretty deep change. It will set up a new age of commerce instead of advertising, which is another pretty deep change in how our media gets monetized. These are all pretty profound changes.

DP: I recall one interview of yours when the CTO of Plantronics, a leading sensor and headset company, used the phrase: "The Age of Context is going to bend the web to you." You also recently interviewed the CEO and founder of Signals, who are making an app that basically makes your smart phone smarter.

Can you tell us a bit more about how technology is going to increasingly be personalized in the Age of Context?

RS: Plantronics is a great example. Their headsets used to have just one sensor on it—a microphone—and today they have five or more sensors so it knows when you walk closer to your computer, it knows when you pick it up off the desk, it knows when you put it on your face, etc. This lets them build much more personal features into the product, and as I mentioned before, we are seeing this exponential increase in sensors everywhere.

If you put on my Plantronics headset and walk towards your computer, it won't unlock it because my headset only unlocks my computer. So these products are going to be very personalized not only in terms of sensors, but also in terms of their owners. Then they will start assisting you in trying to help live your lives. It's tough to see exactly how Plantronics would be assistive, but it might for example say, "Hey, you need to get over here to avoid a noisy area."

DP: You committed to wearing something like Google Glass for the rest of your life. Imagine we're 10 to 20 years into the future. The bugs are worked out, it has reached a critical mass in terms of adoption, and we have an amazing Glass Apps eco-system. What is the experience like and how does Glass potentially interact with other technology, whether it's wearable, in our cars, the office, stores, smart homes, etc.?

RS: Well, in 15 years we are going to have self-driving cars. I say, more accurately, I'm going to have a piece of a self-driving car because I probably won't need to own one. Instead, I will probably just own a piece of a fleet of self-driving cars. When I need one I'll just talk to my Glass or whatever I have on my head and say, "OK, Glass, I need a car in 15 minutes. Take me to work."

And by the way, I probably won't even need to do that because it will know that I need to go to work and just be there waiting for me because it knows my calendar and behaviors. It will know that it is Monday morning at 9:15 and 90% of the time by 9:30 I go to work. And so, it might even communicate with me, "Are you going to work today because there is a bus strike?" "No, I am going to stay home because I moved all my calendar."

It's going to be an interesting world 15 years from now. The prototypes I've seen inside research labs of wearable computers have much sharper screens, much deeper augmented reality than Google Glass has, with much better sensors and cameras. They are also working a lot harder to make voice recognition more accurate.

Today, if you say a place name, sometimes Glass gets it right, and sometimes it doesn't. Right now, Google Glass forces you to go back to your phone, let's say 40% of the time you put in an address. Ten years from now, that won't be true. You will be able to correct and spell it out without going back to your phone.

Today, if you ask Glass, "Where's the best coffee shop in Half Moon Bay?" it doesn't really have an answer. You can sort of hack an answer but it doesn't have an answer to those types of questions. Ten years from now, it will certainly have an answer. Ten years from now, you will walk into the Ritz and they will also have wearables. The staff is going to know I'm coming and they'll go, "Hey Robert, your margarita is ready at the bar and say hi to Joe." Today, they have no clue about who I am and what I drink, and therefore—etc, etc.

DP: A study recently said the average person looks at their smartphone a hundred times a day. I would just assume integrate that experience and basically make Glass the center or focal point of my personal technology ecosystem. Are people still using smartphones in 10 to 20 years, and how does a company like Apple succeed if the smartphone gets integrated into something like Glass?

RS: I think you still need a work surface. I don't think it all goes through Glass so I think you're still going to carry around something that looks like a smartphone. It might be very thin. It might be different than it is today. But you still need to work on a surface. So, I don't see those going away even 10-20 years from now the same way we still have laptops. Just because we have tablet PCs doesn't mean we stopped using our laptops, and the same will apply to smartphones.

DP: It's almost going to become like a secondary device or sort of a personal workspace, more than necessarily something we're thinking of now as a phone?

RS: Perhaps. Also, 10-20 years from now, what is our battery life going to be? Probably longer, but our processors will be more robust. There will be battery-life problems for a while, so putting your cell phone in your pocket, the radios that talk to the cell towers, etc. makes a lot of sense. That will probably not change in the next 10 years, although I'm sure somebody will try it.

That is where it gets hard to guess what the future is really going to look like because you don't know what the breakthrough is around the corner that some research lab or some kid is going to figure out. For example, someone figured out how to throw power across the room. If he is suc-cessful in building a company and this technology out, then you might just walk into a room and your devices charge by grabbing power out of the air. Sometimes it is hard to foresee that kind of innovation or that kind of breakthrough. That is the whole concept of disruptive innovation—the unexpected breakthroughs.

DP: Google has Double Click, You Tube, Ad Words and a variety of advertis-ing and media solutions in addition to its search engine and Google+, Maps, etc. It seems like Google is positioned for dominance in the Age of Context. I'm curious. I know that now you have about 4 million followers on Goog-le+. Do you see Facebook and Twitter still being really relevant in 10 or 20 years or you think + is going to really take the lead as we start moving into the Age of Context?

RS: I never bet against companies that have billions of dollars in the bank and in research. Google is clearly in a power position. They know more about me than most other companies, but Facebook certainly still has my attention every morning. That's a hard question. It requires a lot of variables and a lot of interaction. As long as you have a founder in charge, that is really hard to see happen.

DP: So you work for Rack Space, the leading provider of cloud-based post-ing services. Can you explain to some of the un-technical people who might be reading the book the broader shift to cloud-based solutions and why bet-ter access data in the cloud will be so important in the Age of Context.

RS: Well, there are a few things happening all at the same time. One, cloud computing has made starting a company much less expensive. Ten years ago, if you wanted to start a web company you had a cage somewhere, or a rack—which is why it's called Rack Space, a rack of gear—and it probably cost a million dollars or more just to buy equipment. You had to make that investment before you turned on. Otherwise, if you did get on Oprah or TechCrunch, then your system would melt down and you would destroy your brand and your chance of building your company.

Today, you just swipe your credit card and pay a few dollars for your first server. Then, if the load goes up, you just start opening more virtual serv-ers right from your iPad, iPhone or your Android phone. You don't have to invest that upfront cost into your business, which is just sitting in a cage unused. Now, if you get on a famous TV show or somebody like Walt Mossberg says you are the hottest thing since sliced bread, then you can even programmatically start up new cloud servers and the cost goes up when your traffic goes up, so your business just works.

Beyond that, when you start thinking about what kind of features you are going to put into your system, a lot of them are going to rely on APIs that are available on the cloud. Even if you own your own data center, a lot of people are putting cloud technology into their own data center to make it possible to iterate the codes faster and build new kinds of things. That is really important for the Age of Context, where you are going to have sensors popping up and streaming data to the cloud.

For example, the self-driving car—if it really was happening—collects 750 megabytes of data per second. Let's say only 1/100th gets thrown to the cloud, because they have a little data center in your trunk that filters the data it sees—even if it just sends 1/100th to the cloud—think about what that means for Toyota. Let's say they are going to sell a million self-driving cars between now and 2015. That means there will need to be a pretty sizeable data center just to handle a million cars.

If you are going to innovate and build new things with sensors and you want to collect data, such as what Plantronics is doing with their audio headsets, then you are going to need scalable computer systems that are easy to build—that's where the cloud comes in. That is why we started Open Stack—the foundation is an open source cloud so you can put Open Stack on your own server, your own devices, or your own data center. Then, you are not locked into a single company. You aren't waiting for a single company to improve the infrastructure you depend on. Because it is open source, you can improve it yourself.

DP: I've heard you reference Moore's Law before and joked that basically you just need to be alive long enough for any technology to become affordable.

RS: Yeah, for example, Steve Wozniak showed me his color printer in 1989— it was one of the first color printers in Silicon Valley. At the time it was $45,000, and today you can get a better printer for $70.

DP: What innovations are you reviewing today for the Age of Context that you're particularly excited about becoming affordable in the next 10-20 years? You're seeing a lot of these amazing prototypes—

RS: Robots are coming up pretty strongly, which will bring a new age of manufacturing back to America. Now, it might not bring back the jobs, which is a problem, but I think it will bring a different kind of worker back. There is lots of innovation happening in robots. Right now, even a Skype robot is $3,000, but it would be cool if they came down to $300 or less.

Augmented reality glasses are going to come down a lot. Right now, the military has them and they are $10,000 a pair. In 5-10 years, those are going to be a few hundred dollars. That will affect gaming and entertainment quite a bit. Then, there will be unknown stuff. For example we are seeing new sensors come out every week that sit on your skin and watch things like your blood sugar levels. There are even some sensors that can tell whether you have cancer or not.

You are just going to wear a little sensor pack on your skin—a little tattoo basically—and it will report to your phone all sorts of stuff, which then reports to your doctor. This makes healthcare better. It might play games with you too. For example, if you eat a doughnut, then it will know because your blood sugar level goes sky high. So, it will play a little game— OK. You had a doughnut, now you have to go walk for ten miles—something like that.

DP: I know your son is autistic. A friend of mine Christine Hart works for Autism Speaks and has moderated several autism hackathons. She mentioned one that was funded by the Bing Fund in Seattle, where the group tried to remotely monitor and translate biometric data used in glucose sensors. She saw another possibility of people that might be non-verbal recording physical responses when they might be able to express anxiety or fear. There also appear to be a lot of innovative apps in wearable tech and smart house tech. What might excite you in that area?

RS: Well, we don't understand enough about the brain in terms of why autism develops, what causes it and how to treat it. You certainly are seeing these kids taking to iPads and a range of apps, but that sort of treats the symptom and not the cause or the actual disorder, if we should call it that.

It is tough to know. If my son has a wearable computer on his face that reminds him to look into people's eyes because it knows where his eyes are looking, or it reminds him to do X,Y,Z because he forget about X, Y, Z, then I think that helps him to live his life. That's really interesting.

Take it out of the world of autism—I met a guy who was wearing an exoskeleton the other day. He is paralyzed from the belly down and he was walking around with a robot holding him up. And by the way, that exoskeleton had 30 sensors on it streaming data over to a cloud system so his doctors could watch all of the movements and have a discussion with him. Right now, it only works on flat concrete, but soon that exoskeleton will have a hundred or more sensors. The guys who are building the exoskeleton said, "Next, we want to walk on sand, grass and gravel, etc." That requires knowing contextually where you are and changing the behavior of the robot, but we will get there eventually.

DP: Let's say all of the innovations in tech fulfill their promise. They become scalable and utterly transform the tech landscape—what kind of world do we look forward to? Tell me your vision of what a geek heaven might be like in 30 years?

RS: I'm going to have a car that picks me up because I eat breakfast right now. It knows my favorite breakfast place and it knows I need to get to work. That will likely change car ownership and also radically change the cities. It will radically change what I can do in the car because I don't need to hold the steering wheel anymore. For example, it might not force me to sit forward, so we can turn the seat around and I can have a meeting in my car while I go to work, or maybe watch a TED video or a movie on a nice screen.

That is going to radically change a whole lot of things. For example, it reinvigorates suburbs because people can see themselves living an hour away from the city where their job might be. Start to think about why do you need to go to the office in the first place? But humans are humans. They like to be together. I don't see that changing anytime soon.

We are going to have a variety of devices on us, whether it's an iWatch or Glass of some kind on our face. Or even you stick with an old school cell phone. These things are going to be much more assistive and predictive in trying to improve your experience of them. A lot more is going to happen automatically. If you look at Google+, it automatically makes your photo better and that will seem pretty quaint in 5 years as they have 50 services that are automatic.

We are going to start moving into a world we live in, a world of commerce, and what I mean by that is you are going to ask for what you want and it will serve you. "I want a coffee shop near me." And it will say, "Within 2 miles there is a Starbucks and a Pete's and a Half Moon Bay Coffee Society and X, Y, Z." It will know pretty quickly which coffee shop you like based on your past behaviors, so it will say, "You always go to the Pete's whenever you're in town, so let's take you there."

Then you are going to see an Uberization of society. So with Uber right now, when you click a thing on your smartphone, you basically tell the system I need a driver somewhere and then you see your driver's location. For example, you are in San Francisco and need a cab or a limo. You open Uber and see all of the limos or drivers around town, click a button, say I need one, and a driver starts driving towards you. You see it and his picture, and he sees you, and everybody has transparency on everything.

Take the same experience and imagine you are sitting at a nice hotel. "I'd like another Bloody Mary." You are just going to talk to Glass: "OK Glass, get me another Bloody Mary." One is going to come over to you. Now, that requires a lot of infrastructure to be built out eventually, though it will happen. That gives you a little taste.

Your doctor is just going to call you up. "You better come in so we can check you out because your sensor is reporting something." There might even be an ambulance because the sensor will know you are having a heart attack. The ambulance might just show up. "Hey Robert, your sensor is saying you're having a heart attack." "What do you mean?" "Well let's go check you out." That gives you a little taste.

I don't know what all that means for innovation but this world is iterating. To me innovation is: how fast can you iterate? How fast can you reduce the time to ship new things to customers?

For example, Oakley makes these ski goggles that have a wearable computer in them. These ski goggles did not exist before last June. Last June, Apple came to Oakley and said, "We have a partner who we want to put together with you. We'd like to have you make ski goggles that we can put on our shelves by Christmas." That was last June and by October the product was on the shelf. It sold out at $650. That is how fast it is to build a new product now, and it will only get faster.

If there is any way you can reduce the time to ship something new to your customers, then that means you win. So if you are not using open source or 3D printing, or one of these low-cost computers to prototype things, you are going to lose out to your competitors. This world is starting to move faster and faster. The trick is to see the trends and have systems that help you bring innovation—that the entire industry is bringing in—to your customers.

DP: That sounds like a pretty awesome world.

RS: It does, doesn't it?

Robert Scoble *As Startup Liaison for Rackspace, the Open Cloud Computing Company, Robert Scoble travels the world looking for what's happening on the bleeding edge of technology for Rackspace's startup program. He's interviewed thousands of executives and technology innovators and reports what he learns in books (most recently* "The Age of Context," *a book coauthored with Forbes author Shel Israel), YouTube, and many social media sites where he's followed by millions of people.*

THE COLLABORATIVE ECONOMY

Jeremiah Owyang

Jeremiah's blog Web-Strategist and his Twitter stream have consistently been the best ongoing resource for social media and emerging technologies. When Jeremiah started writing about the Collaborative Economy, I knew that it was imperative to dedicate an entire interview to the democratization of business and the implications of this model:

- Three Internet eras—Brand, Social, and Collaborative Economy
- Why Uber is the next Amazon, and AirBnB is the next eBay
- Collaborative Economy Model—Company as a Service, Motivate a Marketplace, and Provide a Platform
- What the Collaborative Economy might look like in the future

I'm so excited about this material that I am planning a follow-up book called *Beyond Disruption: The Collaborative Economy of the Future.* Congratulations to Jeremiah on founding Crowd Companies, his new venture to help big companies participate in the Collaborative Economy. I look forward to collaborating with Jeremiah again in the future.

DP: You've referred to the social media era as the customer experience phase of the Internet, where there was a fundamental shift from brand-owned channels during Web 1.0 that required a certain level of expertise and resources to create and maintain a website, to a "many-to-many" model where everyone could express their own unique voice and share experiences through access to blogs, Facebook, Twitter, and social channels.

Now, with the Collaborative Economy, this "many-to-many" model is being extended to, and layered on top of, ownership and access to goods and services. Can you tell us a bit about how this signifies an evolution of social business, and how you see the buyer-seller relationship being redefined in the Collaborative Economy?

JO: At a broader level, there are three phases:

First, the early Internet, or Web 1.0, was when very few people could publish because you had to have some technical skills. I refer to that as the Brand Era, because the brand could say, "I talk, you listen."

Next, the second phase or Web 2.0 came along, and we call that the Social Media Era. This is when the customer got what they needed because they controlled the media using social tools–the democratization of ideas.

The third phase is using these same technologies—Internet + social— together in what we call the Collaborative Economy Era. This is when people use those same tools and share ideas, but now they can get products, goods and services from each other rather than from corporations, We're seeing the democratization of business. This means that people can get what they want from the crowd rather than turning to a large company. It also means corporations that do not adopt this business model are disintermediated.

This is the most radical change in business we've seen—social media is nothing compared to this. Social media is just ideas, but take that disruption of ideas and watch it as people don't buy products as much. Many corporations will be extinct because of this next movement. People can buy products once and share them many times with each other—they don't have to buy again and again.

Secondly, in the next phase of the Collaborative Economy, we are seeing people build their own products and services. Look at what you've done with this book, or Wikispeed when they built their own car, or the Maker Movement—people are coming together and acting like corporations. This is the biggest shift we've ever seen in business—the power is shifting to the people.

DP: You've said that companies need to let go in order to gain more, and in your report on the Collaborative Economy you outline an interrelated three-part business model that you refer to as the Collaborative Economy value chain where companies can work with startups and the crowd. (1) Company as a Service (2) Motivate a Marketplace (3) Provide a Platform.

Is letting go to gain more analogous to how companies had to let go of a certain sense of control over their brand in social media?

JO: Yes, it is exactly the same. That second phase is about yielding power of media to the people in order to maintain management of the brand. The people are the brand now. Many companies focus on word-of-mouth because they know that they can't control the conversation, so they let the customers be the voice—this is why Wildfire and Buddy Media took off and got acquired for large sums of money.

The same principle has to happen in terms of adopting social business models and crowd-build products. Each three of those models are examples of the crowd getting more power, but in return companies can decrease costs and increase revenue.

DP: Could you provide us with a couple of examples?

JO: Absolutely. First, there are some bigger trends where people don't necessarily want to own more, population and density is increasing, and so people just want access to goods—they don't need to own them. That's why it's called a Collaborative Economy. As a result, if people don't want to buy goods as much, then companies should not be selling them. Instead, they should be making them available on demand. Don't sell just once and have it consumed—sell that one product 100 times.

Bag, Borrow or Steal allows women (and husbands like myself) to rent high-end purses that cost $3-5,000. You might not buy them, but you can rent on demand. Toyota and BMW now offer their cars as a service—you can rent their cars from their dealership lots in order to compete with Zipcar and all of these other players. In consumer goods, for example razors, kids toys or beauty products—Dollar Shave Club, Citrus Lane, and Beauty Box are subscription models sold once, and then they send products all year. This creates a high form of loyalty because now I'm a member.

Don't sell just one—rent or sell memberships or subscriptions, and then sell it 100 times.

DP: Could you walk us through the three different models?

JO: Sure. First, we have products become services. Second, if you have services, then you need to turn them into a marketplace. Now, you can't own or lead a marketplace. It's very hard to do—eBay tried this for ten years. It means that instead of trying to fight marketplaces like they are doing now, they should enable and profit from them.

So, let's make this a dialogue—who is losing out from AirBnB?

DP: Hotels and existing hospitality providers

JO: Yes, lobbyists are fighting at the local and federal level. Who funds the lobbyists?

DP: The hotel/hospitality industry

JO: Exactly. Now, this is unstoppable. AirBnB is being declared illegal in multiple cities, but it didn't stop it. The only way to stop this movement is to turn off the Internet because most of these businesses are pinned on Facebook plus they have their own social programs. You can't stop it—it's like trying to stop social media. We saw that in the Middle East, and it didn't work so well.

Instead of fighting, Marriott or Hilton should build their own marketplace, invite people to host their own homes, and then take a cut of those transactions. Their guests can go to the local market if they want that local experience, and the host gets trusted customers, access to a supply chain, and can become Marriott or Hilton certified, allowing hotel brands to upsell services such as concierge, maids, and those cool little mints that you get on your pillow.

In fact, if they did this right, they could start to compete with AirBnB. This shouldn't sound radical, since it's what hotels already do—it's a franchise program, but they are essentially franchising their customers.

Now let's look at motivate a marketplace. Patagonia partnered with eBay and encourages people to buy used goods on the eBay community in a program called Common Threads. That's on someone else's site—I'm suggesting people go a step further and build on their own site. Just as we saw the emergence of Jive, Lithium and Chatter building their own communities on their own domains to replicate MySpace, Facebook and Friendster (yeah, I said Friendster), it's the repeat of social business.

Finally, Provide a Platform brings everything full circle. So, if you have a community, then enable them to build your products. If your customers are already starting to self-fund, build, 3D print, and deliver products to each other, then instead of having them do it offsite, enable them to do onsite. Kickstarter, Deliv.co are examples of communities that are already doing this.

Allow crowds to ship and deliver, or store products at their homes. This cuts out manufacturing and retailers. If you want to compete with Amazon, make the crowd your Amazon instead of building an ecommerce site. I think Uber is the next Amazon, and AirBnB is the next eBay. At the local level, the crowd delivers products faster.

DP: One of the ideas in this book is that constraint drives innovation. To what extent do you think the economic recession may have accelerated the trends that you are talking about, particularly with respect to people who lost their jobs and millennials that now face limited job prospects?

JO: The recession definitely kick-started the Collaborative Economy. People didn't have a choice. When I interviewed AirBnB, they said that people were empowered to build their own companies by making their house into a company. We're seeing this now with Cookening, where you can turn your home into a restaurant. So, the recession spurred that on and forced innovation. Necessity is the mother innovation.

Because social media was already mainstream, people could already connect with each other in a frictionless marketplace. The cost of building a company is also cheap—it's easy to start a company and get funding. The cost of innovation is low, whereas the cost of business as usual is high.

Now, the definition of the Collaborative Economy is shared ownership and shared access between startups, corporations, and people—all three, that's a very important point. The crowd can innovate fast with lots of new ideas, but a company has customers, resources, and a trusted brand. If they work together where the crowd becomes the company, and the company becomes the crowd, then everyone wins.

DP: You outlined a three-phase model for how the Collaborative Economy will evolve.

- *Phase 1: The sharing startups will unveil APIs for new growth*
- *Phase 2: A new era of Collaborative Economy Enterprise Software will emerge*
- *Phase 3: Corporations tap the crowd for non-crucial services and goods.*

Do you envision a new era of Collaborative Economy experts, SaaS providers, and this becoming a formative field in the same way as social media did?

JO: Yes, including me—I've already made the jump. Social media and the Collaborative Economy are the same thing—we used to share ideas, now we're sharing products and services. It's exactly the same thing.

DP: I love AirBnB because I like the idea of being able to stay in someone's home and compensating them directly, and I like Kickstarter and IndieGoGo because it makes me excited to help fund someone's creative projects. Lyft and Uber excite me because I know who is picking me up and giving me a ride.

We've talked a lot about the core business aspects of the Collaborative Economy, but I think what excites me most is there is a deep human need being fulfilled. In short, I like the idea of living in a global village, where trust and relationships matter.

How does the Collaborative Economy scale without the authenticity of these experiences being undermined? What role might reputation management, identity authentication, regulation etc. play?

JO: Well, that's a complicated topic. First of all, this is a personalized global experience: basically, localized experiences at scale that are not limited to local geographical areas. For example, you can look into someone's home on the other side of the world and then stay there, getting a personalized, local experience anywhere around the globe.

Second, there are lots of issues with legislation. For example, most of the Collaborative Economy startups are in SF. Relay Ride is opening a lot at the airport, where you park your car and can make money off of renting it, disrupting the rental car companies. Reputation systems will be involved—two ways, rating the buyer and seller. Now, SFO declared ride sharing systems illegal and citizen arrests can be made. It's really complicated, but basically taxi drivers spent so much money on cars and medallions, and are now complaining because they are being disrupted. Medallions are a closed market, and the Collaborative Economy is all about opening up markets.

The public utilities commission is proposing that these ride and share companies should be legal. So we're seeing changes at the business model, city, and state legislation levels. These are huge change. There is another trend here, which is that mayors are driving some of these changes like a city-state. It's not just companies and consumers. Do mayors erode their existing tax base and reduce revenues from medallions in order to make their cities more efficient, or do they tax these new startups and try to put standards around them, which could reduce their efficiencies?

There are some big choices to be made. Now, a lot of these are just tipping for service providers instead of wages, which is a loss of tax revenue for the government. If everyone went to the Collaborative Economy, it's not clear whether we could increase the economy or completely collapse it. There are a lot of variables, and trying to predict how this will all play out is a complicated question.

DP: For the last 20 years, there has been a massive emphasis on bringing people back to cities in pedestrian and bike-friendly neighborhoods, and today young people have less interest in driving. This reduction of our eco-footprint is one of the things that I strongly associate with the holistic values of inclusivity and equality found within San Francisco/Silicon Valley area.

How much of the Collaborative Economy is driven by a new type of entrepreneur that has drank the Kool-Aid, so to speak, where making money is also a byproduct of an intent to create a better world?

JO: First, this is about making money and improving the world. These are venture-backed companies and 36% are funded. There is no question that you have to make money and improve the economy. But at the same time, if that aligns with your mission, then you are doing it right. Now, money is a form of representing value, but value can be measured in many different ways. These have to be profitable, and for the people it has to make financial sense.

To be clear, this is not a socialist environment. It might look socialist, where everyone is sharing everything, but it is actually a free market—pure capitalism. What they are finding is that sharing things you don't use often is the best form of a free market. This is disrupting these business institutions that have been created at local, city or federal level and forcing a free market. For example, look at how Uber is disrupting the taxi medallion market.

DP: When I go to a local resale store to sell used clothes, records, books, music etc. they offer 25% cash or 40% store credit. Store credit is better for me if I am a loyal customer, and it's better for the store because they maximize their profits. It's win-win for everyone.

Based on the companies that you studied, there was an average 20% margin around each transaction. Feasibly the same type of resale-shop model could be applied to create incentives for reinvesting in the Collaborative Economy. What are the broader implications if goods and services start to be exchanged without money changing hands, or if entire communities start to buy in and this reaches mass adoption?

JO: First, a reputation economy can start to emerge, where those with a better reputation for properly sharing and selling goods, or a better social footprint, have more benefits than those who don't. Then the market starts to self-regulate. For example, who regulates the quality of taxis? The city government issues medallions, but they don't regulate the quality of the service. Uber and Lyft have two-way ratings—you rate the driver and the driver rates you. Uber drivers have to maintain 4.6 stars of they risk getting kicked out. The average is 4.3, so they have to be above average.

Second, there is the gift economy. A few examples: 99 Dresses, where you can borrow dresses from other women in your neighborhood. The joke in New York is the closet is now the oven. NYC goes through four seasons, so why own them if you can borrow and trade? There is a point system, where the more you trade, the more points can be redeemed for other things.

NextDoor.com finds neighbors on my block, verifies my location, and makes things available. Just the other day, I put a bunch of cleaning supplies for my car on there, and a woman came by and picked them up, thanking me and saying that her husband would love them. Yerdle is by Andy Reuben, the former Chief Sustainability Office of Walmart, the largest retailer of the world. It's built on Facebook Connect to gift anything that you want for free—all that stuff you don't need you can just gift it for free.

Now you want to talk about disruption—the reputation and gift economy is incredibly disruptive to the economy.

DP: How might the Collaborative Economy help to revitalize local business-es and encourage people to shop locally?

JO: Well, I visited AirBnB headquarters, and I know the investors in Uber. My assertion is that the next eBay is AirBnB. So, eBay first to all is a marketplace itself. Now a marketplace is hard to build, but they've managed to do it. But it's not very efficient—shipping products from around the world is very costly. AirBnB is also a global marketplace of buyers and sellers—they're called hosts and guests—but it's at the local level.

In a recent interview, Brian Chesky, their CEO, said that they are going to look at things beyond beds. So what could be next? Sharing food, renting kitchens, selling services, tourism at the local level. The next phase is to move beyond beds to become a marketplace at the local level, and that will disrupt eBay. Everything is going from global to local—it's cheaper, faster. This isn't simply about sustainability. It's about everything.

Uber is a delivery service. They experimented with delivering ice cream recently. What's next? Blue Bottle Coffee, then Little Star Pizza out of North Beach—high-end products that need to be delivered. Then restaurants, then boxes of goodies for your barbecue, etc. They are building a massive delivery network at the local level. Uber is going to be an on-demand service for everything. Therefore, Uber will be the next Amazon.

DP: On the one hand, the Collaborative Economy could create new job opportunities for people looking for work. Odesk and TaskRabbit are great examples to find freelance workers; Contently is a great example of a col-laborative community of journalists that can be paired with media brands and companies looking for quality storytelling. It also has numerous possible benefits for allowing local businesses to compete, for people to monetize and create new revenue streams from things that they own, to reduce our ecological footprint, etc.

Yet on the other, the increasingly frictionless marketplace could make margins so low that only those who control the means of distribution can make much money. For example, look at how ad exchanges have dramatically cut into margins for publishers in the digital media space.

How does the Collaborative Economy scale in ways that don't turn us into a society of haves and have-nots? What happens to general laborers in a future of highly skilled workers?

JO: Well, that's why it's called the Collaborative Economy, not collaborative consumption and not a sharing economy. Does it create more jobs, and does it reduce unemployment?

The answer is yes for people who use the tools. For example, oDesk and Elance activate smart people from around the world in various opportunity markets that have time and skills. The whole purpose of the Collaborative Economy is to activate idle resources, whether that is space, time or resources.

Now, who is going to win? Does it create "haves and have-nots"? I don't know. That's too far out. It's being highly debated. Look at Denmark or some areas of Northern Europe. They already live this and are doing quite well. The commons are shared. Wikipedia is the commons. Standardize common resources for the crowd; don't own them.

The big change here is a mindset change. When people talk about the economy, they say increase spending. Go shopping this holiday—economic injection. Does that help long-term? Buying mindless stuff to fill your garage? What about reducing overall consumption and investing in things that further grow the planet vs. wasting resources?

DP: During my Ph.D. studies at Princeton I focused on the interrelationship between the adoption of emerging communications technologies and broader shifts in religion, culture, and politics. What I found was that when new ways of communicating reached mass adoption, the real institutional changes tended to occur in the next generations. For example, the printing press galvanized the Reformation and the formation of nation-states; massive changes in publishing in the 1740s and 1800s fueled "Great Awakenings" that were followed by the Revolutionary War and abolitionist movements; adoption of radio and television coincided with the Civil Rights and Sixties Counterculture movements. We're seeing this same pattern today with democratic movements around the world leveraging social media.

What gets me excited about the Collaborative Economy model is that it could lay the foundation for fundamental institutional changes made possible by a shift in how we communicate and share. What you're describing sounds to me like a possible next era in civilization.

Assuming that everything goes right, and an ideal storm of corporate buy-in, insurance, regulations, software, distribution channels, public support etc. coalesce to create a thriving Collaborative Economy, how big of a sector could this be and what is your vision for the future 20 years from now?

JO: This could actually reduce the nomenclature of first, second and third world. It could reduce income and resource inequality—or at least it could trigger that movement. Rachel Botsman who did a TED talk on this topic in 2010 says today it's a $26 billion market. I heard a talk by Stefan Bartscher of BMW at Stanford, who said that by 2050, cities will be saturated with cars and won't be able to fit anymore. Collaborative sharing of cars is inevitable. Our generation will probably live to be 100. My daughter will live in a mega-city that will be 10-20 million. We have no choice but to share everything—to innovate our way towards a vibrant Collaborative Economy and a better world.

....

Jeremiah Owyang *is Chief Catalyst of Crowd Companies, a company he founded in October 2013 to help big companies with the Collaborative Economy.*

Previously he was industry analyst and Partner at Altimeter Group, located in Silicon Valley. His research focuses on the present and future relationship between companies and their customers. His blog, "Web Strategy," shares insights from his research and what they mean for businesses to stay relevant in the future. Jeremiah is often quoted in The Wall Street Journal, TheNew York Times, *and* USA Today *and is a frequent keynote speaker at business and technology conferences around the world. Time named Jeremiah's Twitter feed one of the best in 2011, calling him a "strategist on the front lines of revolution."*

Jeremiah previously worked at Forrester Research as a Senior Analyst focused on Social Computing for the Interactive Marketer. Before that, he was an active pioneer of web technologies on the brand side, launching and managing Hitachi Data Systems' Social Media programs in 2005-2007. He also served as the Intranet Architect at World Savings (now Wells Fargo) and was a user experience professional at Exodus Communications after receiving his Marketing bachelor's degree at SFSU. He recently participated in the Innovation Roundtable at the Aspen Institute, a global think tank that shapes policy.

PART II

ENTREPRENEURSHIP AND LEADERSHIP

SURVIVAL IS NOT ENOUGH

Seth Godin

This was the hardest interview for me to conduct because Seth has had such a formative impact on my views that I did not know where to begin. I admit to have totally drank the Seth Godin Kool-Aid—his straightforward, non-technical, no-nonsense approach and simple narrative hooks just make sense to me.

- Why surviving is not enough and we must all be remarkable
- How we must dance with our fear instead of trying to get rid of it, because fear is a sign that we are onto something
- To innovate you need to be prepared to burn some stuff down
- The opportunities for people who are courageous and brave

Seth makes a great introduction to the section on entrepreneurship and leadership. I spent about three days coming up with questions that he typically doesn't get asked, so hopefully there is something fresh and new for even his most loyal of fans.

DP: There is now what you refer to as a "new normal," where surviving is not enough—companies must embrace change and innovate. What would you tell leaders is the best way to move forward?

SG: We only have two choices: (1) we can either scare leaders into moving forward or (2) we can assume that they have decided to move forward and then give them significant hooks to help them. What we cannot do, and what will not work, is telling them that it is possible to innovate without being frightened and that innovation will work if they do it right, because that's not true.

DP: You said in one interview you had eight to nine hundred rejections to book proposals over the years.

SG: In a row, in one year.

DP: You have obviously pushed through that and reached a point where the rewards outweigh the efforts. In that interview you also mentioned that some ideas for books are eventually written years later, and there is a way in which you feel compelled to bring these ideas into the world. I feel the same way about the approach to my own work, with my next several book projects already pretty well defined.

Can you elaborate on the experience of being a struggling writer and entrepreneur? Was there an "a-ha" moment for you when a vision for your ideas crystallized and you found your unique voice?

SG: I think the hardest thing that most entrepreneurs deal with is understanding that they need to have a unique voice. All of this stuff being pushed on them—the cookie-cutter, follow these steps that will work guaranteed, For Dummies and Wiley books, etc.—is about being an imitation of someone else. It's not about being Richard Branson, Steve Jobs, or Mark Zuckerberg. The reality is that your audience or your customers will say, "The main thing that we want to buy from you is something that we can't buy from anyone else."

It took me a few years before I chose to be me as opposed to an imitation of someone else. Next, I had to learn how to tell a unique story about my work that would resonate with people who wanted to buy it. If you merely stand up and say, "I am being me," no one is interested because no one actually cares about you. When you create a remarkable thing, instead of being just another maker of widgets, the word will spread. The good news is that in this era when conformity is part of the new normal, creativity is scarce and more valuable than ever.

DP: As you got into your writing career, you spent about a year doing re-search for Survival is Not Enough: Smart Companies Abandon Worry and Embrace Change, *which presents an excellent model for success and leadership based upon science and evolution. What does it mean to say survival is not enough, and how should we abandon worry and embrace change?*

SG: Those are really two different questions. First, the Industrial Revolution was all about survival. That is, whether you are making cars, widgets or insurance policies, every day you are going to get more efficient, and therefore what you want to do is survive long enough for the efficiency to kick in. Then you will make a profit. So for the first hundred years or so of the Industrial Revolution, survival was enough.

Today, the efficiency and economy of scale that came with the Industrial Revolution is gone. If all that you do every day is go into work hoping to survive until tomorrow, then what will happen is very soon you will be replaced by somebody braver and younger than you. In times of rapid change, whether we are talking about evolution or business, what we see is that explorers and innovators have an advantage, not a disadvantage. That is a huge shift into the post-Industrial-Revolution.

The second answer involves this idea of embracing change. What that really means is embracing failure. Lots of people like to think of themselves as being innovators and embracing change, but they can't accept the possibility of failure. When things change, we will fail. Failure is inevitable, so embrace it as part of the creative or innovation process. People in big companies hate it when you say embrace failure. But in fact if you say, "What I'm working on is too important, and failure is not an option," then you have also announced that neither is success, because success will always come with some failure.

DP: You have also talked about fear being part of our evolutionary heritage, particularly what you refer to throughout some of your work as the "lizard brain." Basically, our survival instinct is to be risk-averse, to go along with the status quo instead of picking or choosing ourselves and doing what we think is right.

I think that a theme throughout many of your books is to identify these points of resistance and make the choice to confront fear. So how should we approach fear, and what does it mean to pick yourself in a world where we are taught to wait to be picked and accepted by others?

SG: The answer to the first half of that question is: if you are feeling fear in the jungle or the plains, and you want to end up with grandchildren, then you should listen to that fear and run away. On the other hand, if you live in the twenty-first century and are feeling fear, it is almost certain that the fear you are feeling is a vestige of how we evolved. That fear is not a warning; it is a signal that you are onto something.

This falls apart when people say, "OK, how do I get rid of my fear?"

The answer is: you don't get rid of that fear; you dance with it. That is what artists do, and what people who do innovative work do. They dance with their fear. They do not extinguish it; they welcome it, embrace it, and take it to the next level. So if we start this book, this interview, this process of, "How do I innovate without fear?" then the reader has asked the completely wrong question.

The right question is, "How do I find the fear and dance with it?" because the fear is a signal that I'm onto something.

DP: So then how do you go about finding the fear and dancing with it?

SG: Well, we all have it, but our instinct is to rationalize away fear by not acting on it. For example, you're in a class or a lecture, and at the end they say, "Any questions?" and you have a question—every sentient being has a question; you already invested the time to be there—and you do not raise your hand. Why don't you raise your hand, and what does it mean not to raise your hand?

In that moment you have rationalized six different ways about why it wouldn't be appropriate or selfless to raise your hand, and you have talked yourself out of it. That fear you felt, that talked you out of raising your hand, is exactly the fear I'm talking about, and most people feel it every single day, fifty times each day.

The fear that used to protect us is now our worst enemy. Imagine if you did ask that question, asking that question sparked a new conversation, and that conversation led everyone in the room to engage and value your ideas. Take that same simple analogy and apply it to everything in life: the key to dancing with fear is to do things that are safe but might feel risky.

DP: You outlined four factors that create failure: pressure from deadlines, fatigue, fear, and bosses who desire closure, not uncertainty. In contrast to that, you said startups have none of these problems. How can smart companies remove these obstacles to failure so that change is viewed as an opportunity? Can you reflect on how best practices for startups can be applied to manage smart companies?

SG: First, let's understand that if you work every day at a company that makes money by producing something, then you can't afford to blow that up. You can't afford to say, "We're going to stop making the Ford Taurus." You can't afford to say, "We don't do Whole Life insurance anymore. It's what we make all our money on, but we stopped." That is the engine that pays for all the innovation that you are going to have to do.

My argument is: just don't expect people to innovate, because they won't. They are not rewarded for innovating. They don't have time to innovate. Innovation just isn't around the corner for them, not the big-time disruptive innovation that you're talking about. In fact, the big-time disruptive innovation you are talking about would lead to failure in other aspects of the business resulting in them losing their jobs. In most companies there are strong incentives not to innovate.

What you need to do is isolate some people. Put them in an office across the street. Insist that they do not come back to you with interim reports. Leave them alone and only reward them for failing because if you can create that environment, where there is time pressure and intellectual pressure but there isn't that push-push-push from the boss, then and only then is it likely that they will do the kind of work that they do at startups.

The mistake that big companies make is that they say, "We want to be as innovative as a startup, but we want to fail as often as an industrialist," which is zero.

DP: You used the example that in 1906 San Francisco suffered a great earthquake and burned to the ground, and then eleven years later had been completely rebuilt. The idea is that it is easier to replace something that disappears or fix something after it breaks, but it is hard to improve upon what we are currently doing.

If empty lots can be built on from scratch and each presents a new opportunity, then success drives success. How can we identify the empty lots in a business that are begging for innovation, and then inspire people to build upon them?

SG: What I'm saying is that you can't innovate if you are not prepared to burn some stuff down. If there is a clock ticking and it says, "We will not be in this business in nine months, and if you are depending on us being in this business nine months from now, you had better wake up because you are going to be fired," then the team of people who have to replace it will get to work. They will try lots of things that don't work until they find something that does work.

That shift in gears of a talented group of people who trust each other is at the foundation of innovation. If you look at the way certain technology companies have managed to significantly pivot, they don't do it by saying, "We never fail." For example, the essence of Dell Computer is the mindset, "We never fail," and because they had a we-never-fail direct-marketing mindset, they failed.

DP: You outlined a fundamental shift from an economy based on factories to one based on connections. The backbone of the economy used to be middle managers and good-paying manufacturing jobs. Even most white-collar jobs were like factory jobs because they exist to basically turn out the same stuff, which means that they're replaceable.

Now, there are no longer really great jobs that pay you to do what you are told. The new path to success is about becoming someone indispensable that people will miss. Can you tell us a little bit about this shift, why mediocrity is for losers and we really have no choice but to be remarkable?

SG: I would like to say, to anyone who will read my words: I can't change your mind in three paragraphs. But the three paragraphs I would say are:

Culturally, you have been brainwashed, from the time you were two years old, to fit in and do what you were told. School was invented by industrialists to train you to accept the status quo and do your job a little faster and a little cheaper. We do it in second grade, in fifth grade, in college, and we do it when you get to your job. This is so deeply ingrained throughout our lives that you don't even realize it is happening. I should just stop there, because if someone reads this and it doesn't seem true to them, I have no prayer.

But I won't stop there. If, on the other hand, you realize that this is the case and is clearly true, then the question is what to do about it? Once you realize that every time you buy something, every time you hire someone, every time you make an important decision, you are validating my point. You don't buy average stuff, you don't talk about average stuff, and you don't go out across town to eat at an average restaurant.

All the decisions we make are about the exceptional and the remarkable: is it worth paying for? Out of many options, which one is the best choice? So why would that be any different when it comes to your job?

DP: A few years ago, you created an alternative MBA program, and I know that you keep giving back through your books, through speaking, and through doing things like this interview. How do you approach teaching leadership, and what role do you think mentorship has in creating the next generation of leaders?

SG: I think that it is almost impossible to teach leadership. What you can do is create an environment where people will choose to lead, and those are fundamentally different tasks. So when I ran my six-month MBA, or the two-week internship I just finished the other day, the goal is to set the table, create an environment, imagine safely, and then push people to leap, but I can't leap for you.

In terms of mentorship, I think there is a big difference between mentors and heroes. Heroism scales. There are lots of people who can point to someone and say, "I'm learning from that person's actions," whereas mentorship is a little bit overrated because it doesn't scale. As a result we can say, "I would succeed if I could only find a mentor," but of course you can't, and now you have a good excuse to hide.

DP: In a talk to publishers, you had said that in an era in which information can be accessed online, books are now like souvenirs, and so customers need a compelling reason to buy them because the contents that they contain are freely available. I think this same type of model can be relevant to many goods that people want to access, but they don't necessarily want to own.

How is the experience of accessing so much freely available content impacting the way we view products and services? What do you think might be the broader implications of this for the future?

SG: I would say the short answer is: scarcity drives economy—the word economy means scarcity. What used to be scarce were things made out of atoms and molecules, and what is scarce now is trust and connection. The way we acquire trust and connection is by sharing ideas. A book brings with it a combination of sharing ideas and the scarcity that comes from a physical good so it turns out, used in certain ways, it is a very effective tool for building trust and connection. But as an industry it's not clear to me that it has much of a future, because publishing books is built on scarce shelf space and a certain number of retailers, and both of those things are going away.

DP: *There is a great line in the conclusion of* Linchpin: *that we can't profitably get more average and it's our desire to be treated like individuals that will end this cycle. How do you build an organization that encourages interaction, gifts and connections, what might be referred to as a smart company of the future?*

SG: I would reinforce what I said earlier: if your organization is built on a scarcity that is going away, you think that your customer can't get the thing you make from anyone else cheaper, and you are busy defending your retail shelf space and machinery, then you are defending the wrong thing. If, on the other hand, your company built a culture and a mindset around, "How many people trust us? How many people want to hear from us? How many people talk about us to their peers? How many people are likely to define themselves by us?" then I think most of the steps become really clear.

DP: *Imagine you were able to magically go into the future twenty years, and all of the ideas from your books had been institutionalized and ingrained across a wide array of industries. What does a fully realized vision of everyone being artists and linchpins look like?*

SG: That's never going to happen. My ideas are already widely seen, but in a spotty sort of way. In any group of a hundred people you'll find two who feel driven to do this. Now, the reason that I don't think it's ever going to be widely accepted is because it is going to take many generations before we get out of the industrial mindset—I think that the fear that we've had built into us over a million years will probably never go away—and because the rules keep changing.

Now, because the rules keep changing, we have to keep reinventing. It's not like, "Wow, when are we going to get back to normal?" This is normal. We are living in the new normal. There is always going to be a scarce number of people who are willing to be brave enough to play with it. Once a whole bunch of people start doing it, what it will take to be brave will go up. But that is going to take a long time.

DP: You talk about the need to be remarkable, and for products to be so good that people feel compelled to talk about them. When I look across the country, it also seems that there is a strong yearning for authentic connections, locally sourced goods, handcrafted items, and all the sorts of products that are associated with what Chris Anderson has referred to as "the long tail."

How much of what you are describing is something new, and how much of it is a return to the way life used to be before the factories? Have we forgotten who we are, and are the types of ideas that you describe part of a broader trend to have more mindful and meaningful lives?

SG: I think that's an interesting question. I would say that in the Preindustrial Age, you didn't have any choices at all. There was one florist; there was one butcher; there was one baker. If you go to rural France and see how people live, no one talks about how great a loaf of bread was, because it was the only loaf of bread. So that part is new: this notion of so much abundance of choice that we have to make stuff that people will talk about.

I do agree that when the Internet and the Industrial Age commoditize something—when you can go to Target and, for six bucks, get something that used to cost a hundred—then at some point soon it becomes the new commodity. Then the only thing that is worth paying extra for is something that is not six dollars: like a story, like it's local, like it's (I think) better, whatever my definition of better is. So what I'm saying is, as the Industrial Age fades, there is a huge opportunity to step up and say, "I'm making something that is not the cheapest, but it's worth it. I'm making something unique and remarkable."

....

Seth Godin *is the author of 17 books that have been bestsellers around the world and have been translated into more than 35 languages. You might be familiar with his books* Linchpin, Tribes, The Dip *and* Purple Cow.

In addition to his writing and speaking, Seth is founder of squidoo.com, a fast growing, easy-to-use website. His blog (which you can find by typing "seth" into Google) is one of the most popular in the world. Before his work as a writer and blogger, Godin was Vice

President of Direct Marketing at Yahoo!, a job he got after selling them his pioneering 1990s online startup, Yoyodyne.

Recently, Godin once again set the book publishing on its ear by launching a series of four books via Kickstarter. The campaign reached its goal after three hours and ended up becoming the most successful book project ever done this way. His latest, The Icarus Deception, *argues that we've been brainwashed by industrial propaganda, and pushes us to stand out, not to fit in.*

DIGITAL LEADERSHIP

Erik Qualman

Erik Qualman just gets you excited about being a better leader in the Disruption Revolution. You can quickly see why he is referred to as a digital Dale Carnegie. We talked about *Digital Leader*, his follow-up to the international bestseller *Socialnomics*. This interview is packed with practical advice and examples such as:

- How social media creates a digital legacy
- Why multitasking is counterproductive and slows you down
- The importance to fail forward, fail fast, and fail better
- How mission statements and simplification drives success

Erik and I both are alumni of Michigan State University, and he was an Academic All-Big Ten member of our awesome basketball team. That confident, intelligent full-court perspective informs his view of the business world, and there is a sense of clarity and focus on how teams collaborate and work together that shines through this interview.

DP: One of the things that I really liked about your latest book Digital Leader is the way in which you connect digital leadership to leading a happy and purposeful life. I can see, in that sense, why people refer to you as a digital Dale Carnegie.

A lot of critics today say that social media is making us more shallow, undermines authentic connections, and is all about look-at-me cries for attention. Can you tell us a little bit about how creating what you refer to as a digital legacy relates to living a happy and purposeful life?

EQ: No matter what new tools come out, there are going to be people that misuse or abuse them. You saw that with email and search. But over time people get used to it and adjust, and eventually they stop listening to people that talk about me, me, me, so they're actually doing themselves a disservice by misusing or abusing the platforms. Only a small part of the crowd does that, and they quickly learn that no one really wants to hear talk about me, me, me.

The way that it relates to your life and your digital legacy is that we'll no longer look back and say, "What did I do with my life?" because with these tools you're constantly reminding yourself of what you're doing—you are creating a digital legacy, a permanent archive or footprint. Let's say that you're posting on Facebook, "Oh, I'm watching reruns of *Sanford and Son*," but all of a sudden you start to see some other people post, "I'm going down to the shelter to help with the soup kitchen," or, "I'm white-water rafting in West Virginia on a class IV rapid". You are reminded that you only have one life to live, and you need to take advantage of it. I'm not going to look back and say, "What did I do with my youth?" because we're kind of constantly reminded of it, so that's one of the beauties of social media.

The other piece is that you can use social media to lead others. For example, if you were to post to your entire network that you're going down to help Habitat for Humanity build a new house, that can inspire others to do it as well. Because you did it, they want to do it. That's why all of us are little media outlets, or little media beacons, because we now have the ability to broadcast this stuff. That presents huge possibilities when it comes to leadership—to reach more and more people and also to get their feedback to adjust your behavior as well.

You can affect your life today—your life, your leadership, and also your digital legacy—and attract more followers by doing stuff that's considered great. All of a sudden, people trying to affect the world, to change it for good, now have a much larger media outlet and a bigger support base. Think about something like Kickstarter with a social component of helping people fund projects. As a leader, those are the types of tools that are now at your disposal, so that you can get it out to a much broader base and effect many more people—both those that are working closely with you and those that you're directly affecting by the work that you're doing.

DP: Failure is traditionally seen as bad. You not only encourage it, but you compel leaders to fail forward, fail fast and fail better. Can you tell us a little bit about your perspective on how failure relates to digital leadership?

EQ: In this digital age, the only way we can increase our rate of learning is to increase our rate of failure. Most likely, we aren't going to get it right the first time, so it's important to fail forward, fail fast, and fail better.

A lot of people talk about how you gain value or learning through experience. Well, that's not really true. It's not all experiences, but rather evaluated experience. Otherwise you might just continue to practice bad habits, so that's what I mean by fail fast, fail forward. That's the "fail better" part—evaluating what didn't work and how to adjust in real-time based on that experience. In this day and age, the competition is fierce. You're probably not going to get it right the first time, so you need to iterate, iterate, iterate, iterate based on evaluating experiences.

For example, here's a personal story. I lost half a million dollars. Now that I have evaluated the experience a couple years later, I understand that it is one of the greatest things that ever happened to me. How can that be? First, let's put it in perspective: half a million dollars, for me, was almost my entire life savings. Think about that. What it really taught me is to ask: Why would I be saving all of this money?

Saving is good, but at the same time, if savings can get washed away in a minute—whether it's through a bad investment deal; or whether it's the market just gets completely flipped on its ear; you live in a country like Argentina and all of a sudden the money becomes worth nothing, the wheelbarrow's worth more than the money that's in that wheelbarrow, etc.—then why wouldn't I have used that for greater good? Why wouldn't I have donated some of that money to charity; or why wouldn't I have used it to build out my brand as a keynote speaker and an author? Why wouldn't I be buying outdoor boards, signs, places on Facebook, doing book signings, etc.?

Losing a half million dollars led to learning one of the greatest lessons in my life—understanding that this stuff could go away tomorrow. So while saving is good, hoarding is kind of bad. You need to reinvest and get something out there that is tangible. That was a great learning where I failed fast, failed forward, and failed better. It made my business so much better because now

I am more conscious of reinvesting, iterating, and evaluating experiences moving forward.

I use the example a lot when speaking of Gary Vaynerchuk. He owns Wine Library, a shop in Springfield, New Jersey, that sells wines both locally and also on the Internet. He started videos teaching people about wine and no one watched them at the beginning because they were more traditional, soft-spoken. Gary failed fast, but then he asked his fan base what to do, who said:

"Gary, we want the New Jersey Gary. We want you yelling. We want to hear Gary Vaynerchuk. We want to learn about wine in a fun way and that's the boring way, from all the books I have and other people that speak about wine that know no more, probably, about wine than you do. What you have is a way to really get me excited to learn about wine in a fun way."

He made adjustments and in three years went from selling four million dollars of wine to fifty million dollars. That is the entrepreneurial spirit of failing fast, failing forward, and failing better. The one advantage you have as an entrepreneur is you're more nimble and can do that, whereas publicly traded large companies fear failure when they have to report to Wall Street. Failing better levels the playing field for all of these small businesses out there.

DP: It's become the new conventional wisdom today that multitasking is critical in the digital era. In your book, you cite some research by the British Institute of Psychology indicating that checking your email while performing another creative tasks decreases your IQ in the moment by 10 points—a decrease that is equivalent to not sleeping for 36 hours and twice the impact of smoking marijuana.

Why is simplifying and focusing on one task at a time essential to winning, and what does it mean for digital leaders to adopt a philosophy of less is more?

EQ: This was one of the greatest learnings for me, at a personal level, when I did the research for my second book, *Digital Leader*. I thought I was this great multitasker, and then when I went into several research studies, including the one you mentioned, it turns out that from a neuroscience perspective, our brain doesn't function like a computer.

We can't do two creative tasks at once. We're actually switching tasks back and forth, and so when we switch tasks there is a big loss of efficiency. The brain needs to decide what's more important. Is this conference call I'm on more important, or should I be working on this marketing plan that I'm currently writing? When you're switching between tasks, you're not parallel-processing them. There is a loss in efficiency.

We think that we are saving time by multitasking, when in fact we are doing the exact opposite of what we're trying to achieve. The irony is almost laughable—that we're actually becoming less efficient when we try to multitask. Yet all of us, especially in the United States, wear our ability to multitask like a badge of honor.

Now, you can multitask on a creative and a physical task. For example, you could listen in on a conference call and wash your car or feed your baby—I wouldn't recommend feeding your baby unless you have a mute function on your phone—because that form of multitasking uses two different parts of your brain. Actually, the research shows that females are better at multitasking than males. But again, less is more. Eliminating multitasking has been a huge driver to my success. Now, I try to focus on two things that I absolutely need to get done each day. I write them down in the morning and make them happen.

DP: One of the core ideas from your first book, Socialnomics, *is that we need to learn how to navigate in a fully transparent society—that technology is essentially redefining the nature of relationships. Could you tell us a little bit more about what you think are the implications of a fully transparent society? For example, how does this impact product development, customer service, marketing, communications, and other core aspects of how organizations operate?*

EQ: At a high level, what you've seen already, obviously, is that soon there will be less cheating among husbands and wives. Other stuff you'll see are these revolutions being enabled by social communications tools, such as the democratic movements in Syria, Egypt, Brazil, or Turkey. Also, when you think about a business perspective, the dynamic changes to where the relationship between the customer and the company is so deep that the customer is demanding that relationship with the company and vice versa. That's the major shift.

From a personal standpoint, what I talk about in *Socialnomics,* is that historically, especially if you're Gen X or Baby Boomers, we kind of had a work persona, and then on the weekends we could do what we liked. We might have a different set of friends. If we are Al the accountant during the week, we're very meticulous and the best accountant, but on the weekend we are Avalanche Al, we go out bowling, we get crazy. We kind of can lead these two separate lives.

But in today's world we can't do that, and this is not something really for us to argue about anymore. Something fundamentally shifted that is irreversible, and we need to figure out how to deal with both the positive and negative impacts of this shift. A lot of the media like to talk about the negative side, because it's easy and sensational. "Oh, this Olympic swimmer and Prince Harry were almost half naked in the pool in Vegas." That's why I say, "What happens in Vegas stays on YouTube." That's the name of my next book.

But as we discussed earlier, the other side is that you can have a more positive impact. So how do you disable cyber-bullying rather than enable it? How do you become that link in the chain that breaks abuse? Or, how do you, as a leader—whether a political, nonprofit, or business leader—use all these tools to your advantage? The Red Cross can say, "We're human, just like you. We're trying to help human beings out," or a CEO of a company, like Zappos's Tony Shea can say, "This is what I stand for, this is my platform, and my company reflects that."

This is also why companies are taking on the personalities of the people that started them—the entrepreneurs—or the people that work there. Net-net, all this stuff is positive. There will always be negative and nefarious activity, but net-net all of this stuff is positive: when a politician can't lie as much because it is fully transparent, or companies can't be as deceiving as they were in the past. We just saw that with Snowden and the NSA. A lot of people have asked me my opinion on that. I'm not surprised. Look, this is a whole new shift in the world. Privacy is dead. There are a lot of advantages to that. There's some sadness to it as well, but we are in a new era.

DP: You have this great story in one of your TED talks of a turnaround CEO tasked with coming in and reorganizing companies. She says that basically her secret to success is to ask for a list of your 60 best customers and then ask them two simple questions: What do you buy from us? And why do you buy it from us?

I'm curious, in your experience working with so many different types of companies and meeting so many different leaders around the world, are they so focused on generating revenue and responding to the latest trends that they overlook the very basic things: How do they provide value to customers? How important is it for a company to have a mission statement or a sense of purpose that unites the whole team?

EQ: First, it is critically important as a company and also as an individual to simplify. You need to have that kind of one sentence mission statement, or as I call it, your moral compass or your digital compass, to always be there front and center. When I deal with business leaders around the globe, the best of the best are able to simplify, but it's also the hardest thing to do. And so to answer your question, yes, a lot of entrepreneurs and business leaders fail by getting off track and losing sight of the big picture.

For example, I see companies all the time pay and give incentives, internally or externally, for new customers. It might be the cable company is giving you a fifty-dollar monthly rate, whereas the current subscribers are paying a hundred, and they call up and say, "Hey, I've been a subscriber for six years, can I get the fifty-dollar rate?" And they say, "No. That is just for new-time people." So externally, companies do it, and then internally they incentivize marketing teams or PR teams, "Hey, we need to get new customers." And guess what? It costs six times as much to get a new customer or a new client.

The great companies understand it's all about fostering long-term relationships with their customer. They actively cultivate and encourage these relationships. For example, let's say that something negative happens on Twitter and a post goes viral. Well, every company is going to have a meeting at 8 a.m. on Saturday to get that resolved, but the great companies also have that meeting when 80 percent of their clients and customers are posting something positive about what they're doing. They know that long-term relationships are built on doing things that create and add value to their customers.

Think of an offline analogy. Let's say you run a retail store and someone comes up to you and says, "Hey, here's my suggestion card. I love what you guys do. Here's my suggestions on how you can take the business to the next level." If you're in that store and you go "Wait, wait, I've got to run to the back because this new customer might be upset about something," that is essentially burning that suggestion card right in front of your best customer's face. Most of us make these same kinds of mistakes online, but the best business leaders—getting back to what that turnaround CEO does—say, "Look, give me a list of your top clients, and I'm going to ask them, 'What do you buy from us and why do you buy it from us?'"

DP: You're a business school professor and you also teach leadership around the world. What do you say to people who think that they're just not very good leaders or they're not very innovative? Also, how do you teach people to find a balance between being a great leader versus being a team player and following someone else's directions, supporting their efforts?

EQ: Jim Collins showed in *Good to Great* that the best leaders are not necessarily the most charismatic and dynamic. Instead, they are these softer spoken types who would probably say no if they were asked, "Are you a leader?" All of us lead someone, whether that is our family or 5,000 employees. So first, it is important for us to understand that if you turn the video camera on, and you're going to get a fully transparent wall across all of these social channels, what do you want them to see? What will be your digital legacy? How are you leading by example?

The second piece about innovation is the one thing I start a lot of my lectures or discussions off with. Everyone in this room knows something, or has an idea, that no one here has thought about, or knows something that no one here knows. That is basically the power of human beings. How do you leverage that capacity?

All of us have innovation inside of us, but not all of us have it like Steve Jobs, where we can actually make that vision become a reality. And so, a lot of times you have to work together as a team to make that happen, or find someone whose specialty is taking that idea and taking it to the next level.

DP: You say that social media should start with the CEO down, and that all employees across an organization should have a vested interest in social engagement. Why is it problematic to trust an intern or entry-level person to manage social relationships? How do you leverage the strengths of a team while maintaining a consistent balance in terms of messaging across an entire organization?

EQ: Social media is less about technology and is all about living and breathing—it is your customer, your client, so it is essentially going to touch every facet of the business. There are two things that drive the success of any company. First, getting the right people on the team—and think about LinkedIn, a social platform that is completely changing the way we recruit and replacing the paper resume. The second piece is word-of-mouth. Word-of-mouth is now on digital steroids. In fact, I say that word-of-mouth is world-of-mouth because of social media. So these two things have historically driven businesses—getting the right people on the team and word-of-mouth—and now they're all being driven by social media tools and these digital outlets.

The core of the message is simplification. That is why you need a company mission statement so that everyone knows: this is what we stand for and this is what we do. That makes the messaging very consistent across the company. A lot of times I'm hired to come in and I'll ask three questions. "Why do you exist as a company? How do you differ from your competition? If your company were to go away tomorrow, what's the loss to society?" And that's more important for generation Y, especially, not, "What do we do?" but, "How do we do it?"

Most of the time their answers are inconsistent, whereas the great companies will be consistent because they've simplified their business and their message. Everyone knows why they are there, what they are doing and what they stand for. Now, the reason you have your whole team do social and you simplify the message to be the same across the board is because otherwise you just can't handle it. You want to have the right person, in the right moment, answer the question quickly, so if you have five people or an intern in marketing, or just two people on the customer service side, then you're going to be overwhelmed. You won't be able to handle all of this.

The next step, beyond that model, is that you really want your customers and clients to start answering those questions. The great companies have customers and clients post videos on YouTube about how you innovate with their products. They post, "This is how you do this," and so you start to get this relationship between the customer and the company where they almost become one. It's tough to get our minds around that, but that is just where it is all going, and the great companies have already started to do that.

DP: You referenced LinkedIn at the beginning of your last answer. In one of your recent keynotes you mentioned a trend that in many organizations, marketing and communications teams are taking over the management of LinkedIn from human resources departments. I'm curious if you could tell us a bit more about that and also how social media might help visual leaders to shape internal corporate culture.

EQ: On LinkedIn, the reason you are seeing that shift is that a lot of times human resources departments didn't grow up around these digital tools, or aren't used to understanding how to put the best face forward or find talent digitally, whereas a lot of the marketing teams are used to doing it. It is the same concept of trying to get a new customer digitally, so they understand that mindset. That is why, a lot of times, they take over LinkedIn to get it under control. The good organizations have internal teams help train the human resources department, so that everyone can work side by side, as they get it up and running at the right level.

Now, from an internal perspective, tools like Yammer or some of these internal innovation tools can actually even give points and rewards, but more importantly you are also showing that you respect people. "Hey, Susie just sold a deal. Way to go, Susie, that's been the toughest region for us to crack. Way to go!" You're starting to see that internal innovation tools provide a lot of motivation, and that is essentially the influence of social within the organization. Take it a step further—when time and distance can be an issue, now you can blast the same message out to the entire company so it helps motivate that individual but also motivates other people, like, "Whoa, if Susie can do it in that region, then I certainly can do it over here."

DP: You basically tell us that we should all ask ourselves the question, "What is the mark that you want to leave in this world?" I really love this concept that you have of being "flawsome"—that through our flaws we can showcase how awesome we are.

I'm curious, does leadership start from within, and how does being honest with our weaknesses and limitations help us to become more awesome?

EQ: I love that term flawsome, it's from Ann Handley. Think about it on a personal level. No one really likes the guy or girl that is perceived to be perfect. Obviously, no one is perfect, but no one likes the person who is perceived to be perfect. You like someone that is like, "Wow, that person is like me. They made a mistake out here, or did X, Y and Z, so I can relate more to that person than to someone that is supposed to be this perfect person." That is what I like the most about the idea of being flawsome. It allows you to provide faster connections in the sense that you can relate to someone.

Think of the example from earlier: oh, Erik Qualman, that's the bozo who lost half a million dollars! I lost a fair amount of money doing something a little too aggressive. That is the type of stuff where the leader, through flaws, can show just how awesome you are. You can see countless examples in some of my speeches and the book of companies or individuals making mistakes. It all goes back to failing fast, failing forward, and failing better.

"How do I take advantage of this mistake?" Not "How do I hide it?" How do I, being cliché, take these digital lemons and make digital lemonade? As a company and as an individual, when you make a mistake, it hurts and stings in the short term, but all of a sudden put a smile on your face and understand, "How do I take advantage of this?"

DP: You have all these incredible actionable ideas. When I think of things like posting it forward, sort of the online equivalent of paying it forward, and a focus on identifying who you are, who you want to uplift in the world and how you're going to make them feel, I can't help but think that like you're describing an ideal world that I want for myself and my children.

So I'm curious, do you think digital leaders should be more involved in a dialogue about leadership of the world? How might all of the incredible, innovative efforts of leaders like yourself help to shape a better national or international dialogue about solving problems or healing divisions? How can principles of digital leadership be applied to transcending some of the polarizing differences that sometimes appear to be tearing the world apart?

EQ: This is what gets me excited—it's why I love talking about this stuff and writing about it. Like you mentioned, it kind of gets to that utopian ideal. The beautiful thing is that we are never going to get to that utopia, but the closer we can get to it, the better off we can all be. This goes back to Maya Angelou's famous quote "If you don't like something, change it. If you can't change it, change your attitude. Don't complain."

With all these tools at our disposal, more than ever we actually do have the capability to help fix and resolve an issue if we don't like it. I catch myself if I start complaining, let's say, about politics in the US, and say, "The government is me." It's up to me. If I don't like something, I can enable it and effect that change. That is why you are starting to see some of these revolutions around the world. They are not started because of social media, but they are dramatically helped by these digital tools to hopefully make the world a better place in the long-term.

That is the hope we all aspire to, and that is why I get excited about digital leadership. The best thing that digital leaders can do is put their best effort forward. Do your best and forget the rest, essentially hoping that the ones that are following them are also going to have their own tribes, their own followers. And so we perpetuate that with the post it forward, and hopefully continue to make the world better off than we found it, and that is all we can hope for.

Called a Digital Dale Carnegie, **Erik Qualman** *was voted the 2nd Most Likeable Author in the World behind Harry Potter's J.K. Rowling.* Fast Company *ranks him as a Top 100 Digital Influencer and* PC Magazine *lists his blog as a Top 10 Social Media blog. A frequently requested international keynote speaker (42 countries), he has been featured on almost every media outlet including* 60 Minutes, The Wall Street Journal, *and* ABC News.

He is listed as a Top 50 MBA Professor and is no stranger to the executive suite, having served as the Head of Marketing at Travelzoo®; today he sits on several company boards. Yet, he may be best known for writing and producing the world's most watched social media video. Socialnomics *was a finalist for the "Book of the Year." Qualman was Academic All-Big Ten in basketball at Michigan State University and Erik was honored as the Michigan State University Alum of the Year. He recently gave the commencement address to 4,000 people at the University of Texas and has given keynotes for Coach, Sony PlayStation, IBM, Facebook, Starbucks, M&M/Mars, Cartier, Montblanc, TEDx, Polo, UGG, Nokia, Google, and more. He also holds a Guinness Book of World Record for the longest continuous podcast.*

THE FOUNDER'S DILEMMAS

Noam Wasserman

Noam Wasserman's work on the early dilemmas faced in starting a company is essential reading for anyone that wants to found or invest in startups. *The Founder's Dilemmas* is an instant business classic, a mix of practical insights backed up by data from 10,000 companies. We dive into some interesting results from his book, including:

- Why 65% of all failures are due to people problems
- How success increases the likelihood of being fired
- Why contingency plans are like prenuptial agreements
- What investors can do differently based on his research

Noam's class on entrepreneurship at Harvard Business School is one of the best in the world. As a former aspiring academic myself, I consider Noam to be one of those rare professors that teaches because he loves to teach and make a difference. He seems to embody integrity and his commitment to helping founders is a true inspiration.

DP: During your Ph.D. research at Harvard, you came across some interesting statistics in a paper on venture capital that 65% of all failures in startups are the result of team problems. From reading your book and listening to a number of interviews, it sounds like this was a big "a-ha" moment for you that ultimately shaped the course of your work for the last 10 years.

How did this discovery lead you to focus on what you refer to as the founder's dilemmas?

NW: There was a paper published in 1989 by Bill Sahlman, who is now a colleague of mine here at Harvard Business School. It was a long paper in which Bill explored what was back then (and still is in some ways) the black box of venture capital. What do VCs do?

The paper explored all the different parts of the job: How do VCs get deal flow or have potential deals coming in their door that they can consider? How do they do due diligence on those deals? How do they go about crafting and negotiating the term sheets for the deals they want to pursue? How do they join the board and help build company value once they sign on? Essentially, the paper explored the full range of tasks that a VC has to do.

Fortunately, along the way, Bill also thought to ask, "Tell us about the part of your portfolio we'd never hear about: the ventures you won't be bragging about, the ventures that when they hit key milestones, you won't issue press releases; the ventures that were high potential enough to get your check but then failed despite all that promise and the impact that their founders wanted to have."

Within that realm of the ventures that failed, he tried to categorize all the reasons for failure so that he could understand the core factors. In some ways the initial list included a bunch of things you would expect: product-market fit problems, there were problems with functions that had to coalesce to build a product but couldn't, etc. Those factors were indeed on the list, but they only accounted for 35% of the reasons for failure.

The preponderant reason for failure was the team. Accounting for 65% of the failures, the biggest problems involved people: the friction between the founders, or the tensions between them and the hires brought in to complement them. The messy, subjective, "soft," people issues were, in the end, the biggest reasons for the failure of these high-potential startups.

That number hit me like a ton of bricks. When we head into founding, we all hear about the high rate of failure within startups. We can wring our hands about it, but it seems to be something we can't do anything about. We simply take on that hazard of failure when we're founding. To me, it suggests something very different: "Where do we start in terms of tackling this risk?" The 65% number said to me, "This is where we start."

If early on we can understand what those ill-fated people decisions are, then we can diagnose the real risks we are taking when introducing different types of people to our ventures, and find ways to manage those risks or make better 'people decisions' from the get go. This is where we could really move the needle in terms of reducing the rate of failure. We don't have to take failure as a given. We can actually do something about it. We can focus on the biggest reason for failure and find actionable ways to reduce the chances of it being a problem.

DP: What I really like about The Founder's Dilemmas *is that you frame all of these people problems in language that is very easy to understand. For example, you frame addressing things like equity splits as akin to a prenuptial agreement, and you group the important decisions all founders face into categories you refer to as the three Rs: Relationships, Roles, and Rewards. Can you tell us a little bit about the three Rs and the reason contingency plans are important with respect to things like equity splits, particularly in the beginning when there are so many variables and uncertainties?*

NW: The three Rs are a way to capture what the research has shown are the biggest make-or-break early decisions within the founding team. When you are founding, there are so many things you need to tackle, that if we were to say to you, "Here's a long list of other things you need to worry about. You must take care of every risk on the horizon and every uncertainty you might face," that's likely to overwhelm and distract an entrepreneur.

What we have to do is highlight for them the most important ones: "Here are the ones not to ignore. Here are the ones to be learning how to tackle productively." The three Rs—Relationships, Roles and Rewards—have the most impact on whether the founding team is going to become a magical founding team or whether it is going to blow apart, and whether the foundation is solid enough to build a valuable, high-growth venture.

First, Relationships—the prior relationships you are tapping in order to find co-founders. They can range from the people you know socially but not professionally; people you know foremost in a professional sense, though maybe you have also developed a social relationship along the way as colleagues; and finally, acquaintances or people you don't really know well in either a professional or social sense. You go to different places to find each of these kinds of people. There are different attributes that each bring to the team that could either facilitate or hinder developing a robust working dynamic within team.

For instance, lots of research into founding teams has been done on what is called homophily, or the tendency of birds of a feather to flock together. If you co-found with friends and family, there's going to be a greater likelihood that you're going to overlap or be redundant with each other. You might be on the same page when it comes to looking at the world through the same lens, but the skills that you bring are likely to overlap, leaving a lot of holes on the team because of the different skills you didn't seek out. There will be more tension because of the potential overlap between you and people similar to you. There will also be incorrect assumptions you make about each other's abilities, tendencies, work habits etc. Just because you know and like each other socially, does that mean you jointly have the competencies that will build a promising venture?

The data set that I tap in the book covers 10,000 founders in the tech and life sciences industry, the two biggest industries for high-potential ventures. Across those 10,000 founders, by far the most common source tapped to find co-founders is friends and family. More than half of the founding teams within my data set are co-founding with the people that they have a prior social relationship but not a professional relationship. The analysis of the stability within those founding teams also shows that the friends and family teams are the least stable.

This is a microcosm of founding pitfalls: Often, the most common decisions made by founders are the ones that are the most fraught with danger.

For this in particular, the common decision of choosing friends and family is more likely to introduce bigger risks and to cause more problems for you. That's not to say you should never be founding with friends and family, or that you should avoid anyone you have that prior social relationship with! Those teams can indeed be very successful, but founders also have to acknowledge—and act on the knowledge—that they are taking on some big risks and could be hurting themselves and/or their ventures in some ways down the road.

The good news is that there are actionable things that you can do when founding with friends and family to manage those risks and reduce the chances of a team blow up. There are some common actions that I've seen work time after time, but also some that have to be tailored to the specific situation. If you don't proactively take those actions, the analyses and data show that you are likely to become a less stable team than what you are hoping for.

Second, Roles, or delineating decision-making—How are we going to split up the roles within the venture? Are we going to have distinctive arenas where we are each taking charge of leading a part? Or are our roles going to overlap? If you are more similar to each other, then there is a greater likelihood that you are going to have overlapping roles. Overlaps also can introduce tensions related to titles. A lot of founders like to tell themselves or their friends, "Oh, it doesn't matter what title I have," only to later realize that it actually did make a difference, and they then go to the mat to get whatever title is attractive to them. Oftentimes, it's the CEO title that introduces the most tensions within the team.

There are also key Roles decisions at the team level. Are we going to be making decisions where each founder gets one vote? Is that going to lead to ties if we have a two-person founding team? What happens when we have a 1-1 vote? You might only run into that 1% of the time, but you are making so many decisions together, and some of them are pretty momentous ones. If you are grid locking on even some 1-1 votes, how are you going to resolve it without heightening the tensions in the team and slowing down the decision-making process?

Even if you start out as "each founder gets one vote," you need to think through how it's going to change over time. What do you do as you grow to 10 or 20 people? Is equal decision-making going to be able to continue or not? Are you going to have to adopt more of a hierarchy? Are you going to tell your co-founders that they should take less of a role because now we're going to have a person at the top who is the decision maker, where the buck stops, and now they're not going to be involved in a lot of these momentous decisions that the company will be facing? Is that going to cause problems in terms of being able to still have that magical glue you had early on?

These are the types of common decisions that are hard to undo within the roles and decision-making category. Our tendency is to resist making them, but the data and analysis shows that doing so introduces risk and increases the likelihood of failure.

Third, Rewards, namely the equity or ownership stake—representing the potential to gain from the growth of the venture and from its exit. This is often the most important and most sensitive topic, especially in high-potential ventures. It's also an arena in which the easy short-term decisions, where you are avoiding conflict or reducing tensions, often can come back to hurt you in the long run.

"Punting" on the equity discussion—not having it, not having it deeply enough, or not having a serious discussion about the potential pitfalls on the road ahead—is one of the key things that can come back to bite the team. I'll give you some of the data around this phenomenon. Within my data set, 73% of the teams split the equity within the first month of the venture, essentially right at founding, and the majority of those teams then put that equity split in stone. They make it into a static split: "This is what the ownership is."

They are making these momentous decisions during the early heady days, the passionate days, when confidence is brimming over about where they can go and what they can do. They are not considering the bumps in the road they will be facing, the more expected-case scenarios (and almost never the worst-case scenario) that could render an early equity split obsolete, leaving the team without any easy way to readjust the stakes to match the realities of the team's changes, or to replace a founder who has left.

During those early uncertain days, analyses show you are much more likely to apply the "1/n rule," splitting the equity equally among all members as a way to punt on the discussion. But then going forward a team may face a whole slew of uncertainties. On a venture level, there will be ways in which the strategy and the business model will be changing. These strategy shifts will affect the team. Early roles will likely change to adapt to the venture's new and evolving needs. Some team members may not be able to scale or adjust, and may no longer fit their roles. You may need to seek out a new skill set as you move into new arenas, and you may need to free up equity to attract the new hire that has the skill set that will make your pivot success-ful. In sum, there are going to be some dramatic ways in which the expected contributions diverge from the actual contributions, even if every member is sincere about their intentions and commitments.

Beyond the team-related uncertainties introduced by the business, other uncertainties can also be introduced by team members' personal factors.

During the early days, are you making the assumption that everyone is going to be fully committed (100%) and giving their all to the venture? Even with the best of intentions from everyone, at the bottom of the roller coaster ride—as the weight of the world is falling in and you are facing really tough times—everyone's commitment is going to be tested. Are there going to be people scaling back because of challenges at home, or challenges stemming from "the difficulties of founding" entering their personal lives? Or, are they going to have to cut back because of life events that are happening? For example, someone can have the best of intentions early on, but then someone gets sick in the family, or the founder him or herself gets sick and has to drop out or cut back on his or her time. Each of the founders should realize that there is a whole bunch of things—things that are going to test people's commitment to the venture—that they can't foresee in the early days that can precipitate dramatic changes to how members contribute to the venture's growth.

During the passionate, confident, early stage of the startup, if people neglect to give these uncertainties serious consideration, they are likely setting themselves up for trouble down the road. Almost certainly, there will be ways in which the team members' contributions, even with the best of intentions, are not going to match expectations.

Founders need to enact a more dynamic agreement that will articulate the expectations and the principles they'll be using to allocate the equity, while also allowing for changes to the equity should someone fall short. Ironing out the "what if" scenarios before they occur will also likely give the decisions a sense of objectivity, making future changes less personal than they would feel should a change go into effect later. It's a tougher dialogue—a conflict ridden one—to have, but you need to accept as a group the idea that you're going to face uncertainties and changes. This is why I say that accounting for contingencies is analogous to a prenuptial agreement. Though the two agreements are clearly different (and when viewed in context, can imply very different things), they are similar in that they give a team a pre-mediated course of action for when the unexpected happens. Crafting a dynamic and thoughtful founding agreement is also a great way to have proactive discussions about the pitfalls you face and how to proactively deal with them.

DP: One of the issues you raised in the book is that 50% of founders are replaced as CEOs by the time they've raised the series C round of financing, and 73% of those replaced are fired by the board. What I find particularly interesting is that you said greater early success often leads to a greater likelihood of being fired.

Why is it important to think ahead about possibly firing yourself, and why does greater early success actually increase the likelihood of being fired?

NW: This is especially true for a lot of early, first-time, passionate, confident founders. This is possibly the biggest rude awakening that they have along the way: their success can actually breed their demise or heighten the chance that they will be replaced. There are two key ways in which the chances of that happening are heightened. Let's take the situation from the perspective of two milestones (1) the milestone of completing product development and (2) the milestone of raising each round of financing.

During the early days of the startup, the imperative is a technical or a scientific one, where you're developing the product or service to arrive at something customers are willing to pay for, something that is going to be able to change the world. In the early days, the technical or scientific founder is the perfect person to be leading the charge, or a project team, since the knowledge that they bring to the table is exactly what is needed at that stage. As you finish product development—as the molecule is almost ready for prime time, and the system is ready to be shown and sold to customers—at that point the startup has graduated to the next level. You reach this milestone and it is one of the biggest celebrations in your startup's life. You have reached the promised land of completing product development.

Now let's look at the second milestone. During the early days you're cash poor, living the Ramen noodle lifestyle, scratching and clawing your way to get the product developed. Then finally you're able to attract an investor and close a round of funding. You now have someone who believes in you enough to invest in your venture. That's a milestone to celebrate.

But what the data shows is that those two milestones—completing product development and raising the rounds of financing—actually heighten the chances that you're going to get replaced as CEO.

The first of those, completing product development, is a major inflection point in terms of the skills that are needed for the company to be built. It's no longer just a technical challenge you have to surmount. You now need to figure out how to build a sales engine—make sales calls, garner a loyal customer base etc. You don't have any experience in sales. You don't even know how to interview a salesperson or hire them to do that job for you, let alone build and manage a sales team.

That's just one of the new functions that has to be built at this point. You have to understand financial statements and reports for the first time, so you can understand where is the growth, where is growth not happening, and whether you're outstripping revenues by having expenses that are too high. Is scaling becoming a problem for your cash position? Marketing is another example of a function you've never worked in. Now as CEO you have to build out, integrate, manage, and track.

That perfect early leader who excelled at managing the technical or scientific challenge often doesn't have the skills needed to turn this idea into a viable, thriving company. That's why hitting that stage where the product has been completed heightens the chances that there's possibly someone else that should lead the company into its next phase.

Then there's the fundraising side. You're getting "rocket fuel" from the investors to enable the fast growth, investment in the product, and team hiring. That is also going to change the power dynamic within the company. You're now going to have different people sitting on the board with you. You sold equity ownership to people who often have a different view of the company, and a different set of motivations, than you do. At the same time as the requirements on the CEO have changed, these people have a different perspective on how to match the CEO to those new requirements.

When you put together the new stage for the company and the raising of outside financing, the chances of the founder-CEO being replaced go up dramatically.

The board's message that we think there should be a CEO change can feel like a "punch in the stomach" to a founder-CEO, especially for the founder-CEOs who have been succeeding smashingly. (Jack Dorsey, the founder-CEO of Twitter, used those words, "punched in the stomach," when he talked about getting that message.) This visceral reaction is understandable. The founder birthed the idea and made many sacrifices to raise the baby, only to be told, "You are no longer the best parent for this baby."

It's a key inflection point for the company to get the right person to lead the charge, and a key inflection point for the founder personally. There's a very unhappy "fearless leader" who's been leading the charge with all the people he or she brought in and the culture that he or she has built. If the founder is unhappy with this change, it can be devastating, possibly hampering the company's growth and even its survival. This inflection point could be make-or-break for the venture.

That fork in the road is the most dramatic and the most clear example of what I call "the rich vs. king" challenge. It's at this juncture where we could bring in someone else who has better skills to grow the value of the company, though it will mean that the founder needs to leave the throne and take a back seat. If the company can grow a lot more and become more valuable, then the dethroned founder's equity stake might be worth a lot more. That is a tradeoff you might be making in the direction of giving up the reins and letting them bring in a successor.

The flipside is you can choose to remain king at that point, and insist, "I'm going to stick around as the CEO of this venture." You can do this by either resisting the succession, or by making early decisions that prevent you from relinquishing ownership and/or board seats. Those early decisions could enable you to stay CEO, be the visionary who's bringing it to market, translate that vision into actual product, and see the impact. But the data shows that you are going to be building a lot less valuable of a company.

That is the tradeoff: less rich, but king. Going down the other path would mean you probably won't remain king but would have the potential to become a lot richer. It's at the inflection point of the question of founder-CEO succession when rich vs. king tradeoffs are the starkest.

But there are other inflection points beginning very early on that can also influence the rich vs. king tradeoff. For example, the founding team decisions: Should I be a solo founder? Should I be the ultimate king within the venture or bring in co-founders, share a bunch of the decision making, and give up equity stakes? You can play that mindset out through other decisions, such as divvying roles (Am I going to fight to remain CEO, or am I going to give someone else the reins that might be better as CEO?), splitting equity (How much are you going to allocate to the rest of your team?), making your hires (Should you attract all-stars who may outshine you and may be needy on the salary/equity front, or should you take junior folks who are easier to control and have modest expectations for equity and salary?), and financing the venture (Are you going to bootstrap and remain king, or are you going to bring in the resources that you need even though doing so may imperil your control over the venture?).

But the succession stage is where it's the clearest. You can see echoes of how even the earliest decisions you make coalesce in some way to leading you down very different paths in terms of the value of the venture you're going to be able to build vs. the control that you're going to be able to keep of the vision and of where the venture is headed.

DP: If 65% of failure comes from team problems, then ultimately this places more responsibility on investors, who are supposed to be more experienced in leadership, particularly in relationship to first-time founders, the implication being that they invest in the wrong team, not necessarily the wrong product.

Based on your research, how might investors evaluate opportunities differently?

NW: From the investor perspective it's key for them to be able to understand which of these early decisions are going to heighten the risks. When investors are going in, they're not looking for "Let me invest in a team that's likely to blow up." They should be looking to invest in a team that's carefully considered the early decisions, that's built an arrangement that will be sustainable and robust against a bunch of the pitfalls that they might face.

They should, as part of their due diligence, look at the founding decisions we talked about. I'm stunned by a number of investors I've run into who actively try to avoid looking at these decisions. They say, "The equity split is just within the founding team. That's up to them to decide. It's not for me to evaluate whether it's good or not, push back on it, make sure that it was done well, and maybe ask that it be reassessed." That's just one example. Investors need to be able to understand which of these early decisions heightens the tensions within the team.

It's not a good thing for investors to be investing in a team that has latent or hidden tensions that are going to come back to bite the team, and in turn the investors. So from the investor perspective, there are two ways investors should be playing a key role. One, which you were focusing on, is their selection of the teams to begin with, whether they are assessing them correctly and whether they understand the ways in which the early decisions haven't reared their heads yet but could down the road.

However, once the due diligence is completed and an investor decides to go forward, it's important for the investor to stay involved as a mentor, as a guide down the road on which the founder has never traveled. Investors, especially ones who have joined a board, should be a critical input, giving guidance about the key, far-reaching decisions that a startup is making. They should leverage their experience to plug in the portions of the road map that the founders lack.

Back on the founders' side, it's important to note that there's also some conflict of interest that the investors have in terms of playing that mentorship role. Such conflicts can impact some of their objectivity as they advise, perhaps influencing how they paint the pros and cons and the pitfalls that are coming. Investors might not even realize they're going to be misaligned with the founders.

For that reason, I believe that there is a real need for a third-party mentor who can act as an independent board member rather than an investor board member. Such a person will likely be a lot better at being a CEO-mentor, painting the full range of objective advice for the founders. That said, the investors should still play a large role in plugging in segments of the road map that the founders (especially if they're first-timers) lack. This will enable the founders to make better, more informed, and forward-thinking decisions than when they operated without a solid road map.

Noam Wasserman *is a professor at Harvard Business School and the author of the bestselling book* The Founder's Dilemmas: Anticipating and Avoiding the Pitfalls That Can Sink a Startup. *For more than a decade, his research has focused on founders' early decisions that can make or break the startup and its team. At HBS, he developed and teaches an MBA elective, "Founders' Dilemmas," for which he was awarded the HBS Faculty Teaching Award and the Academy of Management's 2010 Innovation in Pedagogy Award. In 2011, the course was also named one of the top entrepreneurship courses in the country by* Inc. *magazine.*

CHOOSE YOURSELF

James Altucher

James Altucher has been up and down, made/lost millions, founded 20 companies, written numerous books, and as his Twitter bio says, "for some reason, I've turned myself inside out and all my guts spilled out onto my blog." We talked about his latest book *Choose Yourself* and how to lay a foundation that empowers success. Highlights include:

- Why Google is an example of how giving leads to prosperity
- Why success all starts with a strong physical, emotional, mental and spiritual foundation
- What Buddy Media teaches us about pivoting and uncertainty
- How failure is just another word for change

James throws convention out the window and gives an unfiltered, honest, intelligent but also candid view of a world turned upside-down. Reading and listening to him is like holding up a mirror—he just shows you how things are, instead of what you want to see. This is a fun and engaging read, and was an absolute pleasure of a conversation.

DP: There's something about your brutal honesty that really evokes this kind of visceral feeling and connection with people. I think you are also particularly vulnerable and willing to talk about your failures, which in many ways, goes against conventional wisdom. Why do you think your ideas of a world out of balance resonate with such a broad audience?

JA: The reason why the world out of balance message resonates is because the world is already turned upside-down. It's not that people are saying to themselves, "Oh, I need to repair myself because the world is going to get out of balance." So when people hear that phrase, they wake up, realizing it's already happening and they need to react quickly.

Right now, we live in a weird economy. The U.S. Economy has, technically, been out of a recession since Q1, 2009, but everybody still feels bad. You talk to your neighbor and they'll say, "Why are we still in a recession?" Nobody realizes we haven't been in a recession for four years. People actually think we're in a depression—they think it's even worse than a recession. The reality is they're both correct and they're both incorrect. What's happened is the world is just turned upside-down.

The Fortune 500 has started firing all their employees and replacing all their employees with temp staffers. This was just on the cover of *USA Today* a few days ago, but it happened to have been written in my book months ago. There is no political blame for this. There is no economic blame for this. There is no policy that needs to be changed. It's just the way of the world.

The idea that living a corporate life in a cubicle is safe was true for maybe a short period of time, but that time has completely passed. I know this from a variety of viewpoints, ranging from my investing to my advising, to my consulting and so on. Also, just from the feedback I get from my readers about my stories.

I've been through a lot of success and a lot of failure, and the failure has been a lot more painful to me than the success has been good for me. If anything, in some cases, the success ruined my life until I learned how to deal with it. What's happening to the world now is like a macrocosm of what happened to me personally, and what's happening to everybody personally. Society is just a reflection of all our individual psyches or souls—or whatever you want to call it—kind of aggregated together.

In a society, you have different factions. Like in Egypt right now, you have the more liberal people who want a democracy, you have the Muslim Brotherhood, you have other groups, and all the factions need to work together in order to have a functioning government that can grow and prosper. Or else, if they really don't work together, there's going to be a revolt.

Well, this happens on a corporate level and this happens on a personal level. So if you grow up thinking that owning a house, going to college and having a corporate job for the rest of your life is going to be the safe way to happiness and success, then there's going to be a revolt. You are going to end up being severely disappointed, perhaps failing at something, perhaps getting really depressed over this failure, perhaps getting sick over this failure—there's going to be a revolt inside of you.

So when you say "disruption," it's one thing to say, "Okay, the middle man is going away." This is a common example of an economic disruption that people talk about. "The middle man is going away—there's not going to be any more bookstores, so there are business opportunities to connect readers with books." In every industry, there is a type of disruption and people have known about this. But this doesn't really help you individually. You still have to deal with the fact that the world, in every way, is different from what you thought it was.

DP: So then what do you do? Where do you begin to start choosing yourself?

JA: First, you have to take a step back. You have to build a foundation to your house and make sure it's a strong foundation. What I describe in my book *Choose Yourself,* and what I had to do when my foundation was no good and my house sank—I mean, I literally lost my house, went broke, lost my family, lost millions of dollars—I had to get up and say to myself, "I still have a family to take care of, how am I going to do this?"

In my head I was telling myself, "I'm broke, I'm incapable of getting a job, I have no potential or opportunity, I'm going to have to kill myself so that my kids will have a better life because of my life insurance policy." So I valued my life insurance policy more than I valued my potential to be a good father. What I really had to do was to take a step back and get healthy. This doesn't only mean eating well or exercising, although that's part of it. You have to be healthy on every level.

I identified four levels I needed to be healthy in—physical, emotional, mental and spiritual: (1) Physical—which is eating right, exercising and sleeping well; (2) Emotional, which means you always want to be preaching to the choir. You never want to be arguing with people who are never going to listen to you. "Once you're explaining, you're losing" is the saying. You only want to be around people you love and who love you; people who inspire you and people who you're inspired by; (3) Mental health, so you always want to exercise your idea-muscle. Your idea-muscle will atrophy just like any other muscle in your body if you don't exercise it every day. If I don't walk for two weeks, I'm not going to be able to walk without physical therapy. If I don't exercise my idea-muscle every day, within two weeks, I'm not going to be able to come up with good ideas.

For most people, their idea-muscle has totally atrophied. One thing that I do is try to come up with 10 ideas every day. It could take a month, it could take six months, it could take a year, but eventually, you become an idea machine. You become like "Super Idea Man," your idea-muscle is that strong. I would say 99% of people let go of their idea-muscle because they think, "I'm in my cubicle, I have my college degree, I own my home, I'm safe." But that could turn out to be incorrect.

Finally (4), in order for everything to connect, you have to have your spiritual body healthy. Which doesn't necessarily mean you have to get down on your knees and pray to God, it just means you have to be grateful for the abundance that's in your life. Even at your worst moments, there are plenty of things to be grateful for. Your body feels better and more present, and more capable of dealing with the issues around you, if you're feeling grateful right now, as opposed to regretting something in the past or being anxious about something in the future. I call that "time traveling," when you are regretting or anxious.

Being grateful and being present exercises those spiritual muscles and adds to your spiritual health. So those four categories—I call them the "four bodies," physical, emotional, mental, spiritual—is what I call "the daily practice" in *Choose Yourself*. And believe it or not, as corny as that sounds, that is the way to deal with the economic disruption that is occurring right now.

From that foundation, you can build the house. You can then say, "I'm going to have 20 ideas. These are the one's that are good, I'm going to know how to execute on them and I'm going to be able to deal with this economic disruption that is happening. Maybe I'll start a business, maybe I'll introduce two other people who are starting a business, maybe I'll be an artist."

DP: I've been meditating for 20 years and I feel like when you have this change in the mind and body, it will radiate out to others like spokes on a wheel. Is it like that?

JA: It's very true. For example, many people judge a book by its cover. They see my book and it's called *Choose Yourself*. Some people will look at that cover and say, "Oh, you're just all about yourself," which is totally the exact opposite of the book's intent. People will say, "You have to help society. You have to deal with global warming or the poor."

The response is two things: (1) If your room is dark, then you need to clean it. And in order to clean a dark room, you have to open the window and let the sunlight come in. Meditation, for instance, is how you open the window and let the sunlight come in. And if you can't clean your own room, you're not going to be able to help the rest of the world. You have to start with yourself; (2) And this is related to regret and anxiety, it takes rain in order for a garden to bloom. If you want your own garden to bloom, then you have to be able to hope for rain because that's how you learn how to handle disruption.

Disruption is almost a bad word, it sounds negative—like an earthquake or something. Disruption is natural. Chaos and collisions are how worlds are created. It's how the human being was created. All life was created through collisions and disruption. So disruption is actually the natural state of things. Raining, so a garden can bloom, is the natural state of things. If you try to resist that, you're going to be stuck in the old, pseudo-comforts of the illusion of safety, and unfortunately, everything is going to pass you by.

To avoid that, you have to get back to a daily practice. I'm not saying this as advice for anyone else. This is the only thing that's worked for me. I have succeeded, failed; succeeded, failed; succeeded, failed, three or four different times—maybe more, depending on how you define success and failure. The only way I've been able to get back up is by doing this daily practice. It's not like I know for sure whether or not I'm going to be able to stick with it, it's a *daily* practice. I have no idea if I'm going to do it tomorrow. I just know that I'm going to do it today.

DP: *As an entrepreneur, you regularly deal with consultants, lawyers, developers, and all these sorts of people who are specialists that are in many ways smarter than you in their particular area of expertise. How can someone be both an extraordinary entrepreneur—and fully develop within themselves as you've described—while still being a great team member?*

JA: My advice is not necessarily to go out and be a great entrepreneur; it's to do this daily practice and then you'll have the tools in place to be creative and entrepreneurial should that be the direction this practice leads you. Being strong within yourself makes you a better team member. For example, it makes me much more aware of what I'm not good at and what I'll probably never be good at. I'm 45-years-old; I'll probably never be good at speaking Chinese. But there are some things I'm extremely good at because I've spent 20 years doing them. So I can focus on those things and if I need to do something in China, I'll bring someone with me who speaks Chinese.

At the same time, if something is important to you, then make sure you infuse a little bit of yourself into everything you're doing. If I'm taking a Chinese translator along, then I'd better know what's going on in the conversation. I'd better know what the cultural "dos" and "don'ts" are if I want to do business in China.

An easier example is, I hardly ever hire a lawyer for anything. The law is not rocket science; I can look up the law and figure out what I need to know. In most cases, in business I've written my own contracts without using any lawyer at all. When I have used lawyers, more often than not, I've had to rewrite their contracts. This is my particular skill, I'm not a lawyer, but I like to play one in the blogosphere. So again, it's knowing what you are good at and what you are not good at.

In terms of employees who work for you, the key to being a good leader is to get them to not work for you, but to get them to work for themselves. This may mean that eventually they learn so much and they get so much better than you, that they go off and start their own business, maybe even a competitor to yours. It might mean that at some point, you take a step down and let them take over your business or parts of your business.

The key then is not to lead people, but to encourage them to be good enough to lead you. As they're empowered, they're going to get really good at what they're the best at, and ultimately you would hope that you've hired the type of people who are going to be better than you. If they're not, then you should probably, eventually get rid of them, which is what's happening across corporate America anyway.

DP: From what I've read, your experience at HBO appears to have been pretty good. There was a way in which you internalized the brand and culture, and that also allowed you to do entrepreneurial things within a larger company. Could you talk a little about the role of mentorship and giving back, and how some corporate environments empower people to actualize themselves?

JA: Think about a beacon. A beacon's only job is to make sure its light is shining clearly. On a foggy night, the beacon has no idea what ships it's helping bring to shore. It might be no ships, it might be hundreds of ships—the beacon will never know. The beacon's job is to make sure the light is on and shining clearly.

For me, all I've ever focused on is making sure I'm physically, emotionally, mentally and spiritually healthy, and then good things will happen for the people around me. I'm getting inspired by them, but they're also getting inspired by me, and then the people around them are getting inspired and so on. It ripples out and the ships make their way to the shore. I don't have to know how I'm helping people, but I know for a fact I am.

It's different for everybody, but for me personally, the outcome was writing my book *Choose Yourself*, doing my blog, helping the 20 or so businesses that I either advise or invest in. Indirectly, I'm helping a million people get paid every month. So again, you have no idea what your effect is going to be, nor can you plan it. All you have to do is make sure every day you're physically, emotionally, mentally and spiritually healthy.

It sounds like a broken record, but that's the only thing you have to worry about and everything else takes care of itself. It's not like you're passive—because your idea-muscle is going, because you're physically healthy, because you're around people who are positive and who are coming up with their own ideas—you're going to be active and doing many things and participating in many opportunities.

DP: You're a big fan of reinvention and have basically proven to yourself and everyone else that reinvention can be both possible and lucrative. Can you talk about how reinvention relates to choosing oneself and how entrepreneurs can reinvent themselves and/or their companies?

JA: Reinvention is almost like the word "disruption." The words "pivot" and "reinvention" almost have a negative connotation, like, "Something bad happened so we have to change." In fact, the natural way of things is for things to change.

When a company starts, even if they have a product and they have polled their customer base, no matter what they do they actually don't know what their customers are going to buy in large quantities. Nobody really knows. In this hi-tech age where so many people are building these innovative businesses, no one really knows if the response to their product is going to be good or bad.

The most striking example is Twitter. Twitter started out as a company called Odeo, which was a platform for setting up podcasts. They had major venture-capitalist investors—some of the best investors in the world were VC investors of Odeo. And then on the side one of their engineers made this platform called Twitter. They got a few thousand users, and they were having fun. So finally, Ev Williams said to the best investors in the world who had invested in Odeo, "Listen, we are going to focus on this thing Twitter. You can totally see it. Here are all the stats, we have 10,000 users, and it's great. If you want, I will give you your money back, and if you don't want, you can stay on as an investor of this new thing called Twitter because we're not going to do this Odeo thing anymore."

One hundred percent of the venture capitalists pulled their money out and allowed Ev Williams to buy them out. One hundred percent—not a single one stayed. So it doesn't matter how smart you are, it doesn't matter how great you've been in the past. A fundamental aspect of every business is that it needs to be ready for change and we don't know really if the change is good or bad until it's already good. We can make our best bets, we can mitigate risks, but look, Thomas Edison had to "reinvent" the light bulb a thousand times before he got it right.

That's the natural course of events. It's not natural if you build a product and suddenly it's a success. An entrepreneur needs to have his idea-muscle fully functioning so that when change happens and is necessary, he is able to ride it as well as he can. Or else it won't be rain causing his garden to bloom; it will be a hurricane that will wipe out the garden. Resistance is futile; you have to appreciate the change that happens.

DP: There's a way in which you describe how choosing yourself directly leads to new business and opportunities. Can you talk about how understanding your own problems and limitations can help to generate ideas for solutions that can be monetized and scaled into real businesses?

JA: I don't think understanding your own problems does that much, the goal is to really keep improving yourself. I don't like dwelling on my problems. If I dwell on my problems, I might say to myself, "Boy, I really need to learn Chinese." That would be a huge waste of time for me. It would take me years and I wouldn't succeed. I think the better way to think of it is to be nimble on your feet.

I was a seed investor in a company called Buddy Media, which was started by a guy named Michael Lazerow. The idea was he had this fake Facebook currency called AceBucks, and by playing games, you could win more AceBucks and you could use them to give virtual gifts to your Facebook friends. This turned out to be a horrible idea and for whatever reason, all the games that Buddy Media was making were being destroyed by the equivalent games that Zynga—which started around the same time—was making. So Buddy Media developed this skill set of building all these tools on top of Facebook.

It turned out that companies like Pepsi needed a way of taking surveys and doing all sorts of things on their Facebook fan page. Suddenly, an immediate, profitable pivot was to charge for the service of creating the tools for Facebook fan pages and Buddy Media had this profitable business among the Fortune 500. But the VC market and stock market don't value a service business very well because the saying is, "All your product goes out the door every day." So Buddy Media took these tools they were building and productized them.

Instead of it being a new product each time a client came on board, the client would basically select from a menu: Software as a Service. Software as a Service is valued very highly in the market and the business eventually sold last year for $900 million. When Mike Lazerow started that business, he had no idea it would end up being Software as a Service, selling things like polls and message boards.

Lazerow is a successful investor, entrepreneur and CEO, who had run a public company and had just sold Golf.com to AOL, and so everybody thought he was doing this AceBucks thing. He had no idea what the final product would be. That's how to be an entrepreneur: never assume you know what's going to happen tomorrow. Do your best with what you have today. You can certainly plan for tomorrow—Lazerow hired the best programmers thinking he was planning for tomorrow—but you can't predict what product the customer is going to want or who your customers are ultimately going to be.

Another great example is Groupon, which started as a way to raise money for charities on email lists and instead became a way to offer discounts to the local McDonalds on email lists. Their product totally changed.

DP: As someone who is a successful writer and entrepreneur, how do you go from coming up with an idea and creating a product or service to telling a story that turns it into a real business? How does storytelling relate to generating wealth?

JA: I always tell people, when you make your list of 10 ideas every day, if you're making business ideas, make two columns: One is the idea, the other is the very next execution step. Let's use Buddy Media as an example. The idea is pseudo-currency on top of Facebook. The first execution step might be identifying what is already out there, calling the person who made it and buying it from them. The second execution step might be raising the money to buy it from the inventor of that currency.

When you come up with the first execution step, then that begins the story. I can't say I want to start a business of mining rare-earth minerals on Mars, because I probably don't know what the next execution step is. Now Elon Musk might have the next execution step if he had that idea, but I don't have the next execution step so I can't start to tell that story for myself.

In one business I started, I had an idea of a social-media site revolving around finance. So I sketched it all out, called up the developers in India and had them make screenshots, pitched the idea to a business that would help me distribute it to their customers, and meanwhile the programmers in India were developing the sites. Eventually, I had a site that was being distributed to millions of customers and I built a very popular site.

So that was the arc of the story. There were a lot of ups and downs along the way like any good story, where it looks like you're going to fail and you come out, and there's a cliffhanger and you come out of that, and so on. And eventually, you either build it up for the rest of your life, you sell it, or it goes out of business.

DP: In Choose Yourself *you say honesty is the only way to make money in today's world. You also talk a lot about giving. Can you talk a little more about the value of honesty and giving?*

JA: Take Google, my favorite example. Google, as a website, I find to be extremely honest and giving. If I go to Google and say, "Google, please tell me about motorcycles," well Google is just a blank page with an entry form on it. So Google will immediately tell me, "James, I don't know anything about motorcycles. But if you go to these 10 other websites that I've identified, these are the best websites that you can go to about motorcycles. If you go to these other three websites, they can also tell you about motorcycles. But I have to be honest with you, they're paying me to tell you that. So 10 of them are really good and three of them are possibly good, but they're paying me."

So Google is encouraging me to leave as fast as possible in order to get more information about motorcycles, and it's being completely honest about what it knows, what it doesn't know and who is paying it—total disclosure. Later on, in the evening, when I want to find out about sexually-transmitted diseases, where am I going to go? I'm going to go back to Google.

So Google is extremely honest, extremely giving, and it actually recommends its competitors trillions of times all day long. And Google's worth—whatever it is—is $250 billion. Imagine microscopically, if you as an individual can act a little bit like Google. If you can mimic Google as much as possible, you're also going to end up having a value—not of $250 billion—but of some tiny, microscopic sliver of that. And that is really how business works. I've seen it with my own two eyes: if people act like that, then they get paid.

DP: You have really embraced the ability to fail and actually encourage people to fail. What is the role of courage in doing what is necessary to succeed and being open to the possibility of failing?

JA: Again, I'm going to use a metaphor. If you plant seeds in a garden and it never rains, by the end of the summer, you are going to have dead grass and nothing is going to grow. You need rain for the garden to grow. I think people are afraid of failure because they think people will look down on them. The problem is 100% of human beings are afraid to admit failure, so we are all looking around at each other, wearing our masks to see who is going to admit it first.

The reality is we all have to admit it and failure is just another word for change. Change happens to all of us and if we resist the change, it is going to be very painful. Parts of our bodies are not going to be working together. Something on a physical, emotional, mental, spiritual level is going to revolt; something is going to happen.

When I've been down on the floor, sad and depressed, it's because at some point I wasn't taking care of some aspect of my health, and so a revolt occurred. I lost money, I would lose a house, I would lose a business. I can't regret what happened because it already happened. The first arrow already hit me and hurt me, but the second arrow—regret—is the one that can actually kill you. That's the one that almost made me kill myself. So you have to avoid the second arrow as much as possible or at least as much as you can, because you are always going to regret a little when you feel miserable.

But you have to then say, "I'm going to protect myself from this second arrow by building up this shield. Again, this is created by being physically, mentally, emotionally and spiritually healthy. This protects me against the second arrow, and allows me to change and be as nimble as I need to be. It also potentially protects me against future failure. I'll regret less and I'll be less anxious about the future, and I'll be more focused on what I need to do in the present moment.

"Did I get enough sleep today, because that might mean I will be less depressed tomorrow? Did I eat well, as opposed to eating junk food? Did I put junk food in my brain, as opposed to putting good food in my brain?" I don't read any news or media because that is all junk food. I prefer to put good things in my brain.

And in those moments that I'm feeling angry—because at least once a day I'm feeling angry about something—if I can try to notice that and replace anger with feelings of gratitude, then my body is going to feel better. All of these things in place will help me ride those winds of change a lot better.

DP: This is all great in terms of ongoing ways of life. Can you switch gears for a minute and talk about your five-year plan for creating wealth and the stages it entails?

JA: It always starts with building the foundation I've been talking about over and over. You can't expect tomorrow to suddenly have good ideas. It takes a good six months, starting from scratch—and everybody is starting from scratch—before you might expect to have a single good idea. Having a good idea, having a good execution plan, knowing how to act on it, this takes some time to build the muscles up to know how to do that. Once you have a diverse number of good ideas, you're not going to be making money the next day. It's going to take another six months to a year before you're even making one dollar from this new business or this new life.

Over the next two years, you're building up and coming up with more and more ideas, and you're diversifying all of your opportunities. Finally, through all of these opportunities and ideas, after two years, you might be making a living. In three years, you might be making a very, very good living. In four years, you might start building real equity. And in five years, there is true wealth that you can either cash in on or live off of. I've seen this over and over again, that type of reinvention and that type of timeframe. Don't expect faster than five years; it's very unusual and very hard.

If I want to be a comic-book artist and I've never done anything with comic books, it might take me five years from now before I see any real successful outcome. That's if I really dedicate myself to it, if I love it, if I immerse myself in it and am constantly coming up with ideas and opportunities, as well as constantly networking, being honest and introducing other people to opportunities. All these combined work together to reinvent.

James Altucher *is a successful entrepreneur, chess master, investor and writer. He has started and run more than 20 companies, and sold several of those businesses for large exits. He has also run venture capital funds, hedge funds, angel funds, and currently sits on the boards of several companies.*

*His writing has appeared in most major national media outlets (*Wall Street Journal, ABC, Financial Times, TechCrunch, Forbes, CNBC, *etc). His blog has attracted more than 10 million readers since its launch in 2010.*

THE MONSTER IN YOUR HEAD

Jerry Colonna

You quickly understand in speaking with Jerry why some people refer to him as the "Yoda of Silicon Alley." It's not simply the depth and breadth of his industry knowledge, but also because he has cultivated a profound personal meditation practice that informs his approach to the lonely and difficult journey of being a CEO and founder:

- The delusional aspects and expectations in entrepreneurship
- The deeper meaning of disruption and "walking into the fire"
- The implications of understanding that most startups fail
- The difference between building a product vs. a company

Jerry is a truly incredible human being, and I'm grateful for the opportunity to engage in such a rich and meaningful conversation. It goes deep into the psychological aspects of the founder's journey, and will challenge and open your perspective on the path that lies ahead.

DP: Working as a VC, you had an opportunity to continually interact with a variety of brilliant and creative people across multiple industries, and I've heard you say in other interviews that you most enjoyed the connection with entrepreneurs. You describe them as passionately optimistic and delusional, this idea that who else is going to risk everything to build the impossible?

Can you maybe tell us a little bit about what you learned as a VC and how that experience may have led you to the work that you're doing now as a coach for innovators and entrepreneurs?

JC: There are things that I learned as a VC and throughout my life that led me to being a coach, but it wasn't necessarily a direct connection or linear path. In fact, it was kind of a circuitous route. What was direct about it was the engagement with entrepreneurs and engagement at the deeper personal level.

What I enjoyed about the work as a VC, and even earlier when I was a reporter, was the opportunity to have conversations that were a mix of very pragmatic, down to earth issues intermixed with existential issues. That conversation, or mix of things, was something that I was always drawn to, and I found myself doing that as an investor and board member, when I played somewhat of the role of the consigliore—the one on the board that the CEO or the founder would go to for council. Becoming a coach became a natural extension of that activity, and it really allowed me to explore that relationship in more depth. It has been very satisfying and nourishing ever since.

DP: I've heard you say that your job is to call people to raise their consciousness—that people are more inspired when they know their leader is real and there is a human connection that inspires them. Can you tell us a little bit more about the psychological dimension of entrepreneurship, and how these human qualities relate to building a great company or great team?

JC: Well, before you referenced a comment about the delusional aspect of a lot of entrepreneurship. We all have a capacity to be self-delusional. Buddhism teaches us that you have to be very, very suspicious of any thought pattern that the mind comes up with because it's almost always about a reinforcement of the constructed ego.

So, if you take that as a natural tendency for human beings, and then you layer into that two corollary but important trends; (1) the expectation around leadership generally; and (2) specifically the entrepreneurial journey, I think you get a very potent mix for the potential for delusion. And by delusion I mean basically bullshitting ourselves, lying to ourselves. There is a necessary component of this extraordinary belief—believing in the impossible, almost to the point that we say a kid can believe in magical thinking. That part is absolutely necessary to the innovator/entrepreneur's journey.

Now pause on that thought. The challenge is that our normal, typical expectations of leadership, coupled with the merging of self with the entity that is at the heart of the entrepreneurial challenge, creates this capacity to bypass our own patterns, believe the stories that we tell ourselves about ourselves, and hide the truth. And the result is—especially when the leader is an entrepreneur or innovator—that an organization can be what I refer to as "highly violent" to the individual.

There are a lot of challenges around trust and learning to deal with the day-to-day. That's why I believe that understanding and seeing our own delusions and making more conscious our own patterns is essential to surviving being an entrepreneur. Then secondarily and equally important is the process of building a trusting and trustworthy organization.

DP: This is the duplicity between the aspiration for greatness and your own internal challenges—does this relate to the title of your blog, The Monster in Your Head?

JC: Yes, The Monster in Your Head. Well, the monster also refers to the belief systems you carry. I did a blog post a few months ago called "Shoot the Crow," which talked about that inner voice that is constantly telling you the work you're doing is crap. There are several monsters that can exist in our head. That's what it really refers to.

DP: It's funny, I've been dealing with that throughout the whole course of this project, because I've been basically interviewing all these people that I just consider to be absolutely brilliant and innovative in their own way, and there's this sort of—

JC: Yeah, watch, I'll call it forth. "Who the hell are you to write this book?"

DP: Yeah, exactly.

JC: Right? "What do you know?"

DP: It's funny, because I can never know enough as the interviewee—they are all the best experts in the world in their area of innovation. So, throughout this entire process there was a constant sense of insecurity and doubt in terms of feeling adequately prepared, am I really asking the right questions, am I getting to the heart of the issue, etc..

In terms of my background, I did Ph.D. studies at Princeton in religion and culture, which is basically the study of worldviews, so I looked a lot at these same types of trends, primarily within the context of the Civil Rights and Sixties counterculture movements up to the present. I studied shifts in language and behavior, particularly in relationship to changes in how we share and communicate ideas.

What I started to notice after the economic crash around 2010 was all these people embracing the term disruption. There was a way in which the rest of the economy was struggling and then of all these innovators, entrepreneurs and investors sort of flipped the struggle into an opportunity. Basically, constraint drives innovation. Cutbacks and hardships created these huge opportunities and disruption became this kind of rallying call, "Hey, let's disrupt everything." That's what I started to refer to as the Disruption Revolution: the idea that disruption became a rallying call that galvanized all of these incredible innovations across the board.

JC: Did the rise of the term *disruption* coincide with Clay Christensen's book?

DP: It did in the late 1990s when he first published it, but I think it really started to be embraced in recent years as tech entrepreneurs and investors began to create real business models, and there were real business opportunities again. I think it really came to the forefront probably when TechCrunch Disrupt came out, and all of a sudden the biggest tech media company is now proclaiming, "disrupt," creating a whole conference around disruption, and I think it became this rallying call for everyone across the board.

JC: So what does disruption mean to you?

DP: Well, I look at disruption as really an effect and an outcome of innovation, and so I feel like on the one hand it's good to talk about disruption in the sense that people are trying to connect what they're doing to some type of goal with real results—to innovation, to creating real business models, etc. The aspiration to disrupt gives innovation a sense of purpose and shapes intentions to be part of a larger movement.

I also think that tying innovation to certain economic incentives and goals encourages a culture of innovation that pushes things forward at a rapid pace, while at the same mitigating some of the risk of there being a bubble that might burst, as in the case of the first dot-com bubble. Disruption in a sense brings the ideas back to the real world.

JC: So you've got a deep meditation practice, and I imagine you've studied some dharma. What's the difference between disruption and impermanence?

DP: That's a really good question. I would say on a much deeper, more existential or interpersonal level, that disruption is a process of breaking apart certain conceptions of what should be normal and abnormal, and breaking apart this sort of duplicity and the things that we're attached to. Uncertainty is more of an ongoing state being and state of existence. I think the foundation of everything is, to some extent, uncertain.

JC: I agree with that, and I think that goes to the heart of the emotional, psychological, existential challenges of people who play in the field of entrepreneurship and innovation. But I'm curious about the word *disruption* and innovation in that regard, and I don't mean to get pedantic with you. Obviously these are terms that we all use, and you are using and defining them in a particular way.

But for me, the word *disruption* implies its opposite. You can't really have a disrupting moment without the implication of things being calm, serene, predictable, as expected. Entrepreneurs love to come in and talk about how they are going to disrupt this business and that business. And I think that's part of the delusional quality.

DP: Absolutely.

JC: What comes to mind is something I often used to say when I was an investor, and my former partner Fred Wilson picked up on it oftentimes, which was if you really want to understand the arc of a particular business, the digital version of that business, you should look at the arc of the analog version of that business.

The reason that's important is because if you are going to step into this realm and say, "I'm going to disrupt the dry cleaning business," for example, then there are certain things that will change with the introduction of new technology. I can go online, someone can come to my house, they can pick up the dry cleaning, I can arrange for it to be delivered someplace other than where I am, I can do all these things, etc. But in the end, someone's still physically picking up the atoms associated with that shirt and subjecting it to a particular process, so that arc is going to remain.

Now, there's all that uncertainty: they can pick up the shirt, it can burn, it can be lost. There's all this uncertainty that exists, but we pretend as if we know what's going to happen, and that's an important psychological defense mechanism against the inevitable variations in life.

I think it's useful to understand: what is it that is truly going to be disruptive? What is truly going to be the application of innovative thinking? And it oftentimes is only a very minute part of that arc, of the experience. And if you blow that, if you miss that, or if you are, as we were talking about that before, delusional, you're in for a hell of a bout of suffering, and you're in for a hell of a ride as an entrepreneur.

DP: A recent study said that science and engineering majors are really popular until students find out how hard they are. And as a result, many students end up changing their majors after receiving bad grades, despite their efforts to do well in classes. I think that the same type of situation appears to be relevant to what we have been talking about in terms of aspiring entrepreneurs.

We have an entire generation now that's inspired and motivated by movies like The Social Network *and shows like* Shark Tank. *They read these stories of billion-dollar exits, and yet they have little understanding of how hard it is to start a company, to build a product, solve a problem, get traction in highly competitive marketplace, etc.*

What advice do you give first-time CEOs to help prepare them for the long journey that lies ahead?

JC: Probably the most useful thing that I help people with in this regard is the understanding that most entrepreneurial ventures fail, or, to use your terminology, most efforts to innovatively disrupt an existing scene or situation will fail. And I don't mean sort-of fail. I mean fail spectacularly. People really need to internalize that.

When I say they're delusional, they actually do not believe failure will happen to them—just like you don't believe you will die—when they start off. Now, that kind of radical, delusional belief in self is absolutely necessary to get the thing off the launching pad. But it's also dangerous because it starts to set up a whole set of feelings that create massive psychological and existential suffering.

The second most useful thing is the notion that most people who are on this journey have a very difficult time. There is a tremendous amount of relief that comes into the eyes of a client the first time I sit down with them and we start talking about just how difficult it can be—especially if they're a first time CEO of an entrepreneurial startup. A tremendous amount of relief comes when they start to realize that the incredibly difficult feelings they are having are actually the norm.

All of a sudden they no longer start to see that this is evidence of their failing as an individual or their incompetency. Their incompetency or competency may come into question, but the loneliness, high anxiety, constant sense of dread and inadequacy—which oftentimes is present in us anyway—gets exacerbated and played out for entrepreneurs. It's tremendously relieving when they discover the fact that it is common. So, second is helping to understand what the journey is like in that regard.

The last useful thing is the challenge that occurs when you merge your own identity with the business itself. For example, I recently did an interview with Jason Calicanis. He was talking about this experience of, "I was Silicon Alley Reporter; Silicon Alley Reporter was me." That sets up a whole dynamic for suffering, and the conundrum is that it's necessary because the leader in a sense is the embodiment of the business.

Those three pieces are probably the most significant aspects that, in my view, the popular media misses. Because we want to celebrate Mark Zuckerberg and think of him as the next Bill Gates. We want to think of David Karp as the next Mark Zuckerberg. We want to think of Bill Gates as the next Henry Ford, or Cornelius Vanderbilt, or Alexander Hamilton. It never ends. We always have these archetypes of successful entrepreneurs who step out into the world and change things, and the myths that arise from them—what is *The Social Network* movie but one big myth?

DP: I want to switch a little bit from what you might describe as the psychological aspect of entrepreneurship to leadership. What qualities make a great leader and how do you empower people to self-actualize and be the best leader that they can be?

JC: I think that my core work is focused on that latter half of what you were talking about: being the best leader that they can be. So it really means understanding who you are and what you believe, and really allowing that leader who, for the most part, is in you, to come forward. So it's actually oftentimes a process of becoming more authentic with yourself.

Probably the biggest question people come in with, implicitly if not even explicitly, is "Do I have to be an asshole? Do I have to be a leader like, say, Steve Jobs?" Because that is part of the mythology that we were talking about before. And what I say is that it is not even as simple as, "No." It's, "You won't succeed, because you are not that person."

So, if you are an asshole, be an asshole as a leader, and if your tendency is to yell and scream then we have got to deal with the implications of that and see if there is a way that we can turn that style into something that is positive for you. My job isn't to turn them into some idealized version of what a leader is. My job is to really help them understand what is blocking their own access to being a leader, and oftentimes it is preconceived notions of what a CEO is or should be.

DP: You mentioned earlier this idea that when your work is incredibly meaningful, there is this merger and loss of the distinction between life and work. I know that this is one of the many driving forces behind entrepreneurship, but it can also come as a risk to the entrepreneur, what I've heard you refer to as "disappearing into the fire." Can you tell us a little bit about what that means?

JC: That is my terminology for this story that I first read in a book by David Whyte. The story is of this ancient Chinese potter who spends his life trying to perfect the most exquisite glaze imaginable. At the end of his life, when he decides his meaningful life is over, he walks into the kiln, or into the fire. The next day, the potter's assistants open up the kiln and take out the pots, and they are covered with the most exquisite glaze imaginable. And that is where the story ends.

For me, it's a story that speaks to the conflict of merging the individual and business faced by all entrepreneurs and leaders. The glaze is exquisite. The potter achieved what he set his meaningful life about doing, but he died in the process. He disappeared in the process. He became one with the glaze, because it was, of course, his own body that became part of what was the most exquisite piece of it.

Sometimes when I tell that story to entrepreneurs, they see the romantic side of that. They sort of nod their heads and say, "Wow, that's so powerful. That's right. Oh, man, right on." And then sometimes, those who have merged and lost things—spouses, estranged relationships with their children, their health—they see the negative side of the story.

The story itself is just a story. It's neither negative nor positive. It doesn't give you any direction as to whether you should do this or that. It is not a parable. So it's something that can prod us and make us conscious of what our choices are. Are you walking into the fire consciously, or are you doing it because of, as we talked about before, these unconscious patterns that dictate your life?

Are you doing it because you have this overwhelming sense of inadequacy, and you think that disrupting an industry and coming up with the most innovative way to deliver dry cleaning is going to somehow redeem you? Or are you doing it because of the sheer joy?

Again, I don't mean to imply judgment. I can hear in my own language almost a judgment there. That is not my intention. I just think that the risk for a high degree of existential suffering is greater when you move through these choices unconsciously, asleep, as opposed to being awake to what your mind is really up to—to what you're really up to.

DP: You mentioned earlier that most startups fail. I know that traditionally failure is viewed as something that is bad, but in startups it tends to be viewed as a learning experience that shapes better entrepreneurs in the future.

JC: Yeah, we say that. I don't know that it is always what we feel.

DP: In a lot of companies today, there are many approaches, such as the lean startup movement, where failure is in a certain sense encouraged, the idea that you should be shipping imperfect products, learning from failure serves as a form of testing and rapid prototyping, and that allows you to optimize performance and iterate faster.

JC: I think it is a slightly nuanced difference. It's not so much that you should fail. It's that you shouldn't let failure stop you from shipping the product, which is a little different. You're not seeking to build a product that will necessarily fail. Because failure is an inherent part of the process, you might as well fail quickly. You might as well get it over with.

DP: Could you tell us just a little bit about how entrepreneurs should approach and deal with failure?

JC: First, understanding that the received wisdom that failure is an opportunity to learn, failure is a good thing—those stories that we talk about are actually true. For example, you'll see lots of famous investors stand up and talk about how it's great to meet an entrepreneur with a great idea who learned on OPM: other people's money. What we would talk about as investors is, "Go fail over there with that guy's money, and then when you're done learning, come to me and I'll back you." So we talk a lot about failure being acceptable, and I think that is true, that it is an aspirational value.

But I think that there is a corollary. We also believe that our experience should be like Mark Zuckerberg's experience. Now, I don't know if he has personally experienced failure or not, but the mythology is one day he was at Harvard and the next day he is a billionaire. That is the mythology. Because of the persistence of that myth, we actually struggle to internalize the acceptability of failure. It doesn't matter how many times people say, "It's okay to fail," we still take it personally.

DP: To build upon that, Steve Blank and others have talked about how there used to be this assumption that startups are essentially smaller versions of big companies—that they need a five-year business plan, teams with clearly defined roles, there's this waterfall model of development that makes polished products and then pushes them onto the marketplace, etc.

In contrast, startups today are often a series of untested hypotheses in search of a business model. I'm curious if you could tell us a little bit about how you approach people when they have to embrace this sense of uncertainty, and basically approach building a company as testing these hypotheses, versus going out and doing something that's been done before.

JC: The one thing that occurs to me about this phenomenon is actually less prosaic. I would ask: are you building a product or are you building a company? Most people today think they are building a company but in fact are focused on trying to build a product. And when we build products, we don't worry necessarily about business models, or exits for the investors, or building the team, and so on.

Using my construct of that same question, what I will do with a client, or even somebody in a workshop, is take them back to their original goal. I will ask them to go back to their original epiphany idea. Was their epiphany idea a better way to make a light bulb, or was it a better way to build a new GE?

The reason why this is important is because you start to get into purpose. Why are you in business? Why are you making all these sacrifices? That sense of purpose and original intent start to become compasses for navigating ahead during these times. One of the most difficult times in my coaching work are the day or two after Instagram or Tumblr gets sold for a billion dollars, because everybody comes in and they're filled with this angst because they're not there yet. They don't understand it. They are not really a company—it's really just a product.

The only way to navigate through that is to stay very, very focused on what it is that you intend to do. And again, I don't mean to make judgment. If you just want to build a product—if you want to swing for the fence in the hopes that Google will buy you—then go for it, because a lot of people make a lot of money doing that. In my observation, just like a home run hitter has a much lower batting percentage and much lower on-base percentage, those who swing for the fences are almost always going to deal with a lot of strikeouts.

Go for it if you can deal with that, but if what you are really trying to do is build a new platform, a new company, that has a series of products, a series of technology innovations, then that is a different process. You have to change your expectations and you have to change the whole business. Unfortunately, in the mythologizing that goes along with the startup businesses, we tend to conflate those two things—building a product vs. a company—and it gets very, very confusing for first-time CEOs.

Jerry Colonna *It was 2005 and I was sharing office space with Fred Wilson when I met a young man who changed my life. Fred and I had been friends since 1996 when we'd started Flatiron Partners. In 2001, we parted ways as partners but remained friends. I joined JP Morgan in 2002 and, within months, was miserable. The existential questions that had been haunting me for years were so loud, so relentless that I had no choice but to pay attention.*

When I told my colleagues I was leaving, I said I wanted a business card with no company name, no title. I wanted to understand who I was stripped of any persona. And so for the next few years, I sat on boards of directors, consulted here and there but mostly, I read, and sat, and learned to be still. I learned to listen. Derek Walcott's poem Love After Love comes to mind; I learned to love again the stranger who was my self who had loved me all my life, whom I ignored for another, who knows me by heart.

Then one day a young man came to see me. He wanted to leave his law practice and join a startup. Someone suggested that seeing the former VC would be a good first step. After asking him why he'd become a lawyer in the first place, especially considering he obviously hated his job, he began sobbing. I realized then that, through the act of listening, I had found my own way. Those years of sitting still began to pay off; I had to coach. And I've been coaching ever since.

PART III

INNOVATION AND THE ENTERPRISE

SCALING INNOVATION

Shail Khiyara

Shail Khiyara considers innovation to be our birthright, a perspective that informs his work with some of the largest companies in the world, numerous nonprofits, TED and even the United Nations. As CMO and Chief Customer Officer of Spigit, the leading innovation platform, he is the ideal person to kickoff the section on scaling innovation:

- Why innovation is a birthright and lifeblood of organizations
- How rewards, incentives, and gamification drive innovation
- Innovation tools and platforms formalize and standardize processes to maximize productivity and results
- Using strategic objectives to streamline innovation

This interview serves as a poignant reminder of how innovation needs to be part of an organization's DNA. Innovation tools such as Spigit will continue to play an important role in facilitating the exchange of ideas and formalizing innovation processes that are already occurring in email exchanges, post-it notes, social media and white boards.

DP: You are CMO and Chief Customer Officer for Spigit, the leading innovation software company, and in your personal life organize TED events and sit on the board of several nonprofits trying to find innovative solutions to problems.

Why are you so passionate about innovation? What is it in the field that excites you?

SK: There is a lot of talk about innovation being an overused word. The question is, can it be taught or is it intrinsically learned?

I'm of the belief that innovation is actually a birthright. People are intrinsically innovative, and it is really about creating value. It is the lifeblood of any organization. Innovation is mission critical to all modern brands and organizations out there, and it has really become the industrial religion of the late twentieth and twenty-first century—the life-blood of any business. Businesses see it as a key way to increase their profits and market share. In fact, governments reach for innovation when they are trying to fix the economy.

There's another market ripe for innovation that's often overlooked. While innovation is often used in the public and private sector, it is often neglected in humanitarian work. Innovation has a chemistry, an alchemy that comes together to create innovation at personal, business, community, society, national and global levels. It is in fact, an intrinsic human desire that requires more attention in far-flung corners of the world. Humanitarian innovation, for example, has the power to transform lives and make a real difference through efficient, effective and creative solutions.

DP: You're responsible for communicating about innovation to a broad range of clients. In terms of talking about creating a culture of innovation and role for innovation within a larger company, why should an enterprise company that is already market leader embrace innovation?

SK: It's an opportunity for a business to reinvent itself whether it's in incremental innovation, product innovation, or even business transformation. For example, one recent study found that the overall rate of return for seventeen successful innovations that came out in the 1970s averaged 56%. Compare that with 16% average return on investment for all American businesses over the last thirty years. That gives you the power of what innovation can do for an organization. That's why enterprises, even if they are market leaders, should continue to embrace innovation. Apple has done it fairly well, as one example, in the recent past.

DP: Throughout the course of these interviews there has been a consistent theme that constraint drives innovation, the idea that if you cut back on budgets, resources, and teams, you need to generate new revenue streams and develop more innovative products in order to remain competitive. How did the economic crash of 2008-2009 impact innovation? Do you think it was a catalyst?

SK: There were two catalysts.

Companies are comprised of two things: people and everything else. Up to 75% of an organization's costs are its people. Over the course of the economic downturn in terms of cost cutting and optimization, companies and CEOs have optimized their property, plant, and equipment rather well. But they have not optimized their talent within their organization or within their ecosystem. In fact, over 86% of the organizations are dealing with disengaged or detached employees to a large extent, which is costing the U.S. economy approximately $350 billion a year in lost productivity. So that is one catalyst.

The second catalyst is that in this time frame there has been a Renaissance in social media, which has led to adoption of enterprise social tools, or dial tone tools as I call them, and companies have realized that not only did they not have structured innovation processes but also the playing field is now non-linear. That is, you can't put raw materials in one end and get a widget out the other. That is still possible, but innovation as we know it can come from anywhere: from your employees, your customers, your suppliers, your vendors, and, in some instances, your competitors. Those are the two key catalysts that have contributed to the impact on innovation in enterprise.

DP: When the downturn first happened, we were all bracing ourselves for possible cutbacks. I was working in social media, and we were increasingly getting a seat at the table. We saw a huge shift where social media transformed from being an experimental budget to something that most brands were interested in and needed to use.

SK: Isn't that amazing. Then, fast forward that to today, where Social ROI, rather purposeful Social is top of mind in many organizations.

DP: Businesses are increasingly under pressure to respond to shifting expectations from their customers as a result of social media. At Spigit, you actually use social media tools to facilitate innovation and encourage companies to use them internally.

Could you elaborate on how social workflow impacts the enterprise?

SK: That's an interesting question. Social media has democratized information and the Information Age. Social workflow has had profound effects on the enterprise today and will continue to do so in the near future.

Take communication as an example. Marketing has grown long ears with Social Media. It's no longer a push strategy but a capture strategy in marketing. What I mean by that is actively listening to the social workflow of one's customers, partners, and competitors, the conversations that are ongoing. This also includes determining when and how to respond to those discussions and conversations.

Another example of social workflow would be activity streams. Dial tone social software, or basic first-generation social software can help enterprises stay abreast of all the activity pertinent to their particular customer or user. Fast forward that to integrated activity streams, which can actually show you transaction data for multiple systems coupled with HR or sales data, and that brings in a whole new spectrum of how information can be gathered and decisions can be made. The point of need for a customer with social workflow is now determined by a mouse click as opposed to times when a customer used to walk into a store. So that's completely changed the landscape of how workflow like this can impact the enterprise.

DP: *Statistically speaking, 1-3% of people have been labeled innovators when you look at the larger distribution from innovators to full adopters. Is innovation something that you can really teach? How can enterprise companies encourage innovation for people who might not consider themselves innovators? How do you essentially galvanize an entire organization around innovation?*

SK: I do see innovation as a birthright. I'll explain that briefly and then get into your question here. There's a term I've been using a lot in my Twitter streams over the last two weeks: "transient exuberance." For example, what's going on in Egypt at the moment is democracy in transient exuberant. It's there. It's gone. Is it going to come back again?

What transient exuberance really means is that there are neurons formed in one's brain between the time the person is born to age six or so. A lot of those neurons by the age of eight or twelve are gone, and permanent connections are made. In that context, your brain is really innovating itself with all the information that is coming in.

Fast forward to your question about how companies encourage innovation...innovation is about creating value. Sometimes innovation means that it is important for organizations to make it one of the core values and assets inside the organization. It takes the mindset. It takes a process. It takes positive output. So innovation can be taught if you're willing to have a mindset, follow a process, and define and measure success accurately.

DP: In terms of the entire organization, what role does the crowdsourcing of ideas and feedback play in innovation? Is this role the same when it is applied internally within the enterprise as when it is applied externally like running a crowdsourcing innovation contest with consumers?

SK: Much like the democratization of information in the Information Age, crowdsourcing democratizes innovation's ability across the entire board. The role is the same whether you are running an external or internal crowdsourcing innovation contest. P&G, Starbucks, Dell, Best Buy, and Nike have all created digital platforms allowing customers to help them create new products and messages. In fact, Starbucks launched a proprietary online forum called My Starbucks Idea. Have you heard of it?

DP: No, I haven't.

SK: They launched MyStarbucksidea.com and received 17,000 coffee ideas in the first 14 months since the launch of this proprietary online forum. The company is actually using it internally and externally. Spigit has several instances like these for internal-external innovation programs. We've seen deployments to the tune of over 300,000 people using it at one customer across 97 countries with thousands of ideas generated.

DP: Everyone knows that innovations occur in the realm of products. How does innovation reach deeper into the realm of processes, customer relations, and client services? Across the enterprise or more broadly, how does innovation impact all aspects of the customer life cycle?

SK: The taxonomy of innovation can be product, process, or business model innovation. It can drive incremental breakthrough, or insubstantial growth.

For example, Cisco has used Spigit to tap into the human network to identify their next billion dollar growth opportunity. DPR construction has increased engagement and efficiency by 20% using an innovation platform from Spigit.

Subsequent to the tragedy at Sandy Hook Elementary School in Newtown, Connecticut, the Poway Unified School District felt compelled to do more than merely evaluate issues of campus security and safety then foremost in the minds of the public and educators. They also took the opportunity to implement an entirely new and innovative method of tapping into the creativity and innovation of the broadest segment of their stakeholders.

They used our software to power an initiative dubbed Innovation University, the District was able to break down traditional knowledge and communication silos and engage ALL employees, generating nearly 100 new ideas to improve on-campus safety and security.

DP: Innovation is easier said than done, especially within larger companies where people are accustomed to doing something a certain way. How do you implement a platform like Spigit and get people across an organization to use it? Could you talk a little bit about the sorts of innovations required to get people in a large organization to use the platform?

SK: From a technology perspective, the software is very easy to use and implementation is minimal.

Often companies struggle with establishing the Innovation charter, defining and building an innovation culture. Having access to Innovation leaders who can guide them through the pitfalls and best practices of establishing, sustaining, and growing a successful social innovation program, is often a need within some organizations. Over time, the programs we build with our clients become mission-critical parts of the enterprise, driving a stream of opportunities for organic growth, business model and market disruption, novel process efficiencies, differentiated product streams, and ultimately a steady source of new value throughout the enterprise.

Customers can indeed get the platform and start using it immediately. For those customers that need it, we offer services to those customers that need it to get their communities up and running, to drive rewards and recognition, and to construct their innovation challenges (questions) very effectively.

DP: Some companies have Internet policies where they actually discourage people from surfing the Internet and participating in social networks. I've read a lot about responsible Internet usage within a company, and that incentives and rewards tend to only encourage innovation among top performers.

Could you explain the concept of idea management and responsible Internet usage, and how it might integrate within a more sort of holistic approach to innovation?

SK: A lot of companies already acknowledge that their business outcomes are tied to how well their employees engage. As I mentioned earlier, disengagement is rampant and a *pandemic* across many organizations in the country, so introducing gamification or game elements to their business processes gives them a new way to encourage much higher levels of engagement.

There are a number of ways to do this. For example, we encourage focused challenges, so we have a purpose for the challenge and a time dynamic (the length of time the challenge is open) represented by sort of a game board. You go from step 1 to step 2 to step 3 and so on. And then gamify challenges so having a storyline around the challenge, incentives, rewards and recognition, different levels, reputation rankings for employees who actually participate (who are voting up or down—looking for the positive and at what is the discerner's score inside of your organization and why is it that way). Those are the kinds of gamification aspects we bring to the table to drive more adoption around innovation.

DP: There are different types of innovation, for example, incremental innovation, which occurs over time, and disruptive innovation, which tends to be an entirely new way of doing things that comes on the marketplace. How do enterprise clients find a balance between responding to external demands in a marketplace and incremental innovation based on the evolving needs of consumers?

SK: On an ongoing basis, incremental innovation, if tools are provided and with an innovation culture, will continue to occur within organizations. Again there's a big if there. Are the right tools provided? If you look at the edges of the organization, there is a whole army of customers and employees who may not be aware of the organization's strategic objectives, or, if they are, they don't know how to contribute. The old suggestion box doesn't necessarily work very well.

To provide organizations with a tool like Spigit, where you can very easily log in and put in your ideas, track your ideas, get your reputation scores, see who's voting and not voting on your idea, helps you drive that incremental or transformational innovation on a regular scale on an ongoing basis.

Take for example United Health Group, that launched their innovation program called Ignite in 2011. The program has grown significantly and has over 40,000 users, 44 communities, with a healthy number of focus initiatives, generated over 138,000 views of and interactions with ideas and over 8500 ideas generated in the system using Spigit.

Messaging and communication across the organization are key. If a person doesn't feel they are an "idea" person, then I think you need to look at your program and the message you are communicating. If you are solely looking for "big ideas" or focusing on the sole ideator in terms of participation and engagement, then I think you have to expand the idea of Innovation to include other roles for people. Finally, is the person you are talking about a high contributor? Are they already highly engaged and providing 50+ hours of work to advance the goals of the business? Are you expecting them to contribute above and beyond their high level of contribution? I think for these people the business needs to weigh the needs of that individual to perform in their current capacity with the needs for their participation in innovation. For these people I think either you need to offset some of their work so that they can engage innovation or you need to accept the value they already bring to the business and fill the innovation gap with contributions from others. Google does a pretty good job with that, as an example.

There are many examples of how innovation can come from the edge to the point of transformational innovation. For example, "We want to increase our profitability by 15%" or "How do we transform our product to get higher adoption" or "How can we increase our customer satisfaction in a particular region". Challenges can be defined in that fashion. Challenges can also be defined such that they are open to the entire crowd or to a selected group of experts. That's how companies find balance in innovation inside an organization.

DP: A lot of times, things like innovation can appear somewhat abstract or elusive to C-level executives that want to quantify the value of investment. How do you set short and long-term goals, identify different key performance indicators, and, in a larger organization, map innovation against the way that they do business to measure success?

SK: Roughly $280 billion worth of investment goes into R&D across the globe annually. If you step back and ask organizations, how do you actually measure success out of that, many don't have a way of defining what that looks like. A lot of people can say I launched a hard disk drive project, for example. But if you ask how much did that actually cost, it's very difficult for organizations to identify the entire structure or innovation process that went into it and what that cost was.

You need to lay out the strategic objectives and make innovation critical in the organization, because innovation is already occurring. It is occurring in an unstructured fashion within emails, meeting notes, and yellow post-it notes, but many of those ideas are not captured and there are many whose time may not be there today are lost and never come back again.

This is why tools such as Spigit were designed—to provide companies with a structured way to not only capture ideas but also involve your crowd in soliciting ideas and voting on those ideas. At the same time, you have an idea bank, a repository that stores these ideas from which you can pull at a later stage. So it's that structured processed innovation that really helps organizations get more and more excited and drives ecosystem and employee engagement. The tools to facilitate innovation essentially become integrated into the daily routines and workflow of an entire organization—this is purposeful social with a high ROI.

DP: I've read that 80% of knowledge tends to not be shared within an organization. You spoke to that very well in terms of putting into place different processes. The social web tends to generate an enormous volume of unfiltered data.

How do you leverage social data to make it actionable and create more innovative products?

SK: It goes back to providing business context and relevance to that data. Being able to connect data to what we call challenges inside an innovations platform is key. Then how do you create gamification elements that help drive people to galvanize communities or crowds, to galvanize around and start contributing to that challenge? The key here, and many analysts talk about this as well, including some in your book, about providing purposeful social, with business context and relevance and with a high ROI.

DP: The greatest fear of a larger enterprise company is that a more nimble and able competitor is going to come along and radically disrupt their business, so how can enterprise companies stay ahead of the curve and protect themselves?

Innovation is a daily process. It's not something that you put on a shelf and say, "Well, we're going to innovate from July 5 to July 10." The proof is out there in terms of the metrics I shared with you earlier. Organizations that have a structured innovation process continue to grow and see significant returns as opposed to organizations that don't. How can companies stay ahead of the curve?

Make innovation part of your DNA. Sales pipelines and Financial reports are not a coincidence. They are built systematically with a consistent process. Such is the nature of Innovation and Idea pipelines. While companies continue to value innovation and in some instances make it their core brand proposition, they still struggle to derive innovation leverage from their employee, customer and supplier networks. At Spigit, I drove a study that examined Fortune 50 companies to see just how big of a role innovation plays among the leading organizations in the U.S. We took a close look at company demographics, such as location and size, in order to hone in on any interesting patterns, as well as how 'innovation' was used in the company branding efforts. I did this as part of our 'Deconstructing Innovation' series: *Deconstructing Innovation—To analyze and identify the essential elements for repeatable crowd empowered innovation and engagement.*

We found that a lot of companies are actually still using innovation in their taglines, Over 65% of larger companies (>100k employees) mentioned innovation in their branding efforts, as opposed to 29% of smaller companies (>100k employees). They're using it in the 'About' section of their website. They're using it in their videos. But then, you go deeper into the organization, and you say who's responsible for innovation? Or how do you measure if you are Innovating? Fingers become pointers. Only 6% had appointed a Chief Innovation Officer or similar C-suite position with core focus on innovation.

What is interesting in the course of the last many years is there's been a rise in the Chief Innovation Officer role. There are about 600 of them across the United States today. These are some of the ways companies are staying ahead of the curve. They are making innovation part of their DNA, they're rewarding innovation, and they're putting someone in charge of innovation inside their organization—more importantly they are making Innovation a daily process, a move from a closed, exclusive concept of who can engage or participate to an open and inclusive concept.

When do you know you are an innovative company? When you stop asking that, it's a cultural tipping point.

"Have you Innovated today" for example, is a great tagline.

DP: Imagine you're the head of a company. You want to make your company more innovative. Where do you start? If I were to start something tomorrow, I want to be a more innovative company 2 or 3 months from now, where to start and how do you go from 0 to 60 in the fastest way possible?

SK: It goes back to establishing a mindset, having a process, and creating or defining specific measurable business outcomes. Those three parameters are key. Setting the mindset is important from the perspective of involving the broader crowd and making innovation core DNA inside your organization, which requires you to have a process that is transparent, easy to use (e.g., Spigit), and accessible across the organization. Then having challenges that are defined around that process to measure specific business outcomes is key.

....

Shail Khiyara *is the CMO and Chief Customer Officer at Spigit and brings 15+ years of executive and marketing experience with a track record of proven success, leading marketing teams at some of the most recognized brands in Silicon Valley.*

Shail has worldwide marketing responsibilities including increasing revenue and brand awareness of Spigit. He joined Spigit from Taleo where he was the SVP and CMO and drove significant successes leading up to the acquisition of Taleo by Oracle. During his tenure the company grew successfully, established a robust pipeline and drove significant new customer acquisition and revenue growth. Prior to Taleo, he was the SVP and General Manager for EVault, the Cloud services business of Seagate Technologies where he drove significant revenue growth through innovative product positioning, branding and channel marketing.

Previously Shail drove the European sales and marketing efforts to position the Verisign brand in multiple geographies, drove revenue and significant customer acquisition of F1000 companies. An avid humanitarian Shail actively serves on multiple boards in the Bay Area with organizations focused on education, innovation and economic development. Shail holds an MBA from Yale University, Exec Education at Harvard Business School and has an MS in Engineering.

....

BUILDING A GROWTH FACTORY

Scott Anthony

Scott Anthony lays out a straight forward, easy-to-follow view of how innovation can be standardized and structured the same way as in manufacturing to build what he refers to as a growth factory. As managing partner of Innosight, the leading innovation firm founded by Clayton Christensen, Scott brings years of experience to tell us about:

- Using a set of systems and processes to formalize innovation
- Creating a growth blueprint, and going from strategy to action
- Managing innovation like an investment portfolio
- The innovator's dilemma and lean-forward management

This interview with Scott Anthony made me rethink the significance of how corporations can solve global problems by providing scale, resources, and infrastructure. My background in startups shapes a bias that disruptive innovation comes from the bottom-up, but there are significant strategic advantages for larger enterprise companies that will play a critical role in the Disruption Revolution.

DP: In your latest book, you talk about a company needing to go beyond isolated programs to develop what you refer to as a growth factory. Could you describe what you mean by that term?

SA: The basic notion is that more and more companies recognize that the pace of change in their markets and their industries requires that they really get systematically, programatically good at innovation. And if you really want to do that, and not just introduce a single new product or a single new service, but introduce a steady stream of new products and services, then you have to approach innovation the same way as a manufacturer approaches producing things. This means thinking about not a single thing that you do, but a set of systems that come together that we call a growth factory that makes the pursuit of growth or innovation as reliable and repeatable as the production of a widget in a factory.

One of our observations is many companies recognize the problem of innovation, and they try to solve it by doing a thing. So, they might launch an idea contest or they might create rewards for people that bring them ideas, or they might create an open innovation program or new growth group. All of those things are good, but because innovation is a systemic issue, a point solution just doesn't work. So those individual efforts are doomed to disappoint unless you think structurally and think systematically about the problem.

DP: So what happens when a company stops growing?

SA: Once a company's growth engine stalls it almost never restarts: 90% of companies that experience a stall where growth begins to slow and level off, they never start growing again. And in today's world, if you're not moving forward, you're moving backwards, because the rate of change and disruption in so many industries means that if you just keep doing today's operations better, you are falling farther and farther behind. So, if you don't get this right, then you suffer the fate of Eastman Kodak, of Blackberry, of Nokia, of General Motors, and on and on.

DP: The first step in building a growth factory is to create a growth blueprint. This requires pursuing multiple layers of growth at the same time, identifying distinct types of growth and innovation, and creating a set of common definitions.

Can you walk us through the process of creating a blueprint? Where do you begin, what are the steps, and how do you prioritize growth and innovation types?

SA: The first step is a recognition that you have to approach innovation and the growth that comes from innovation in a structured and strategic way. A lot of times, that is a big shift for a corporation who believes that innovation is about letting a thousand flowers bloom, not put any constraints around it, and trying lots of stuff. So first you have to recognize that you have to approach this strategically and thoughtfully.

The second step is to really get grounded in what is the goal of your innovation efforts, and the way that we generally suggest doing this is to calculate what we call the growth gap, which is you might look at 3, 5, 10 years or some cases longer than that; what is our aspiration? What do we want in terms of revenues, profits, whatever factor matters? Then, you take an honest look at what your core business is set to deliver, and what your ongoing growth efforts are set to deliver, and if you're honest about it in 90% of circumstances you will see a gap between what you are currently doing and investing in, and what your aspirations and your targets are.

The third step then is to come up with a plan to go and address that growth gap, and that plan should identify different types of strategies used to attack it. Like any good investor you'll want a portfolio. You will want some that involved current today's business and some that involve creating tomorrow's business. You will want to think specifically about what involves tomorrow's business, what are the greatest opportunities for growth. You want to then as precisely as you can set targets and allocated resources for each of those efforts.

So those are the three steps: first recognize the need to approach it strategically, calculate the growth gap, and then begin to come up with a plan to attack it.

DP: There is a common misperception of innovation being led in bits and spurts by a few visionary geniuses, but in your book you say that unfocused innovation efforts tend to struggle. Can you tell us a bit about how to create clearly defined goals and guidelines in order to transition from a growth blueprint to actual growth building?

SA: One of the biggest mistakes that we see senior leader make is that they approach innovation like a cowboy approaches the Wild West. They think it's good to say, "Let anything go. Let's try lots of things and see what happens." What ends up happening is that there is a lot of confusion of efforts, and a lot of random things. As a result, they tend to stay pretty small. If you look at the things that made Steve Jobs great, he was ruthlessly focused—he only did a few things incredibly well.

One of the easiest pieces of guidance is to put constraints on the problem. Research on creativity shows that constraints and creativity are friends. You think that they are an enemy, but the more you focus your attention, the more you are likely to get an uncommon answer. So, one of my simple rules of thumb is to ask executives to tell me five obvious things that you won't do: five boundary conditions that might surprise your staff.

Then give me five things that you might be open to in the right circumstances. This might be geographies, new business models, new commercialization approaches or brand strategies—it could be lots of different things, but explicitly take at least five things off and put five things on the table, and this puts some guidelines around the things that you are going to do.

DP: How does a company find a balance between core or incremental innovation that improves upon existing offerings vs. investing in adjacent or disruptive innovations? Could you tell us a bit about the different types of innovation?

SA: First, just about every organization defines things differently. For example, in the book we describe P&G and its four categories of innovation (1) Commercial that involve different types of promotion, packaging and marketing (2) Sustaining, everyday enhancements that make toothpaste taste better, laundry detergent work better, etc. (3) Transformational that up-end existing categories and (4) Disruptive that create new categories. That is one typology. Other companies might use core, adjacent, and white space, for example, so it varies.

The important thing is to have at least one type of innovation that purposely goes beyond the boundaries of today's business. How far beyond depends on the leadership team and industry circumstances, but you need to have something in your corporate portfolio that stretches, pushes, and promises to create tomorrow's business.

Second, approach innovation like a portfolio. There is no one answer—every company is different based on its circumstances and growth aspirations. Generally speaking, most companies spend between 50-70% of their time strengthening today's business doing incremental or core innovation, 20-30% pushing into more adjacent businesses where they bring something new to customers, and the remainder from 0-20% really explores new marketplaces.

Last, be careful about how you stage investment in anything new. One of the biggest failure mechanisms is a company invests millions of dollars and has thousands of people do this because they want to enter new markets. Instead, you want to approach like a venture capitalist. You make seed investments in small teams and have them go demonstrate an opportunity. Then, you invest the next round of capital and realize that opportunity.

DP: You identify four stage of innovation:

- *Stage 1—Spot Opportunities*
- *Stage 2—Design Solutions*
- *Stage 3—Test and Learn*
- *Stage 4—Scale*

Can you walk us through these stages, and are they standardized across all types of innovation?

SA: So the answer to the second question is yes. Emphasis and degrees of iteration might be different, but the process and stages are the same.

The first part is identifying a problem to be solved. Next, develop a solution to that problem at least at the hypothesis level. We typically call this blueprinting to imply that it is not just a product or service, but a business model that you are bringing to the problem that you are trying to solve.

The next step is to test, learn and adjust, where you go to run as close to market experiments as possible to work out some of your critical assumptions. This stage can be very quick if it's close to your core business, or it can take years if you are really pushing the boundaries, but at some magical point you really understand what is the essence of the business and business model you are trying to create—your key assumptions are addressed, there is a good fit between the offering and the market, and you have developed a good business model—and then you go to scale it.

DP: Many readers of this book will be familiar with the concept of an incubator for startups. How do incubators work in larger organizations to incubate higher-risk ideas? For example, how do they serve as separate, safe spaces

to incubate high-risk ideas independently of being criticized by manage-
ment, while still maintaining purposeful linkages with the core business?

SA: The biggest challenge and opportunity for large companies is to take advantage of all the unique assets that they already have. It could be technology, licenses to operate in a market, sales force, established brand identity,
etc. The key is to identify what is it that we have that the rest of the world
lacks? How does our growth effort tap into that capability? It's a very careful balancing act. If you look at research by Clayton Christensen and others
about why companies struggle with disruptive change, a root cause is they
are held captive by their own capabilities, so they don't stretch and buy new
businesses and create new business models.

If you do this right, then you create a growth group within your organization
where you collectively borrow from the core business. You can also forgo
the things that might hold you back, and learn some of the new things that
power success. That is something that has a degree of separation, but also a
form of connection. For example, we have been very interested in watching
efforts by Clark Gilbert, CEO of *Deseret News* in Utah, by doing exactly this.
He has been very thoughtful in creating what he calls a capabilities exchange–
a formal mechanism to selectively share business between the legacy and
new business.

So, for people who know what incubators are like in the wild, you would see
some things that are familiar—separation, ability to move quickly, rapidly
prototyping, etc.—but you also get to leverage some very unique, powerful
capabilities without being crushed by the legacy issues that come with those
capabilities. It's tough, but when it works it can be quite magical.

DP: One of the things that I've learned working with startups for the last ten
years is that innovation can be all about timing. If a product is too ahead of
the curve, consumers might not understand it, while there are key advan-
tages to being first to market. Can you tell us a bit about rapid prototyping,
testing, and the decision processes involved in scaling innovations so that
they align with an ideal market fit?

SA: First, when this transformation happens and you have this magic moment breakthrough that really takes off, particularly within the context of a
larger organization like many of our clients, the magic happens when three

things come together (1) you have a latent job to get done, a problem in the market that you might not be able to articulate but exists (2) a technological or societal trend that begins to expose or make possible doing that job (3) a catalytic corporate capability, something unique to a particular company that really few others can replicate.

As an example, think of Apple's iPad and Amazon's cloud computing service. In both cases, there was a latent job that needed to be done. With Apple, people wanted to enjoy simple computing when I'm not sitting in front of my laptop. For Amazon, businesses want to effectively manage their IT spend. There were clear technological and societal shifts that made both innovations possible (increase in bandwidth, computing power, etc.). Finally, Apple had its brand, design and previously existing product lines, etc. and Amazon had developed powerful IT systems that allowed it to move into a new market.

Second, recognize that every growth strategy will be partially right and partially wrong. You want to get really good at understanding the underlying assumptions that are behind success—consumer adoption, feasability of scaling, revenue model, etc.—and then test those assumptions in as close to market conditions as possible. You might be wrong with those things, so you need to be ready to study results of experiments and be ready to course correct.

To return to the Apple example, the iPad looks like an overnight success story creating $10 billion dollars in sales during the first year, but it actually traces back to a product in the early 1990s that failed. Apple learned from that effort, refined its technologies, and was then ready when the world was ready for a tablet solution.

DP: You mentioned Apple and talk about Apple in your book. Apple launched four successful billion-dollar platforms—the iPod, iPhone, iPad, and its retail stores—and its success has been covered exhaustively. Yet one of the hidden stories that you mention is the critical role that a few strategic acquisitions played in its success. Can you tell us about how M&A and partnership engines can be a driving force of innovation, even within a company like Apple that is a widely recognized leader in innovation?

SA: Any smart company recognizes that they don't have a monopoly on technology, talent or business models. If you look at any company that grows through acquisition, you will find people that recognize the need to tap into ideas that exist outside of the organization. In the case of Apple, key-underpinning technologies such as the touch interface, voice recognition, microprocessors, etc. have led Apple to do a number of acquisitions to enhance their capabilities. In fact, some of their complete new businesses, such as advertising in the case of Quatro Wireless, come entirely from acquisitions.

People need to approach innovation in a balanced way. Don't try to do it all organically or try to buy their way in—like in all things success happens when you find that magical balance between anything you're trying to do.

DP: Companies typically have hierarchical reporting structures, yet in the case of innovation sometimes more junior-level employees may have innovative ideas that could add significant value to an organization. How do companies facilitate and encourage innovation within the context of their management practices that can ensure a growth factory runs efficiently from the top-down, while also allowing ideas to bubble up from the bottom to the top?

SA: First, recognize that you want to manage different types of ideas in different ways. Now, this is one of the biggest challenges because most companies have dominant mechanisms by which they govern the company—decision rights, control mechanisms, templates, tools etc.—that exist to maintain today's business and they do that quite well. However, when you are trying to discover tomorrow's business, you need different mechanisms, which require a different type of discipline.

Second, try to create clear mechanisms for clearing houses to gather ideas wherever they might be. Spigit is a great example of a tool system that a company can implement to capture ideas wherever they might be.

Finally, all of this gets helped if you clearly communicate the problems that you are trying to solve—clear growth strategy about what is on and off the table, identify the opportunity areas that are most important, and then cascade this through the organization. Then you create a mechanism for the junior-level people that are closest to the front lines interacting with customers to say, "Oh, I've been thinking about this too!" This notion of parallel disciplines, specific mechanisms, and being clear about the problems you are trying to solve ensures you can get great ideas wherever they might be.

DP: You mention that most seasoned investors understand the importance of having a diversified portfolio to reduce risk, and yet they often fail to apply the same principles to their own companies when managing investments in innovation. Why is this? What are other common blind spots that you perceive in your work with the world's leading innovators?

SA: The primary reason is that there is a difference between an individual and a collective. Any individual with any degree of investment sophistication recognizes that portfolio diversification is generally good, and you evaluate different types of investments using different criteria. So, investing in a house is different than choosing a college, investing in stocks is different than investing in a friend's business, etc. An individual gets that, but the challenge in organizations is that everything gets systematized. Processes and mechanisms translate things into rewards systems, so while individuals understand individually, the systems don't support taking a true portfolio view. This gets back to what we started talking about, which is that you need to look at innovation in a systematic way.

The single biggest blind spot that I would point to is a false belief that a spreadsheet represents reality. So, you'll see in many companies, everyone is bowing before numbers on a spreadsheet and making very big decisions based on those numbers. The reality is, when you go into a new business the spreadsheet is often a bunch of made-up assumptions. They are best guesses. I know this especially from our Venture Capital activities in Singapore.

Whenever I see a leadership team for a new growth business that has any numbers to the right of the decimal point, I get worried because it is false precision—not reality. People obsess about the numbers and don't think about the story, the people, the strategy, and all of the other components that allow growth to happen.

DP: So what does it mean to be a "lean forward leader," and how do things like mentoring and forming the right teams contribute to creating a culture of innovation?

SA: A lean forward leader does not simply sit around and review a PPT at a desk. They are out talking to customers, participating in pilots, using new solutions, getting involved at a deeper level. Steve Jobs was a great example of this—incredibly detail oriented, working on every pass of design, touching the prototypes, etc. Now, a lot of people have been critical of his leadership style and the psychology of Steve Jobs, but touching, feeling, and participating is so important in part because the top leadership in large companies got there by participating in yesterday's business. If you're trying to get into tomorrow's business, you need to invest time into that.

In terms of the formation of teams, mentoring etc. innovation is a highly human activity. It is done by human beings, and that will be true for the foreseeable future. In most companies, it remains an unnatural act—it doesn't fit the existing systems and culture, so the role of the executive is to demonstrate through their behaviors things that might be counter-corporate culture must be encouraged. It's a critical component of getting this right.

DP: Failure is often viewed negatively, particularly within larger organizations, and yet within the context of innovation it is often perceived as a learning opportunity. How do you encourage innovation without unintentionally punishing prudent risk taking and smart failure? What types of incentive or reward systems can be put in place to reinforce and identify innovators?

SA: First, people recognize that failure is an important part of the journey of innovation. Rita McGrath frames this well. Basically, any new idea you get two good outcomes (1) you have a commercial success (2) you learn something that sets you up for the next commercial success. Many things that might be considered failures have very important key learnings that enable the organization to do new things.

Second, leaders can use the spotlight that often shines on them as a vehicle to humanize failure. AG Lafley from Procter & Gamble does this particularly well. He regularly talks about his personal failures, what did and didn't work within the organization, and how it impacted his life. Leaders that do this make it feel safer within the organization to take risks.

Third, on the performance systems, the single biggest thing that I suggest, borrowed from Michael Mauboussin who researched this in his recent book *The Success Equation*, about how you can measure performance in something like innovation. It's a lot like playing poker or hitting a baseball or investing in stock. Success or failure in any single event is a mix of luck and skill.

What he found was that you have to look not at the results that are achieved, but the process or behaviors that are followed, because in the long run following the right process and behaviors you'll succeed more often than you fail. Now, that is incredibly easier to say than do at scale in a larger organization, but it is what is necessary if you want to have performance management systems that encourage the right type of risk taking, failure and learning.

DP: One of the monumental paradoxes that Clayton Christensen cites in The Innovator's Dilemma *is that the root cause of corporate failure is often good management practices. They do everything right, and then a cheaper, better solution comes along in the form of a disruptive innovation.*

Can you tell us a bit about the relationship between good management and disruptive innovation, or what Clayton Christensen refers to as the innovator's dilemma?

SA: The paradox that Christensen identifies is that you are taught to prioritize opportunities that increase profit margins, produce better service or outcomes to the best customers, and focus on things that enable you to run your business better. All of that is very good guidance when you are trying to incrementally improve today's business, but they can cause a leader to deeply discount someone who comes in and changes the game by making it simpler, more convenient or more affordable.

It's interesting because today Kodak is just emerging from Chapter 11 bankruptcy protection. The people who ran Eastman Kodak were very smart, disciplined managers, and the discipline and skill that allowed them to build one of the world's great businesses proved to be challenging when Kodak tried to transition and transform into new businesses and new business models. It's not because they are dumb or want to run their businesses in the ground—it's just really hard when the game changes and you have to manage it using different rules.

So, to go back to this theme of a portfolio is absolutely critical if you want to not succumb to the innovator's dilemma.

DP: One final question. You mention that fifty years ago, it was a common belief that manufacturing processes were random and unpredictable, and that has since changed to improve the quality of manufacturing, Today, innovation is viewed as a similarly random and unpredictable process. Fifty years into the future, how might a fully realized vision of the world look like if all of your approaches to innovation have been adopted?

SA: You would predict that if people really approached innovation in a disciplined way that you would have companies able to more systematically and reliably deliver growth to their investors, stakeholders and employees. This means that instead of going through these unending cycles of boom and bust, where they realize one opportunity and build a great business around it, and then collapse when the world changes, they would be able to reinvent themselves and power into new markets.

I think this would be a tremendous thing for the world. I think a tremendous amount is lost when a great company like Eastman Kodak is lost because in the creative destruction a lot of smart people lose their jobs and lots of technologies take longer to realize their full potential. I love entrepreneurs—we invest in them, and they are an important part of the world's economy—but there are some things that only big companies can do.

Look at the big problems like access to affordable healthcare, climate change, feeding billions of people—these require the assets of a big company to solve. As the innovation revolution continues, and as people can be more predictable and reliable as it comes to some of these problems, we have a greater chance at putting a dent into some of these problems, which I think is a very good thing.

....

Scott Anthony *was elected Innosight's Managing Partner in 2012. He has led Innosight's expansion into the Asia-Pacific region as well as its venture capital activities (Innosight Ventures). In his decade with Innosight, Scott has advised senior leaders in companies such as Procter & Gamble, Johnson & Johnson, Kraft, General Electric, LG, Credit Suisse, Ayala Group, and Cisco Systems on topics of growth and innovation.*

Scott has written extensively about innovation. He is the coauthor of the new eBook Building a Growth Factory *and author of "The New Corporate Garage," which appeared in the September 2012 issue of* Harvard Business Review, *as well as* The Little Black Book of Innovation, *published by Harvard Business Review Press in January 2012. He is the co-author of the* Harvard Business Review *article "How P&G Tripled Its Innovation Success Rate." He co-authored* Seeing What's Next *(2004) with Harvard Business School Professor and Innosight founder Clayton Christensen and was the lead author of* The Innovator's Guide to Growth *and author of* The Silver Lining. *He has a regular column at* Harvard Business Online.

Scott's passion is in enabling innovators around the world to realize their untapped potential. In early 2010 Scott and his family relocated from the United States to Singapore to take advantage of the booming opportunities for innovation in Asia. He has spent significant time on the ground in India, Singapore, Korea, and the Philippines, and believes these and other countries are poised to be true innovation powerhouses.

Scott chairs the investment committee for IDEAS Ventures, a SGD 10 million fund Innosight runs in conjunction with the Singapore government. Scott has served as an active Board member for two companies incubated by Innosight (Village Laundry Service, a laundry service company based in Bangalore, and Guaranteach, a US-based online education company), helping those companies develop and execute their strategy and raise external expansion capital.

BUSINESS MODEL GENERATION

Alex Osterwalder

Alex Osterwalder's *Business Model Generation* was a huge inspiration for writing this book—an international business bestseller, self-funded and self-published, highly disruptive and incredibly innovative, it inspired a global movement and entirely new approach to business model innovation based on visual language with huge implications. Highlights include:

- Business models expire and need to be tested and reinvented
- Why the most innovative companies disrupt their own business models
- The questions you must constantly ask to remain competitive
- How business leaders should use tools the way a surgeon operates on a patient

With over 700,000 copies in print in 26 languages, and 5 million users of his Business Model Canvas, Alex has succeeded in creating a global movement that is a critical component of understanding the Disruption Revolution. I would highly recommend all readers to integrate his methods and approach into your business toolkit.

DP: Why is business model innovation important?

AO: For a few reasons. First, there is more competition than every before through globalization and technology. Everybody is competing against everybody. The arenas are not clear anymore. We used to call it industry. If you take the work of Rita McGrath, we now call them arenas. For example, Google, Apple, Amazon, they are all competing against everyone so industry boundaries are disappearing and everybody is competing with each other in the same arena.

Second, business models are expiring faster than every before. We know this from the music industry, the publishing industry, the news industry. But now it's happening to any kind of arena. If you take the pharmaceutical industry, if you can still call it an industry, their business model has expired and they need to come up with a new one. And probably, some of the dominant players today won't be around tomorrow. These are some of the things that we know from technology and mobile phones, but we're not as swift in things like banks and pharmaceuticals.

Third, I like to say that business models are like yogurt in the refrigerator— they expire, it's inevitable. Managers used to manage one business model over their whole career. Today, it's not unusual for one person in the same arena has to manage different types of business models. One expires, and they have to come up with the next one. And if you don't, you can see what happens with companies like Nokia—you can go from the top to the bottom very quickly.

DP: So what makes business model generation disruptive and how would your approach relate to broader trends in innovation such as the adoption of social media or the Collaborative Economy model?

AO: I don't think that we have a lack of ideas and concepts out there—wonderful, amazing concepts like disruptive innovation—and we were not the first to write about business models. I wrote a Ph.D. on business models and built upon a foundation of previous work. But, we did a lot of things differently.

If you look at Google trends, the Business Model Canvas is straight on a path to replace (if you want) the search term "strategic plan." Now, that's pretty impressive, this is a very broad term. So why did the Business Model Canvas succeed so much while we were not the first to talk about business models?

I'll point out two main reasons why the business model canvas has been successful.

First, it's visual. As human beings, we're inherently visual. It's just genetics. We used to see a lion on the savanna, and we ran away—it had to do with survival. Now today in the boardroom, it's not about survival as much as it is using visual tools to enhance the conversations that we're already having.

So, when we have a board meeting, and you just talk, you're violating the rules of genetics and evolution. We're visual people, so what you really want to do is use tools like the Business Model Canvas to discuss your business. It leads to better conversations, from startups and their boards up to senior executives in large companies like GE. The visual aspect changes the game.

Second, it is ultra-practical and relevant for people in their daily conduct. While there are a lot of great business concepts out there, and I'm a big fan of business concepts, very few of them take the time to turn concepts into practical tools that a manager or entrepreneur can use on a Monday morning. We help translate the concepts into tools that they can use. Many business books stop at the idea and don't turn it into a tool that a business practitioner can use immediately.

For example, we came up with a Value Proposition Canvas, a new canvas that can zoom into parts that are too small to sketch out on the Business Model Canvas. We had this thing that looked like the Business Model Canvas, and what we realized in using it with practitioners is that they would narrow it into greater detail. So my cofounder and I at Strategyzer figured out how to shape a better user interface. Now, it might sound silly, but tell me how many management thinkers have time to figure out a better user interface for their tools?

Once we figured out the shape and we tested it, we had a breakthrough with the method. While we have experience designers for websites and products, we need the same things for business tools. Why should we expect less from the user-interface and user-experience of a business tool than we do from a website or product? We're talking about elevating our investments and value propositions, so we should maximize the utility.

DP: Your current work is based on Ph.D. research. As a former Ph.D. candidate at Princeton myself, I remember the lonely life of a graduate student writing papers that maybe only 2-3 people would ever read. Jump ahead today, and you have 700,000 books out, 26 languages, 5 million canvas users = one big movement.

What made you want to study business models, and how has your thinking evolved since you built such a large global community around your work?

AO: The initial spark was my interest in the entire company—understanding all aspects of a company. In all of my studies, I never found the answer. I did marketing, management information systems, accounting, etc. and yet nobody ever showed me how these pieces all fit together. Then, I had this opportunity to do a Ph.D. thesis with Yves Pignuer on business models, because he needed a researcher on business models, so the initial idea came from him.

Then, I had another opportunity with McKinsey. Now, life is funny, because the McKinsey interview was a bomb, and then I did the Ph.D. with Yves Pignuer because the topic was interesting and it allowed me to study the entire aspect of the company. Coming full-circle, the business model canvas is used by consultants around the world.

It's really about looking at all aspects of the company very quickly, and today I can see in my workshops and as a team that this is what people are interested in—seeing the big picture on one piece of paper. What interested me at the beginning is actually a very relevant problem. Today, people don't see the big picture anymore, and the big picture changes. If you can't manage that big picture and your business model expires, what are you going to do?

It's not marketing or operations that are going to save you, it's the big picture. Nobody knows how to do these big changes anymore because we don't have entrepreneurs at the head of these large companies. So, it's interesting to see what interested me at the beginning turned out to be a relevant problem that went mainstream today—understanding all aspects of a company in the quickest possible way.

DP: There can be multiple business models for the same product. You've said that we should test out business models by asking ourselves tough questions. What types of tough questions should we be asking?

AO: There are two types of testing of your business model: (1) inside the building and (2) outside the building, inspired by Steve Blank's work on customer development and Erik Ries's work on the Lean Startup.

First, inside the building—ask yourself: Do you have the best business model design possible? It has nothing to do with the market; it has to do with design of the business model. For example, you should ask yourself "Can I create more recurring revenues?" Transactional revenues are more costly to produce. Can you move from transactional revenues (selling something) to recurring revenues?

One of my favorite examples is Nespresso. They turned an entire industry selling coffee from transactional to recurring revenues.

Or ask yourself: What would you do if you couldn't earn money anymore from your bestselling product or service anymore? Now, for most people that question sounds crazy. But, in many industries this became reality. In the telecom industry for phone operators, when Skype arrived their revenue from international calls went to zero. When Google Maps became popular, look at what happened to all of these map companies. So, these very tough questions become reality.

How can you get others to do the work for you? Look at the business model of Facebook—they have one billion free employees. The value of Facebook, for users, is not the platform but the content, and the content is generated for free by a billion users. So, Facebook built a business model based on free labor—everyone that uses Facebook turned Mark Zuckerberg and his employees into billionaires. That's great for them—they figured it out and built a business model based on a free product.

Asking yourself these tough questions moves you beyond competing on products to compete on business models because business models are harder to copy. Have you seen a copy of IKEA? It's hard to copy. This is an ultra-profitable business model. Economic theory would say that it should be copied right away, but it's much harder to copy business models than to copy technology or products.

DP: Most companies tend to think of their business model in terms of a simple product-market fit because they think that they are basically building products for a particular market. This is basically what you refer to as a level zero understanding of business models. What does a level 2 or 3 business model understanding look like?

AO: Level zero is about companies that mainly focus on what in the startup scene we call the product-market fit. What they don't realize is that today you compete more on business models, or worse you create products with the wrong business model and totally flop. To come back to Nespresso, they almost failed and went bankrupt with the same machine and a different business model because they were trying to sell to the wrong market, and then they came up with a different business model.

Take any Fortune 500 company or FT 500 company, and look at where they spend money—R&D, research and development—and that's great. We shouldn't replace that. But the success of most products today is related not just to great products, but also to a better business model.

Nintendo with the Wii is a great example of a company competing on a Level 2 business model. When they first introduced the Wii, all that we saw was a technology innovation—controlling game console with motion control—yet if you look at its impact on the business model, it's pretty spectacular. Basically, they used an inferior technology to address a totally different market with a totally different value proposition. It's not just that which is important in terms of creating the product-market fit.

Because they worked with inferior technology but a better value proposition, they could reduce their spending on R&D and reduce subsidies that the entire industry spent on game consoles, and in the process address the larger market of casual gamers that led to insane profits. So, here you have a company that builds a better business model based on an inferior technology. That's something companies don't do—it's totally counterintuitive. Today, some people are talking about reverse-innovation.

They are a Level 2 company instead of Level 3 because they waited until they would disrupt their own business model. Level 3 are companies that build great business models but don't wait for the market to disrupt them. They start coming up with great business models while they are successful and on top. Nokia and Kodak didn't do that.

Apple is a great example. At every stage they started to invent a new product with a new business model behind it. So, with the iPhone they deliberately accepted that they would disrupt or cannibalize their iPod sales. When they introduced the iPad, they knew that they would cannibalize and disrupt their laptop sales. So, they disrupted themselves while they were successful. At each stage, the business model changed as well. When they introduced the iPhone and disrupted the iPod, that was a totally different business model—

it's a different industry, they built the Apps Store. The same with the iPad; they started to move into advertising.

Same with Amazon. They continue to build new business models while they are successful. When they introduced Amazon web services, the analysts said that they were crazy. Now, with the Kindle and Kindle store they are starting to disrupt the entire publishing industry. Level 3 companies are successful because they understand one thing: they improve their existing business models and invent new ones at the same time.

If you look at Rita McGrath's book *End of Competitive Advantage*, she writes about this fact that the best companies that can improve business models and invent new ones at the same time. The truth is it's hard to do. Inventing requires an entrepreneurial logic of experimentation, while improvement requires the execution logic of a larger company. Large companies don't know how to invent because they stopped experimenting and they are too afraid to fail.

DP: You made a successful transition from academic to author and entrepreneur. What is your vision for Strategyzer, the business model generation and platform—what might a fully realized vision of mass adoption look like 20-30 years from now when entrepreneurs and CEOs are all applying your tools across their organizations?

AO: First, I wouldn't say that they all use our tools—just that they simply start using tools, like an architect or engineer uses CAD to design when they design buildings or airplanes. That doesn't mean just our methods, like the Business Model Canvas and the Value Proposition Canvas to start with, but all of them together.

Imagine if surgeons would operate with the same kind of training and experience that people have with strategy and innovation, we would never go to a hospital for surgery. Imagine if your surgeon said, "I read this book last weekend and there is some cool stuff in there, so I'm going to start snipping away." Of course not—surgeons are trained to use tools in a very rigorous way. There is no one-fits-all tool and they are trained to use all tools together.

So, in the same way as we have the canvases and tools that we developed, we'll have canvases and tools for culture, vision, etc. and we'll use them together and be trained really well. It will be commonsense in the same way as a doctor comes out of university training and goes into a hospital and learns like that, people in strategy and innovation will be the same way. It's going to be normal to use these tools. Today it's not, and it should be that way.

Today, we are good at doing things right—operations, accounting, project management, etc.—but we're not good yet at doing the right thing. Figuring out what's the right business model, what are the right value proposition, customer development, lean startup, etc.—the methods are there but when it becomes normal to use them that's when we will really get somewhere. So, my vision is that people will want to use Strategyzer and these tools will be so common that if you don't know about them, then people will not think you are a serious professional.

Now let me give you the really geeky part of my vision: when we have project rooms where every wall is a touch screen, and we can play around with our tools in a digital way instead of a paper-based way. We'll enhance paper with technology. Today, they still use paper and pencil in CAD, but that seamless moving back and forth between paper and digital to enhance creativity is the future that really excites me.

Alexander Osterwalder *is an entrepreneur, speaker and business model innovator. Together with Professor Yves Pigneur he co-authored* Business Model Generation, *a global bestseller on the topic of business model innovation. His Business Model Canvas, a tool to visualize, challenge and (re-) invent business models is used by leading organizations around the world, like GE, P&G, Ericsson, and 3M. Alexander is a frequent keynote speaker and has held guest lectures in top universities around the world, including Stanford, Berkeley, MIT, IESE and IMD.*

The Business Model Foundry, his current startup, is building strategic tools for innovators. Strategyzer.com and the Business Model Toolbox for iPad are the Foundry's first applications. Alexander holds a PhD from HEC Lausanne, Switzerland. He is recipient of the Innovation Luminary Award 2013 awarded by the EU Open Innovation Strategy and Policy Group. He is also a founding member of The Constellation, a global not-for-profit organization aiming to make HIV/AIDS and Malaria history.

CUSTOMER-CENTRIC SOLUTIONS

Paul Wittenberg

Paul Wittenberg has a gift for making incredibly complex software and services that might cost $100k-$1mm or more seem like a bargain because he knows how to frame them as solutions to more expensive problems. We talk about how customer-centric approaches are critical to selling innovation and how to implement these strategies across teams within the enterprise:

- How smart questions guide customers down a decision path
- Marketing and sales can be an extension of the same process
- The unique challenge of selling innovations that your target customers might not understand
- Segmenting products and services into tiered offerings according to market needs

Paul Wittenberg and I worked together at Visible Technologies. He taught me how to market and sell solutions instead of products and services, how to create and manage sales pipelines, and overall had a formative impact on my view of how large companies are run and operate. I guarantee that you will sell and market more effectively as a result of reading this interview, and your customers in turn will like you more.

DP: What does it mean to be customer-centric? How does this type of approach impact the various parts of the enterprise like management style, product development, sales and marketing, client services, etc.?

PW: Let me tackle this question in two ways—first by looking at customer centric from the selling perspective, and secondly, from a more corporate wide perspective and as it relates to social media.

From the sales perspective, you are looking to help your customer solve a problem, reach a goal, or fill a need. In this context, you are in discovery mode when you talk to your customer. You ask questions about their situation, the background and their objectives, in order to co-create a solution. If you come in wanting to talk about your product first, you're already headed in the wrong direction.

While it will feel very unnatural for a seasoned salesperson, your intent is not to sell, but to identify a solution. By focusing on the solution, it is going to feel much more comfortable to the customer that you are talking to. They will be more open with the information that you will need as a salesperson. Understanding the customer's issue at a deep level is going to give you all of the information that you need to sell. Now you just need to wait for the right time.

Once you've agreed upon a solution to the issue, you can begin to describe how your technology/software/service fits the needs of the customer. You are no longer talking about the speeds, feeds and features of your product in hopes that they actually are relevant to the customer's issue, but now you can specifically tailor a solution that is designed to meet the needs of the customer, which is the solution that you and the customer have previously jointly agreed to.

There will also be times when you work with a customer to define a solution and you realize that your technology/software/service is not a fit. At that point you should drop the opportunity and move on. Customers have access to a vast amount of information today and they generally understand the capabilities of each of the vendors that they are talking to. They will know as well as you, and sometimes better, if your solution is a fit. If you try to push a bad position, it will only waste everyone's time.

The second point in your question regarding what it means to be a customer-centric company revolves around social media. As I just mentioned, customers have access to greater and greater amounts of information today. They are very knowledgeable buyers. And this is where the concept of a customer-centric organization comes in. Social allows every department in the organization to have a focus on the customer. If nothing else, everyone can listen to the voice of the customer using social media listening technology. Those organizations that keep the customer top-of-mind are the ones that will ultimately win those minds, and hearts.

From a management style, the organization needs to be much more open and accessible. It needs to have a transparency that heretofore has not been the model under which most organizations operate. This means that there needs to be a significant cultural change in organizations, and this change, and leadership, needs to start at the top.

Lastly, while sales, and the process that you use as part of the sales function, is something that can be executed in a customer-centric fashion for some time now, because you are directly engaged with customer, other functions have not had this advantage. However today, with the use of social media, you can engage customers and potential customers in many of the internal processes of an organization. The concept that we've used in sales is now applicable to the entire organization.

DP: Your background is in sales strategy and consulting for a variety of innovative enterprise technologies that clients often need but might not necessarily understand how to use or implement. What are the unique challenges in selling innovation?

PW: It is interesting that many vendors want to sell innovation to their customers. Everyone is creating products that will equip companies with a new set of capabilities which will allow them to innovate in either what they do, or how they do it. The capabilities that their products provide are generally beyond both the level of detail that can be communicated in a sales cycles or comprehended by the customer, but also, they are generally beyond the capability of the organization to implement once the sale is completed. So there are challenges behind both the selling of the vision, and then the customer actually receiving the value that they were expecting.

In the sales cycle, you need to address a few core items in order to make sure that you are getting your message across. First off, you'll need to tie the innovation back to the need/want/desire that has been expressed. Secondly, don't over sell. Product offerings today can be very comprehensive and carry many features. We all often get stuck in the trap of explaining all of the bells and whistles that exist in the product. But if these features do not address the need/want/desire of the customer, the message is probably creating more confusion for the customer. Keep focused with the message and stay on point with the issue that you are looking to solve.

More and more, we find that organizations will have a new role titled Chief Innovation Officer. This role is focused on helping the organization make greater strides with either their products, internal processes, or both. If the product or service that you are selling is one that is going to make a major shift in the way that a business operates, the Chief Innovation Officer will need to be one of the people that you are talking to.

Now I'm going to bring this back around to being customer-centric. Selling innovation, or innovative products and services is great, but I would not necessarily suggest that you sell "innovation." As a salesperson, you still need to be helping the customer define a solution. Many times, this means that you need to help your customer create a vision for what is possible, or even extend the vision that the customer has started with. As a salesperson, we are generally more knowledgeable about the industry segment that we sell into and will be able to paint a vision for the customer, which is beyond what they have created for themselves.

Lastly, I want to talk to the point in your question regarding implementation. It is important that the sale is not just focused on selling, but on success of the customer. When I worked in the Big 6 (now I call it the Big N, where N is one to many) I had a Partner that would remind us that we are like the airline industry. We don't celebrate takeoffs; we celebrate landings. In this context, the sale is the takeoff, and the overall success of the customer is the landing. But in order for the customer to be successful, we need to ensure that they have all of the other support necessary for success bundled into the deal. Without this, customers can struggle with their implementation and have difficulty in finding value with your product or service.

DP: The way in which companies communicate with their customers is critical, particularly when dealing with innovations that the customer might not understand.

Why is asking intelligent questions so important?

PW: In sales, as it is in interviewing, I find that the best thing you can do is ask an intelligent question. You can talk all day about your products and services, but the moment you ask a really smart and insightful question that the customer hadn't thought about, which indicates you were listening, and is relevant to what the customer is doing, you will engage a customer. They will immediately understand that you have a command of the problem set and can apply a solution that specifically meets their needs. This is the best way that I know to demonstrate knowledge to a customer.

I think that's why the probing question is so important. It's more valuable than any other approach you can take. So, a customer-centric approach is wrapped around finding a need, want, or desire. Now, they might not be things that are in the forefront of the customer's mind. It may take some probing questions to get the customer to realize that there are opportunities for them that they have not yet realized, or conversely, that there are competitive threats in the marketplace for the kinds of services they are selling. Either one of these heightens the customer's understanding of the market.

Without uncovering one of those needs, wants or desires, you are really not selling against a particular objective. You're trying to push a product and selling against no particular need. You might have other customers who are more readily capable and understand the domain space you're trying to attack and you could more easily work with those customers than the one you are currently talking to. Part of the objective here is to spend your valuable time with those customers who "get it".

Many sales people will tell you that if they can't identify a specific customer objective (want, need, desire), they just very quickly walk away from that deal. And that's the way I would approach it too. If the customer is not "getting it", and through your intelligent questioning you can't uncover a want, need or desire, then I would move on and find the customers where you can.

DP: Can you tell us a bit more about how to qualify a lead? What are a few examples of probing questions and how do they move someone along a decision path?

PW: Much of the lead qualification that takes place today holds up in the customer-centric model as well. These are all of the standard questions that we've been asking already regarding budget, timelines, responsibility, and compelling business events, etc. While these are necessary and valid, I would take a second tact as well.

Sales cycles are as much about selling as they are about educating the customer. Asking the right questions about the solution itself will give you a better sense of how far the customer has thought through the problem. If the person that you are talking to is limited in their understanding of the scope of the problem, then you probably need to be looking for others in the organization that need to be included in the sales process.

Innovative technologies can span a much greater number of departments in an organization beyond just the one that you may be talking to. When you get large leaps in technology, such as corporate adoption of the Internet in the 1990s, and Social Media today, you need to start looking across the organization. These types of business-related evolution will fundamentally change the way the businesses will function.

DP: Asking questions and talking about solutions can sound very philosophical and abstract. How do you take a customer-centric approach to sales and map it to critical milestones in a decision process, making the sales process more objective and easy to manage from the perspective of a sales manager. For example, how does saying "yes" to certain questions mean that a lead might be 40% or 80% towards closing?

PW: You make a good point here. I think that solutions can feel a bit abstract for some customers, but these are not really abstract concepts. If a customer has thought through the problem that they are trying to solve, you will find quick alignment with them and none of your questions will feel foreign to them. For customers that haven't completed their own thought process, they will find your questions educational, as they will provide a roadmap for them, defining the additional items that they need to consider. If you find your customer finds your questions to be in the clouds (not the technology kind), you either don't have a deal, or you have a very long sales cycle ahead of you.

From the process perspective, there are a number of discrete steps that are taken as part of a customer-centric selling approach. These are clearly defined and each of them indicates that a salesperson has moved the process further to a sale. These are quantifiable steps that allow sales leadership to have a common language and understanding for where a deal is in the process. Given that each market segment is different, I would suggest that each company define their own percentage complete thresholds that best fit their industry segment and tune these as necessary.

DP: How does customer-centric selling relate to things like pricing and seg-menting products and services into different solution sets for different tar-get markets? For example, let's say I'm a software company with 10 features, and I want to offer all 10 to enterprise clients at $10,000/month, 6-7 of them to small businesses for $1,000/month, and 2-3 features in a free version. How do you create pricing models, package features into solutions, and then position them in the marketplace?

PW: The segmenting of products and services for the purposes of tiering the market offerings will need to be done in a way that is consistent with the market's needs. Most companies will be more focused on a single market segments until they become more mature. If a company's offerings are go-ing to be segmented, I would do it along the line of solutions to start with. If these solutions fit the specific needs of small, medium or larger enterprises, that's great, but it doesn't always work out this way. Generally, each of these segments have similar needs and it is just a question of scale or size. So packing should start along solution lines first.

This is why the scale of cloud software has been so great. In general, it scales in two directions. Everyone starts with the same base functionality. It doesn't matter how large or small you are. But from there you can order the number of seats that you need, which directly scales to the size of your organization.

The second scaling item is functionality. Everyone has a unique business with specific needs. This is where app exchanges play such a big part. You can easily scale the functionality of the solution that you've purchased by adding the modules that are specific to your needs, and only pay for the ones that you want. The solution that you build will be specific to your business, allowing you to pay for just the right amount of capability, and for just the right amount of people.

So, this is all to say that I wouldn't suggest that customer-centric sell-ing influences the pricing and packaging of products, but the other way around. The fact that technology now allows us to customize solutions to this level of detail requires that the sales person be much more of a consultant to their customers, helping them build a solution that fits their needs.

DP: Sales people are often the ones closest to customers. Lots of times in enterprise sales, there is a disconnect between the promise of what is sold and the actual functionality and value of the product. How can a more consultative or customer-centric approach to sales help address these disconnects, and what steps can companies take to integrate feedback from sales into product development to ensure solutions align with the needs of customers?

PW: While there may be struggles with the selling of capabilities that are not in fact inherent in the product, I think that we are moving further and further away from that as a core issue. What I see more these days is that customers are having a hard time with achieving value from the technology. And this is not a technology issue. While technology will always have its bugs, it is generally very solid and robust. This issue comes in when the customer needs to derive value from the product. As example, I have Excel on my machine, and while it is an incredibly powerful tool, I don't nearly get the value out of it that I could, and I would guess that this is true for most people. This is not a technology issue.

Where the salesperson needs to be focused is in "selling success". This is no longer just a product question, but a solution question. This is why customer-centric selling is so important. A salesperson needs to define the entire solution for the customer, and can't just walk away and hope that everything will be a success. Conversely, the customer can't just assume that the lowest price option is the best, or that the product is the only component that they need for their solution. Consulting resources, executive sponsorship, education and training of staff, organizational realignment and many other changes to the organization may be necessary in order to achieve success and realize value from a new technology.

DP: We have been talking primarily about the sales process up to this point. How do you take a customer-centric approach to lead generation, and take advantage of web, social, email, events, and other channels to generate qualified leads?

PW: If an organization is listening to its customers and potential customers, not just via sales calls and round tables, but on the web and in social, they will have a good idea of the solutions and innovations that customers are looking for. This is the great part of social media. Everyone is connected and everyone has a chance to provide their input regarding the products and services your organization produces. Once an organization is listening to all of the channels that are available to them, they can better support their customers, and this starts right at the beginning of the sales process, at the lead generation stage.

In lead generation, you want to provide value to the community that you are focused on. It is a value exchange, where the company is providing valuable information through these channels to both their customers and potential customers. In exchange for some of this content, customers will provide an email address or a social ID. This exchange provides value to both the producer and consumer of the content.

There are a number of metrics which can be followed regarding frequency of the messaging and the content, so it is not always a solution-focused message, but when it is, it should target the customer needs that you define and discuss later in the sales cycle.

All of these digital and social channels allow a company to begin to build a relationship with their customers early in the process. This relationship helps establish the company as a thought leader and a valued member of the community, and helps to maintain the relationship with a customer throughout their lifecycle.

DP: Can you maybe talk a little bit about the concept of the customer lifecycle. For example, how does a focus on solutions allow companies to continually up-sell and cross-sell additional products and services after the initial point of sale? Does a customer-centric focus help to increase retention rates and drive more revenue?

PW: Once you get through the initial sale, then you are into deployment, meaning that a customer has taken your product or service into their operations. There needs to be a compliment of this phase where you don't completely leave the customer—some type of methodology that is part of the overall customer journey that continues ongoing support to the customer. In this sense, the sales cycle only begins once and never ends.

Instead, the sales life cycle becomes part of an ongoing process. In order to up-sell or cross-sell, you need more products and services that are tangential to what you've already sold. These offerings are going to bolt on and extend the value of a previous solution. Doing this requires an ongoing process of identifying needs, wants or desires and having services and products that actually fit for the customer.

This all goes back to the importance of asking intelligent questions—how are things going? What problems are being solved? What new challenges are you facing? Because the reality is that the best way to generate sales is to sell additional products and services to your existing customers by constantly adding more value. In this sense, customer service becomes an extension of the sales process, and to a certain extent the sales process never ends.

Another component is that you are always selling in a competitive market— innovation wouldn't be a requirement without competition. We would only have one company per market that would produce all of the products for that market, and they wouldn't need to do it well. So, as competition continues to be more innovative and customer needs continue to evolve, it is equally important that feedback from sales and customer service teams is funneled back into the development of better products and services. This is why it is essential to put programs in place that institutionalize innovation—it should not be a haphazardly executed function.

DP: I think this relates to a larger question, which is that often times there is a risk in larger companies of operating in silos. They require planning and a cohesive internal workflow, and by nature tend to be resistant to change.

How do they implement and encourage a culture of innovation?

PW: That's a really good question. I think you can stratify this at different levels.

First, there are repeatable operational elements that you need to put in place and retain. There is also a whole layer of what I would describe as middle management that tend to be younger, newer, and come from other organizational backgrounds with different institutional processes. I think there is a real challenge and opportunity to more quickly integrate knowledge from middle management into the organizations—because ultimately these people will rise to the top and eventually run the company.

Part of building that culture can be the use of technology. Whether or not that's an innovation platform that is deployed that specifically works on pasturing, vetting, disseminating, etc. those ideas or whether it's things like social technologies that allow for individuals to collaborate across silos doesn't matter—these kinds of technologies can allow people to be innovative and do the kinds of things that need to be done to move an organization forward from a new product, service or operations. Innovation isn't limited to the external components of a company—it can be any component of an organization.

DP: Innovative technologies can provide companies with a continually evolving toolset to remain competitive and gain strategic advantage. What steps do you take to identify essentially the best tools in the marketplace, and then how do you integrate them into daily workflow and leverage for strategic advantage?

PW: There are two parts to this (1) identification and (2) operational. In identifying products, there are continually new products and services on the market that any company could use to evolve its toolset. And secondly, once you acquire these tools, how do you get your organization to change? How do you get everyone to use these tools effectively?

First, identification—you need to have people that are continually evaluating technologies, processes, services, etc. available on the market that can be used for competitive advantage. Most companies do that relatively well with respect to their existing products because that's the way they build their products.

It's a little more complicated when you're talking about operational elements internally because you get any number of managers, directors and vice presidents across the organization looking at these things differently. Each realize it would be effective for their component of the organization, but innovation touches a broader swath of people, so the real challenge is how do you operationalize this across the entire organization?

First, you need to have the correct level of executive sponsorship in order to move things forward. This is the level of support that is needed to break down silos and drive innovation across an organization. Secondly, oftentimes these changes requires the execution of a cross functional team to provide the overall governance and processes. This includes creating common definitions so everybody has a say in how changes will get rolled out, but also has a seat at the table. That way the various vice presidents and managers brought in can help guide the processes in a collaborative way.

....

Paul Wittenberg *is a technology professional, helping customers enable their organizations to best leverage leading edge technologies. Paul has held senior positions with IBM, BEA, KPMG and Salesforce, where he focused on technologies such as Telecommunications, Mobility, Internet/ecommerce and Social Media. Between building the first local Internet practice at IBM, running the World Wide Telecom practice at BEA and leading the social media strategy delivery at Salesforce, Paul has continued to look at the application of new technologies in support of business objectives.*

Paul has been recently looking into the application of these technologies to assist regional governmental entities with the services that they offer to their communities.

When not working, Paul has one marathon under his belt; 95% of a pilot's license; plays guitar in a rock band, banjo in a Dixieland band; and is rebuilding a 65 GMC pickup.

....

THE ROI OF ACKNOWLEDGMENT

Dr. Natalie Petouhoff

Dr. Natalie Petouhoff has spent her entire career being an internal champion and advocate for customers. As an engineer, management consultant, research analyst, marketing and PR strategist, and customer service expert, she has held leadership positions in every seat of an organization, uniquely qualifying her to communicate the ROI of acknowledgment:

- Why customer service is really customer retention
- Crossing the chasm to engage pragmatic business leaders
- The importance of mapping ROI to traditional business metrics and KPIs
- How to quantify the value of acknowledgment and customer experience

Dr. Natalie breathes fresh air into an often confusing and convoluted area: quantifying the value of things traditionally considered intangible such as being heard and acknowledged. Calling herself a "Margaret Mead of Tech," Natalie's intelligent, human-centered approach should be useful to anyone that wants to scale and sell innovation.

DP: In a couple of your talks I watched in preparation for this interview, you mentioned an experience in your first job out of college that involved turning lead into gold. It's a great example of the challenges many innovators face in larger companies—can you tell us the story?

NP: At the GE division I worked for, we made tungsten carbide tool bits. We coated them with two different types of coatings: Aluminum oxide (white in color) and Titanium Nitride (a shinny, gold color.) This was one of my first engineering jobs. As I sat in a meeting with sales, marketing and engineering, our goal was to figure out which coating we should make more of.

Sales said, "Look at the numbers. We should make more of the gold ones because they are selling better." They cared a lot about their bonuses. The engineers responded by saying, "But the white-coated ones are more durable and last longer than the gold-coated tool bits. Maybe we need to market the white ones better so sales will increase. Our reputation is at stake."

As I was observing these different points of view, I saw both sides of the story. I wanted to show that I could contribute to the decision-making process. I asked, "Did we ever ask our customers what they think is better or what they want to buy?" The room got really quiet and then everyone started laughing out loud. Devastated, I wanted to crawl under a large boulder and hide forever.

But then I heard my grandpa's voice in my head. He said, "You're a smart girl. Follow your instinct." His acknowledgement was enough to give me the courage to take the next step. Even though I was completely embarrassed, my gut told me that knowing what customers think *is* important. I asked my supervisor for a gold and white tool bit to take to some machine shops to ask their opinion. My boss looked at me like I had three heads, "You're still on that? Wasn't it enough that you got laughed at?"

I stared, holding back the tears. Seeing my determination, he said, "You can have the tool bits, but clock out. I'm not paying you to talk to our customers. That's ridiculous!" Feeling resolute, I followed my gut instinct to talk to customers. As I entered the machine shops, I held out a white and gold tool bit and asked the machinist, "Which one do you like better and why?" It was a very simple focus group. The answer? They liked the gold ones better.

I said, "But you know the white ones last longer, right?" They shook their head yes. I asked, "Why do you like the gold ones better?" They replied, "The gold ones make us feel happy." That wasn't the response I thought I would get. And that made asking the next question even more valuable. I questioned, "Could you tell me more about that?" The machinist exclaimed, "Look around us, Natalie. Everything in this machine shop is gray. The floors are gray; the walls are gray; the machines are gray. We've been doing these jobs, some of us, for 30 years. We don't care if the white ones last longer.

The gold ones make us happy. They are the one shiny thing we have to look forward to—everyday."

I wasn't sure if it was worth telling my managers. Part of me thought it was crazy to say anything; and it was crazy if I didn't. I did tell them. And though I thought the information was "golden," they didn't care. They told me to mind my own business. That experience left an indelible mark on a very young and impressionable engineer. How could "we" as a company not care what our customers think? And that's how my engineering career began. The ROI of acknowledgement? It's about the return on the investment for when someone acknowledges you—like my Grandpa did. Though I didn't get the acknowledgement from my bosses at that job, it did set me on the path to be dedicated to understanding what customers want and need, and how to set-up systems to go beyond the basics and provide them things they didn't even know they wanted. The ROI of my grandfather acknowledging me, my ideas, my principles? Priceless.

DP: You were an early adopter of ideas like customer experience, which have started to become mainstream recently with the rise of social media. You have been sitting between two groups—the early adopter/innovators who are super excited about social media, and the early-majority pragmatists who are unsure what the excitement is about. How do you help the early majority see what you see and reduce their resistance to adopt social media?

NP: I became what I call a Chasm Crosser. It's a term I coined to describe the ability to bridge the gap between the *early adopters/ innovators* vs. *early majority*. Studying the adoption of change via work by Geoffrey Moore, Everett Rogers, John Kotter and Thomas Kuhn, I realized there's always a chasm between the two groups. Moore's book *Crossing the Chasm* coined the chasm terminology we use today.

As I observed the current business issues, I saw the way the early adopters/ innovators were talking about social media was actually turning off the very people who were in charge of increasing the budgets—i.e., the early majority. As part of the early adopters/ innovators group, I knew we just were excited about the possibilities that social media could bring to a company. And in many ways "right" what's been wrong with Corporate America i.e., the pattern of not listening to customers and providing horrible customer service because the contact center is thought of as a cost center. That's wrong, by the way.

The reason for the chasm? The people who create new things—like Web 2.0 and social media—are the early adopters/ innovators and "get" the inherent value of social media; they don't need ROI models or business justification. On the other side of the chasm, the early majority are very pragmatic. Many early majority executives said to me, "Honestly Natalie, don't tell anybody, but I don't get social. I know my kids are on it. They share pictures of what they ate for lunch or things they bought at the Mall. But as a business, I don't understand why we're doing it or what the budget is *really* being used for. I'm unsure why people are reporting things like Impressions and Likes. It feels to me similar to Advertising. We know we have to do it because everyone else is, but I'm sure of the true business value."

DP: Innovators and early adopters embrace change and are often excited by challenges and new opportunities, whereas many business leaders and C-suite decision makers tend to be more risk averse and pragmatic in their approach to innovation. I would place myself in the camp with the innovators and early adopters, and in my experience selling and marketing enterprise software to global agencies and Fortune 500 companies, I often found that the things that were the least interesting to me were the ones that ultimately helped to close deals.

How do you help to facilitate communication between the two groups, and how can innovative companies eliminate their blind spots and remove obstacles in the sales process? For example, are ROI models and identifying KPIs critical to scaling growth?

NP: I realized the early majority executives were my new "customers." It wasn't about me trying to change the early majority's mind. It was about me changing me; the way I talked about social media and innovation. Being customer-focused, I had learned the process of solution selling. I was taught to ask, "What does the customer want? What do they value? What are their objections?" Contemplating those questions, I saw the best way to help the early majority see the value in social media and cross the chasm was for me to talk their language. The early majority wanted know the cost / benefit of jumping over the chasm. They wanted numbers. But most early adopters/ innovators didn't have the numbers or proof. Excitement without proof, makes the early majority skeptical.

Looking at Moore's adoption curve, the cavern between the two groups is as deep and wide as the Grand Canyon. Even Evel Knievel's son Robbie used a motorcycle. The early majority's "motorcycle?" Numbers/data/proof. I think what most early adopters/ innovators don't realize is how much of a gap there is. Or that most of corporate America and the senior leadership is made up of the early majority. Without data and a process to show proof, social media and the value it brings can die.

I got really busy creating social media ROI models. With hard data and ex-amples, I changed the way I talked about social media. I asked executives, "Do you want to make money? Do you want to decrease costs?" Their re-sponse was very different. I was speaking their language. Dollars and cents. What I learned was that the most important aspect to facilitating change is to meet people where they are, not where you want them to go to.

I like to look at history, because it's helpful in informing the future. You'll often hear me say, "The more things change, the more they stay the same." To me, social media is essentially what Edward Deming was saying in the 1950s. *Listen to your customers and employees, and integrate that feed-back into your products and services.* If you do that, then you will have a better company—better products, services, more loyal customers and em-ployees who will work harder and stay longer so can you retain all of that knowledge required to make better quality products. All of that leads to an increase in customer lifetime value, higher revenue, profits and margins, if done right.

Edward Deming tried to help the American Auto Industry. They weren't in-terested. The Japanese invited Deming to Japan. Flash forward 25 years. The American Auto Industry needed a government bail out. The Japanese Auto Industry followed what Deming said and by doing so, it flourished over those 25 years. Deming was an innovator/early adopter.

I realized that if I was going to contribute and really move the needle in business, then I would need to be able to converse with executives about the business value of social. And not make jokes about it, "Would you consider calculating the ROI of giving all your employees phones? Would you calculate the ROI of your mother or of putting your pants on in the morning?" But to provide real, concrete business value to the pragmatists.

Without some proof of concept, without something that seemed concrete to CEOs and decision makers, I could see they wouldn't buy-in to social media. And for me, there wasn't anything more important than executives really understanding the value social media brings. If decision makers didn't cross the chasm, then the potential of what social media and Web 2.0 could bring would be lost. And the changes that need to happen in the corporate world would slip out of our fingers, fast.

DP: You were one of the first people to calculate an ROI model for social media. Can you explain how to go about quantifying the value of things that a lot of people think are intangible? How does what you do now with social media ROI models relate to the work that you did before the rise of social media?

NP: Calculating the ROI for social media is not for the faint of heart. It requires three basic components:

1. Your traditional business goals and how you measure them
2. Your social media goals and how you are measuring them (Most people don't have goals or if they do, they are measuring metrics– Likes, Impressions. Metrics are important, but KPIs are not ROI.)
3. Knowing how social media affects your traditional business goals

Being able to give attribution to how social media is affecting in the business is not easy. You have to use software to measure and track attribution. But it's not just about technology. It's also about strategy. And Chasm Crossers must have the ability to see both sides of the conversation. That's why I created a 7-step framework and a methodology for executive business success for social media ROI— it gives a point of reference for both sides.

Most companies started in social media with a tactical approach. Creating a Twitter handle and a Facebook page, they said, "*Happy Monday and buy our stuff.*" And then were disappointed in the business results. Why? Most companies don't have a point of reference to know if what they are doing will drive better business results in Customer Service, Marketing, PR, Innovation.

DP: Imagine that a potential client approaches you to create an ROI model. I like what you did for client X, and I want the same thing for my company.

Can you walk us through the process? How much of your approach is stand-ardized and repeatable, and to what extent is it customized and unique to the needs of each client?

Some of the approach is standardized and repeatable. But it does need to be customized to a certain extent for each customer. Every business is different and how they have approached social media is different. The 7-step process and ROI models show how social initiatives, integrated with traditional business operations, provide real results. My goal with the 7 steps? Clear up the hype about social, benchmark the company's social media capability maturity and show executives how it can drive business results. Here are the steps:

Step 1: Insights. Most people start at what I call *Step 5: Interaction.* But they need to start by gaining insight (Step 1) into their audience, their competitors and how their company is perceived. Companies with negative sentiment find out quickly when they launch into social and it results in a field of #fail messages from customers. You can't sell to people who are mad, so you have to listen to figure out what's right, what's wrong and what would be better if...

Step 2: Benchmark and Measure. Social media innovators didn't ask for permission; they asked for forgiveness. But today the only way to get, keep or expand budget is a business case. When senior leadership is asked for more money, they respond, "*You want more money for WHAT?*" Budgets are stuck; social software vendors are jockeying for position with similar promises. It's confusing at best. Companies need to benchmark themselves compared to their competitors, best practices and set up business goals/measurements; i.e., Step 2. The key is to give attribution to how social is affecting traditional business metrics. Without it, companies can't explain why they need more resources and budget for social or show an ROI.

Step 3: Target Audience and *Step 4: Content.* Part of the value of social is the relevant, exponential reach of customers and brand ambassadors (Step 3) who share content (Step 4) with your key audiences that drives awareness, lead conversation rates and solves customers' problems; done well it creates—advocacy, referrals and loyalty. But to do Steps 3 & 4 well means you've done a great job with Steps 1 & 2.

Step 5: Interactions. Without Steps 1-4, knowing how to personify the benefits of your products via storytelling content to drive social engagement, interactions are dull, ineffective and don't hit business goals. But companies who do follow this type of structured strategy and chose the right technology to scale interactions are delivering ROI/business results.

Step 6: Organizational Alignment. Corporate politics? They should simply be a white-collar crime. They waste money, time and resources. The issue? CEOs are delegating social down into their organization. Politics are thick; who should interact with the social customer is more complicated than ever. Businesses need strong leadership and organizational change management so that Steps 1-5 don't end up in political quagmires and stalemates.

Step 7: Iterate and Pivot. Without a clear plan in place and a way to evaluate its success, it can be difficult to iterate and pivot (Step 7) real-time so businesses can do more of the right things, quickly.

DP: An executive comes to you and says that their sales are incredible, but they have a high churn rate and don't understand social media or its ROI. People are buying products but not using them. Once you get corporate buy-in, how do you get people to change their habits?

NP: Change for humans in general is not easy. Think about the twenty pounds you just lost. How many times have you gained and lost it? Work is not that much different. The idea of listening to customers/employee and change isn't new. *The Cluetrain Manifesto* predicted in 1999 there'd be a time when the customer and employee's voice would matter. That time is now.

Consider a company that is listening to its customers; employees and making changes. Then consider one that isn't. Over 5 years, the first type of company will have innovated its products / services. The second type? They will become the DECs, Tower Records and Circuit Cities of the future. Social Business is as simple as that. The question is, what type of company are you?

Unless you can show a company why they should change, they will keep doing things the same way. In using the 7-step framework, as I walk a client through it, they come to the conclusion that they want to change. Nobody really wants to do anything poorly once they know that they are doing it poorly. At that point, the change is self-motivated. And I have accomplished my goal as a Chasm Crosser.

....

Dr. Natalie Petouhoff *is a business strategist and a futurist. She has spent her careers looking at how businesses interact with their customers and their employees and she provides companies with social media ROI models, best practice assessments, a scorecard, a report and long and short-term with the best way to create environments that foster loyalty, motivation and innovation.*

While at General Electric, General Motors and Hughes Electronics she spent time as a product engineer, manager and innovator of an integrated product development process created to guide technical engineers, as well as financial pros, sales and marketing to collaborate. Next she went on to be a management consultant and software systems integrator at PricewaterhouseCoopers, where she matched strategic advice on reaching business goals by correctly choosing, implementing and using Customer Service and CRM technology to scale and improve businesses.

As a business analyst at Forrester Research, Dr. Natalie focused on Customer Experience and social media, writing the first social media ROI model. Realizing that a long-term career in leading social media would mean understanding the role of PR, Marketing and Communications, she joined Weber Shandwick as the Chief Digital and Social Media Global Strategist. Today she helps executives cross the chasm and deliver ROI on social and traditional business objectives.

....

PART IV

MARKETING AND COMMUNICATIONS

THE CONTENT IMPERATIVE

Steve Rubel

Steve Rubel has a way of cutting through the noise and clutter to distill the essence of trends in media and culture. His LinkedIn influencer posts are essential reading. What Steve refers to as the "content imperative" signifies a fundamental shift in how brands and media partners will work together moving forward, making it an ideal starting point for the section on marketing and communications. Highlights include:

- How social media impacted PR and expanded the industry
- Why paid and sponsored content symbolizes an evolution of supply and demand
- When the lines blur between journalism and branded content
- Best practices on how to identify and map out trends in media and culture

Special thanks go to my old roommate from Princeton, Marisa Biaggi, who now works with Steve at Edelman PR, for introducing us. Since my graduate work focused so much on emerging communications platforms and shifts in publishing, this interview was one of my personal favorites. The content imperative in my opinion marks one of the most significant, irreversible shifts happening right now.

DP: In one of your LinkedIn posts, you advised recent college grads to remain digital natives for the rest of their lives–advice that you said was basically applicable to anyone at any stage in their career. In that same post, you had a passage that I think brilliantly captures one of the main themes of the book, which is that disruption is the new normal and businesses that are able to shed the outdated vestiges of the past will be in the best position to succeed.

What does it mean from your perspective that disruption is the new normal?

SR: The Internet was such a transformative once-in-a-lifetime event. At the beginning of the Internet, we compared it to the advent of TV as a medium, but, over the last decade and a half, we've seen that it's way more than that. It's truly a transformative event that has since gone through different stages: the desktop age, the social age, and the mobile age. The next wave will be the even more mobile age, which is going to be like a wearable age. Who knows? Maybe in ten years there will be an age when it just becomes nano-tech.

All of these waves have been disruptive, creating all kinds of changes across different industries. It wasn't like the Internet was just one wave of disruption. A new disruption occurs every year now, so we have to just anticipate. Where disruption was a slower process in the past or at least a seemingly slower process, now it's accelerated.

You have to be comfortable being uncomfortable because you just don't know where the next one is going to come from. People who think, for example, in our field that with social media there is not going to be anything else that they need to be concerned about for five years should probably just be watching the broader horizon both for opportunities and threats.

DP: Ok, so if we could break that down a little bit...first there was blogging followed eventually by platforms like Facebook, Twitter, YouTube, etc. that were incredibly disruptive to traditional publishing. Next, lots of magazines and publishers freaked out about the future of content, and social media went from a hodgepodge of experimental tools to share content to become a formative field.

In the process, the lines kind of blurred between PR and marketing. Can you tell us a little bit about how the rise of social media has impacted public relations and changed the way brands tell stories?

SR: Social media has really expanded the industry. So many people just think of PR as pure publicity. Media relations is and will definitely continue to be a big part of it, but in the last 15 years, it's expanded beyond that towards public engagement, or building a closer rapport and relationship between a business and its stakeholders.

With blogging and the dawn of social media, I was one of the early people in PR at least to recognize what an opportunity that was to do something different. I wasn't the first. There were many. We recognized that there was now a way to go direct that was not available to us before and not as democratized as it was at that time. What that has done is create a track that's moving PR beyond its media relations roots into a bigger net, building relationships.

Next, social came along and made that easier to do at scale and more efficiently. What it's done is fed into or off of inherent characteristics of the field, such as the need to be real time, conversational, and two-way. It came along at a time when the PR industry was starting to make its own transformation out of this sole focus on media relations to become much broader. This really was transformative in part because it allowed the skill sets that we had to be used in new ways.

DP: My experience was that when the economic downturn of 2008-2009 hit, budgets were cut dramatically and shifted from traditional media buying into social channels. As a result, social media agencies like where I was at the time boomed, as did a number of different self-service solution providers.

We all kind of braced ourselves for cutbacks, and then, within a year or so, everyone appeared to be embracing disruption and making lots of money. How did the crash impact public relations?

SR: We were beneficiaries of that trend. The crash made businesses double down on relationships as opposed to taking only a brand-building approach. They recognized that they needed to build a closer relationship with the people who were still going to buy from them during a tough time. They needed to be seen as trustworthy and credible. During that time, there was also a series of scandals that upended a lot of the public's trust in institutions, and businesses recognized that they needed a way to build greater trust with their audience. Social was one way to do that.

DP: There are now a billion people on Facebook, and social media has arguably reached mass adoption. The sheer volume of content created and shared can be daunting, and as a result, it appears that we're seeing a shift from mediocre content produced to go viral to higher quality premium content that stands out from the noise.

Does this signify an evolution of the social Web, and do you think content will always be king?

SR: I don't think it's an evolution of the social Web but rather an evolution of supply and demand. I tend to look at this very simplistically, which could be to a fault. Let's call supply "quality information and content" and demand "attention or appetite for that content or time with that content." Somewhere in between fall marketers.

In the pre-Internet days, the demand for content was high, and the supply was limited. There were few options because the cost to produce and distribute content was high. The evolution of the Internet in the 1990s increased the number of options but not to the degree that it outstripped demand, so demand for content increased. People were spending more time with information. Supply was increasing but not so far ahead of demand. They increased in unison. So there was enough to benefit everybody.

Then the social revolution happened, and content has exploded, particularly in the last six or seven years, not just because of social but also because the overall costs involved in creating a content operation have dropped. So content exploded with options vying for attention and into micro-niches. There are also multiple players in the same major niche. Time and attention for content has increased as well because we have pockets of time we never had before where we use our cell phones, for example, to get it.

The problem is, supply of content is increasing so dramatically, including from brand marketers that have decided to go direct. So that has to be reconciled. The only group that benefits is readers or viewers. They have lots of diverse sources they can choose from, but for the companies that make their money on content, that can be problematic due to competition. The marketers are depending on those companies to deliver some sort of scale of audience. That can be difficult. No one outside of readers or viewers is immune, so everyone has to work harder now at how that gets reconciled.

That is what's going to set up the next wave of growth in the PR industry. More and more, the media companies are saying bring us your content and pay us, and we'll amplify it in a very significant way that we didn't do before. It's an outgrowth of a historical model that worked well in print and TV, and is now going to become the norm in many media companies.

At the same time, it's disruptive because of the way it is accelerating, but it's necessary to align the interests of the marketers and the media companies in scaling. Whether or not it provides any value to the audience remains to be seen, but that's the next wave. The key trend is the supply and demand issue: the supply of content choices and the demand for that content. That's what now seems to be inescapable and accelerating

DP: In another LinkedIn post you advised any company to create a content engine. You listed five lessons from The Art of Storytelling:

(1) adopt a newsroom mentality, (2) handcraft your content for each venue, (3) cultivate superstars who have a POV, (4) be relentlessly data driven, and (5) let constraint fuel creativity.

Can you elaborate on the idea that a company should create a content engine?

SR: The reality is that there is too much content and not enough time. You have to have a car in the race, so if you're not in some way instilling the resources to tell your story in a holistic and balanced way then either A) somebody will tell it for you or B) you'll get lost in the sea of noise. So now the pressure's gone up dramatically to be in the game, and there are new options, but being in the game is required, whereas before maybe there wasn't as much pressure to do so.

DP: Media publishers took a really big hit when the economic downturn came because brands cut back on advertising budgets, and, in recent years, they're taking another hit as a result of innovations like programmatic buying and ad exchanges.

Can you tell us a little about how these changes and the ad budgets that are being conserved are impacting PR and advertising agencies?

SR: For media companies, the classic revenue streams are changing, so the advertising revenue stream is under more pressure from programmatic ad buying and that puts a squeeze on the ad prices. There are continuing cost pressures because of the number of platforms and innovations they have to invest in to tell the stories and convey the information in a way that the public wants nowadays. There is an inability to go to subscription revenue because the number of people they can charge for content is still very small.

Then you have appetite by brands and marketers wanting to go direct but still maybe can't do so on the scale that they would like because it's hard to build from scratch, especially with a high interest company.

All together, this is a perfect storm disruption. This is encouraging them to take a model that was there for years, which was advertorial and sponsored content, or paid placement of content, and turn that into a revenue driver or a way to offset their losses to start with. This bends the marketing ecosystem side of things too because it's a mix of skill sets. The folks who are very good at media buying are not as good at journalistic storytelling, and the folks who are good at journalistic storytelling and creating content that will work in an editorial environment are not as good at media buying. The way to resolve this is to seek out who is going to get what first and how.

The media companies themselves are also looking to ensure that the quality stays high in sponsored content because they risk losing audiences if it's not good. So that has led some to put it in their own hands. That in some ways could disintermediate agencies at least in that part of things by setting up their own studios to serve marketers. Everyone is looking at content marketing and native advertising, and what people lose sight of is why this is happening now, what that might look like as an evolution, and how different skill sets may come together.

DP: I listened to one of your recent talks in which you described three models for response syndicating content. The way you referred to it was basically (1) the advertorial reinvented, essentially monster pieces of content (2) an integrated model kind of like product placement for the Web; and (3) actual co-creation of content jointly between the brand or agency and a website, creating a new topic. Can you expand a bit more on how you see this playing out within the context of media properties?

SR: Those range in complexity from the simplest to the most complex. They range in complexity in terms of cost. The value exchange in each of those is also different and evolving, so the real question is: Does display advertising become so automated and so effective, and programmatic become so effective in optimizing, that media companies try to do that in such a way as to remove the friction from the process and do it at scale?

The notable thing about those three models is that the last one is the best because it's a triple win for the reader, the advertiser, and the media company. It's also the hardest to do, and do consistently well, and the hardest to experiment with. In contrast, the first model is the easiest to experiment with: It could potentially be a self-serve platform or one with minimal checks and balances. It could become more scalable but risks alienating readers more because they may not read it and the quality of content is out of your control. So I don't think this is the end of the chapter. This is just the beginning.

Others will seek new models that lie in between those or even dust off other ideas. But that's not a direction media companies want to go in. They are doing it because they have to go in this direction, especially in the last six to twelve months. It's also a reflection of a belief that this approach worked in other digital channels.

For example, a sponsored story on Facebook is to a story, just as a sponsored post is to a post. They see that something worked and is automated, and that turns out to be a pretty big business, and so then they send it out to another ring. Google found a way to create a demand-driven advertising platform that is closely aligned with a demand-driven editorial product and that has become a successful business. That's the hope of the media firms here: this becomes a viable or firm way to have revenues in addition to the classic two. Some of us believe that those will not be as strong as they were before.

The level of need to move to these business models is directly related to the other two revenue streams. A *Wall Street Journal* or *Financial Time*s, for example, are very successful digital subscription businesses with very successful digital advertising businesses because of the nature of whom they reach. They may not need to move in this direction as quickly or in a very limited way. Others may have to because they are too beholden on the banner ad. That's going to be the really interesting dynamic here: which part of the marketing services ecosystem will do this and do this well.

Ethics are going to be very important here, which could favor the PR industry. Not that the ad agencies don't have ethics. They do, but I don't know if they have as many experiences navigating complexities like this. Changes to the ecosystem become more like a programmatic buy, and then, that changes things. But quality will be a real issue. The sponsored content editorial stream has got to be really good, balanced and authoritative. Otherwise it's just not going to be consumed. I also think that's why the media companies create content. This is a really interesting idea because as the content creators they control their own destiny this way.

DP: One of the concepts that had a big impact on how I think about the evolution of technology and culture is this idea of a creative class. As we shift to a more narrative storytelling around brands, do you think this could lead to the creation of new kinds of goods, services, or experiences? For example, could different features come to the forefront (e.g., design) and actually change the way that we market and produce products? How do we transform our experience of the world? How might this trend continue in years to come?

SR: We're going to have to underscore the logical and emotional, handling both sides with equal dexterity. So how do you create? What kinds of stories evoke sharing versus what kinds of stories evoke consumption and where do they overlap?

That's going to be an important thing to watch. I also think the role of analytics will be very important in getting us real-time information, helping us make decisions about what kinds of stories will resonate the best. But the basics don't change. There are certain laws of humanity that remain.

DP: You touched on some of the ethical implications, so this is sort of the flipside: the aspiration of a creative class versus the potential ethical downside of this model. If media companies are essentially in a position where they need to do anything to survive or close to it, then basically an ethical gray area starts to emerge around journalistic integrity and sponsored content.

For example, one of the prominent examples that comes to mind occurred during the BP oil spills. There was constant coverage of how a multibillion-dollar company had destroyed the environment, and then basically the TV and Internet were covered with BP stories about how they were doing everything right.

How do we maintain balance when, as you mentioned before, PR folks might have an upper hand in this area?

SR: No good comes out of getting this wrong. In other words, everyone's invested in getting this right. The media has a lot riding here to make this work. The marketers want to make this work because of the lack of scarcity and difficulty in scaling with enough resonance. The reader and the viewer have a lot to lose, too, because there could be a quality deficit, but they don't want to pay for news, and they want it to be available to them from brands they love.

It's kind of like when you're driving on the highway. You're driving on the highway, and 99% of people don't want to have an accident. There's too much at stake, for example, your money and your health. People make mistakes all the time, but most of the time, 99% of the time, those mistakes are not made with malice. We are in this kind of covenant together called the road: I'm not going to run you over, and you're not going to run me over, because an accident would injure us both. There are rules that guide that, so everyone is aligned in their interests, but the one that has the most to lose is the reader.

We need to make sure that the interests of business and government are first and foremost aligned with the interests of the audience. I believe this will happen, but that discussion has to start happening now.

DP: As Chief Content Strategist at Edelman PR, the largest independently owned global PR agency in the world, you're balancing relationships with clients and best practices in terms of what platforms to use. Can you tell me just a little bit about how you make decisions regarding what platforms are appropriate for clients? How do you shape best practices for implementing innovation across a global organization? For example, at what point, did something like Facebook, Twitter, or Tumblr go from being experimental to something where you feel confident having a brand presence? What were the decision processes involved in formulating this idea around a content imperative?

SR: First, I don't have an operational structure. So I don't have direct reports. I'm designed to be watching out for disruption and understanding what could be on the horizon that could change our business, and then advising our senior management, our team, and our clients on what that looks like. That is a byproduct of great leadership here.

Our number one characteristic is that we are independent. We are fiercely independent. We have 5000 people. We've been in business for 60 years.

We have no plans to go public or become part of a larger holding company. Management is committed to that, which allows us to invest time, energy, and money to go chasing things we think are relevant.

Our number two characteristic is that we are pretty entrepreneurial. So there's opportunity for a lot of debate and for different opinions to surface and be discussed around critical issues. There's a tremendous amount of focus on IP, which in our sense is research, whether it be data-driven or qualitative research. We're not afraid to put a point of view out there nor are we afraid to change. We have a culture where every person here is an account executive. We all still do the basics: my CEO still brings clients to see reporters. I still go see reporters all the time. As we rise here, we don't like to lose sight of the day-to-day of the business because that would mean also losing sight of what's going on.

All this maps nicely with my skill set and I have been really set up by design to be watching out for what disruption is next that's going to impact our business. The process I go about to do that is a formal part of my job. I feel like there are many people who are way smarter than me, and what I do is I try to find them and pick out what I can from them to form pieces of a puzzle. What occasionally happens is that I get an idea for that puzzle, and there are other people here who then help shape it and provide input. I think our independence makes that happen though.

DP: My last questions are more related to technology. Platforms like Snapcat have become popular recently. They are impermanent in the sense that stories are shared and then erased within a certain amount of time. Also global tablets and now Glass are making content more visual and instant.

I read in one of Edelman's recent trend reports that 63% of respondents stated that they viewed video on mobile phones and other devices more than they did a year ago. Can you elaborate on the possible implications for storytelling? There's this sort of shift from permanent to temporary or written to visual or Web to mobile, tablets, and other devices.

SR: I don't think it's an either or. Some stories are ephemeral. We don't remember them day-to-day. Others we remember for a lifetime. The conclusion is, you have to do it all. You have to think about what's going to be ephemeral or at least create enough rain. The ultimate goal is to create enough rain on people to make them realize they need to buy an umbrella. That requires leveraging every means to create surround sound. Eventually, the stories that are ephemeral and disappear might form a mosaic of memory. No easy task.

DP: So to wrap up, and we touched on this in the beginning, you advised people to always remain digital natives. What kind of parting words of wisdom might you have to continue to remain relevant on an ongoing basis in this era with disruption as the new normal?

SR: You don't know what you don't know. The more you can know about what you don't know, the more you'll be successful. Just know what it is. If you can identify what you don't know, you can then segment it into things that you think you need to know and things you don't need to know. So for example, I know that I don't know anything about finance. I also know to stay away from it. Also, it's easy to draw conclusions very quickly, including the ones I just rattled off, and what I'm learning is not to be so sure. Having a hunch and chasing it is okay. The fun is in the journey and seeing where that's going.

For example, I didn't know in 2004 when I helped certain clients launch blogging sites that they would become a much larger phenomenon called social media. I had no idea. Much as now we're talking about sponsored content, we don't know if this is going to be a multibillion dollar business or if this is going to be a flash in the pan and a new way will emerge. But we see some underlying things that are happening that we kind of think are indisputable. What I'm learning as I get older is not to jump to conclusions but to follow hunches. Then to try to figure out what you don't know and try to acquire the knowledge from people closer to it than you are and also sometimes further away.

The last piece is just to be really organized and detailed in how you keep and maintain your own information because harvesting information is so critical now. Being able to make sense of it, correlate it, and then pull it up at a moment's notice is critical because having your own personal Internet is super important. That allows me to cultivate my own view of things among the old texts, my social network, and Google. So I think there's many levels to that. Being really organized and harvesting information is going to be critical in the years ahead on a personal and professional level.

Steve Rubel *is Chief Content Strategist for Edelman–the world's largest independent public relations firm. In this role Rubel is responsible for creating and cultivating best practices in content strategy and for piloting innovative media partnerships that blend paid, owned and earned strategies. He serves as a strategic advisor to both the firm's Executive Committee as well as its clients.*

While with Edelman Rubel has served in a number of senior advisory roles. He helped evolve both the firm's thinking and strategy around the rapid advance of social media and, more recently, disruptions in the broader media landscape. As part of his remit, Rubel publishes regular reports that are based on in-depth interviews with executives and thought leaders in the media, technology and entertainment industries. He also represents Edelman on the World Economic Forum's Media, Entertainment and Information Industry Partnership.

Rubel is one of Edelman's most visible industry thought leaders. He has written a monthly column for Advertising Age *since 2006. Further, he was one of the first marketers picked to join the LinkedIn Influencer content network. He is followed by 80,000 on Twitter.*

Prior to joining Edelman in 2006, Rubel worked for 15 years in a variety of marketing communications positions in corporate, non-profit and small/mid-sized PR firms. He joined Edelman in 2006 from CooperKatz where he lead some of the earliest social media programs in both consumer marketing (for Vespa) and in corporate reputation (for the Association of National Advertisers).

BEING AWESOME

Faris Yakob

Faris Yakob is incredibly ahead of the curve in terms of understanding the significance of trends, and yet he makes them easily accessible through concise examples and clearly articulated strategies. This rare combination of insights and ability allows him to bring the future into the present in a way that is actionable for brands and agencies:

- What the agency of the future might look like
- How media is technology, and technology is media
- Tools and experiences can be similar to traditional advertising
- Why being awesome—inspiring awe—leads to success

As former Chief Innovation Officer of MDC and now head of his own planning and innovation consultancy GeniusSteals, Faris has a deep understanding of the process and workflow required in the production of scalable solutions. I consider him the best in the world at innovation in advertising, and I was super excited to conduct this super geeky interview .

DP: What does a Chief Innovation Officer do within advertising?

FY: Well, there has been a lot of debate since that role manifested a few years ago. The first key responsibility is to keep looking at the assumptions that underlie the operations of the agency, and trying to unpack those embedded assumptions so that you can encourage people to do more than what they did yesterday. Next, it involves innovating for the agency itself—understanding that the needs of clients are evolving, disruption is becoming ongoing and iterative, and thinking about product developments in the same way as an innovation person at an enterprise company thinks about products and services.

In an agency environment such as New York, that might be creating a content group as opposed to an advertising supply chain, or a social or software group, and at the same time facilitating new types of processes and ideation. For example, I did a lot of work with workshop processes so that the agency process didn't just assume that advertising is the answer to every question.

DP: Imagine that a billionaire wants to start a new global holding company and brings you in. What does the agency of the future look like and how might you approach building one if given unlimited resources?

FY: That's an interesting question—the fresh start is always appealing, the idea that you can start with a new beginning.

The agency by its nature doesn't make anything. What I mean by that is agencies are kind of intermediaries that germinate and broker the production of solutions. In a sense, the agency model is really robust because you can make any kind of solution. The challenge is that they are used to making specific kinds of content units as solutions to all problems, and so a lot of the thinking gets kind of linear that way.

You want to start with a group of people that have a relevant set of diversities, bringing all types of things to the table without an inherent creative hierarchy. One of the challenges of agencies is that the creative department has a large amount of weight purely based on their opinions. You want to start with a group of relevant people that have different elements of content and solution-development—tools, utilities, software-type thinkers as well— and then I wouldn't segregate them out necessarily into different tribes of production specializations.

I think the model we're moving towards in terms of an "agency of the future" is two-sided, and you can look at it through the lens of experiences and stories. The campaign model is a certain kind of solution to certain types of problems and it is still very relevant in lots of situations, but advertising and content are two sides of the same idea. Advertising tends to be by its nature very promotional. Content tends to be something that people choose to engage with, so thinking about the allocation of attention and how you either apply it or earn depending on the needs is quite important.

On the other side, there are what might be called actions and tools—brands have massive scale and can provide solutions to people above and beyond what their products can do, and it is into that space that I think we are moving. So, brands create massive actions that function like advertising—actions like sending a man into space and getting him to jump out of a satellite with a parachute. And then tools. People tend to think of tools as software and utilities. I think tools can be all kinds of things. Anything that helps make anyone's life a little bit better can function to create attention and function like advertising historically did, but in a different type of way.

DP: Your blog and consulting practice has a tagline "Talent imitates, genius steals," based on this belief that ideas are new combinations, and nothing comes from nothing. On your site, you have a great line about innovation that is worth sharing (or stealing)—"the best way to innovate fast is to select the best of that which came before and combine those elements into new solutions." Can you tell us a little bit about that?

FY: Yes, this is part of the innovation process that I've been trying to develop and my work is based on this thinking. Originality is a romantic notion and in some sense is also a handcuff—nothing is truly original, nor is originality necessarily important. Innovation just needs to be effective. The best way to get to ideas faster is to have the right stimulus, because ideas are new combinations.

There is a certain space in which ideas are appropriate—what Stephen Johnson refers to as the adjacent possible. This is where good ideas come from, or kind of an idea space. Now, within the limits of that space there are ideas that are wrong—ideas that don't solve the problem—but within that space the further you get from the most obvious, the more interesting things tend to be. Finding more diverse elements to recombine becomes the challenge—looking beyond just traditional sources of inspiration such as film, music, and other kinds of content families.

It's this notion of combined elements that leads you much faster to new kinds of ideas. This is to some extent what all creative processes are about. You find inspiration and apply that inspiration to the problem at hand. Sometimes that moment of fusion happens at a subconscious level, but I think you can do that in a very practical way with people by providing the stimulus and direction around the right kinds of ideas.

DP: You mentioned that even brainstorming is a recent phenomenon.

FY: Yes, brainstorming was an idea invented by John Osborn—the O in BBDO—and it took over the entire creative industry, this idea of group ideation. One of the reasons why brainstorming was important is because hierarchical systems in the 1950s and 1960s made it difficult for people to say things that might sound stupid or out of turn, so you had to create a space that disrupted their norms and allowed them to be more free.

But I think it's important to understand that innovation is a lot more important than just putting people into a room and talking about ideas. It is about structuring an environment and a process that allows innovation to happen. I think the challenge is in knowing when to use the right situations and the right tools together.

DP: A lot has been written about digital natives and the significance of the next generation growing up on the Internet. You wrote a paper around 2010 that the next generation is fundamentally different because of the way they consume, manipulate and propagate ideas, and that brands need to express themselves differently in response to this new idea consumer.

One line jumped out at me: "The future is already here, it's just not evenly distributed."

FY: Yeah, that's a William Gibson quote.

DP: Yet our perception of the future is usually flawed. For example, if you go shopping before and after eating, and then compare what you took home based on whether you were hungry or full at the time.

FY: Yes, the bias of presentism—you can't help that.

DP: So, if the future is already here but our perception is flawed, then how do brands plan for the future?

FY: I have been thinking about this a lot lately. It is almost like there are two sides. First, all strategy is by its nature planning for the future, and things are constantly moving and working in real time. But second, there is some sense that we have gotten locked into a certain way of thinking about the future, and maybe we need to focus more on developing different things now instead of waiting for the next generation to solve problems.

Regarding digital natives, I used to think it was just sort of a bimodal media consumption base, where people who grew up with television were passive consumers of content vs. people who grew up with the finger on the computer mouse are far more interactive in relation to content. But I think it is much blurrier than that now.

Negroponte said in *Being Digital* back in the 1990s that each generation becomes more digital than the previous one. It's not even generational anymore—the rate of change is moving so fast that every few years there are distinct media habits emerging. That is the part that agencies and brands have a hard time with because you have to keep learning and adapting to these new platforms.

DP: Traditional advertising was built upon a model that benefited from the privilege of how the means of production were controlled–they were able to plan campaigns and advertising a year in advance, there were a limited number of things that they could sponsor on TV and print, etc.

How has the democratization of technology that has occurred with the rise of platforms like Facebook, Twitter, blogging etc. changed the agency world?

FY: Previously, the production of content at scale was a massively privileged act. Nobody could do it outside of the government, the media-industrial complex, advertising agencies and their affiliates. Then, almost overnight everyone could produce content at incredible speed and scale, which changed the uniqueness of what agencies could offer.

The difference between doing something vs. not doing something is infinite– but the difference between doing it well vs. badly is of degrees, meaning there is lots of content out in the world and the difference now is whose content is better. Agencies tend to refer to other people's advertising as clutter, but you could equally understand all content is competing for attention. Now there is also an infinite amount of content competing for attention, most of which is coming from friends. The content of people's lives is a way of passive communication.

Agencies began to move into a content production space, and work at how they can move much faster, which set up two different systems (1) the ad production model, which is relatively slow and expensive; and (2) content that is shot and cut to be put online the next day, which can be made much more efficiently, but it is fundamentally different—it looks and feels different. The key is that if all agencies continue to do is produce content then they could become less and less relevant. This goes back to what I talked about earlier in terms of actions and tools, producing things that might function the way advertising traditionally did but focused more on creating unique experiences and functionality that adds value beyond just content.

DP: I remember around 2009-10 after the economic crash when social media appeared to be the answer to every brand's problem. Facebook started to replace destination websites, YouTube provided free video distribution, Twitter became this 140-character PR platform. As social media reached mass adoption, content consumption habits changed and now there is so much noise competing for attention that you need really great content to stand out.

I'm curious, now that social media has reached mass adoption, do you think there will be a return to premium content and some of the things agencies traditionally did very well?

FY: It's a combination. The media system as it exists now should be considered as that—a complete system that interacts with itself in lots of different ways. The premium-level content is one of those things that brands can do that most individuals cannot do, and therefore provides a kind of scale advantage, but I also think that the threshold of expectations changed because of social media. It isn't just about the marketing and communications: it's about how people interact with companies.

There is some expectation that companies will respond in these channels. The customer service aspect gets confused with the marketing function. Who is supposed to be controlling what? Brands would rather use social media as a broadcast channel because they can just keep pushing things out, but more often people would rather have it as a customer-service channel and respond almost in real time, putting a massive burden on the operational aspects of companies.

DP: You talk about how everybody is becoming a technology company. One of the things that you have written about before is this idea that we have a limited view of technology that we associate with robots, frenetic media, and things that we don't understand, and then there is the stuff that encompasses the basic aspects of our daily life that we take for granted. For example, writing and language is a form of technology that we use to structure our own thoughts.

What does it mean to think of media as a function of technology?

FY: I think media is technology, and technology has become media. To a certain extent it always was to a point—it is simply about habituation. Stuff that is in the world from wherever you are just seems like it is normal, but because Moore's Law drives exponential shifts in very specific areas of technology—computing, mobile, etc.—that change is very fast and people can see that change. At a certain point, to paraphrase Douglas Adams, basically anything that comes into the world after you turn 30 seems a bit scary, whereas anything that comes into the world when you are a teenager is inherently exciting and something you want to be involved with.

There are two ways to think about this. First, media and technology are two faces of the same idea. Media is a conduit for ideas connecting people together, and technology is the facilitator of this. Moore's Law drives bandwidth through better technology, and bandwidth creates these infinite amounts of space to populate with media.

Second, I think that you can use technology to express ideas in ways that don't just simply use pictures and words—solutions to problems that have emotional resonance but are created through technology, such as IBM's Watson project or the WWF file format that is like a PDF format that can't be printed out so you don't waste trees. So, there are pieces of technology being used in ways that media has been used.

DP: You use a lot of historical examples in your talks and writing. If you were a historian looking back on the present, what are the fundamental shifts that you would outline that are going on right now?

FY: I think each generation has a similar response to new technologies. Every time something new happens that increases the speed of communication and/or changes the way that people interact, people get frightened about it, starting with the ancient fear of writing destroying memory and so forth. Everyone kind of worries about media in a certain way, and you can kind of see this on a continuum throughout history.

Right now, the big piece is twofold. The latency issue is really interesting. Speed has become this weird sort of determinant, which you can see in how news is functioning. Everyone is trying to keep up with the speed of Twitter. Peer reviewed news stations are making massive mistakes because they can't compete at the speed level. But I think that results from a misunderstanding of what journalism is about—news and journalism are two different ideas.

I also think there is going to be an increasing drive towards literacy of computing. I'm not so sure it is absolute. There are people who talk about how coding will become a new form of literacy, the way that writing previously was only done by scribes and became universal, and perhaps coding will be the same thing. I'm not sure that is entirely the case, but understanding computing at a deeper and conceptual level will be a huge shift. Douglas Rushkoff says program or be programmed—that may be extreme, but unless you understand how a machine works, you never will really be able to use it outside the constraints that it has given to you.

DP: You've talked a lot about the concept of experience maps, and the idea that there is a baseline of experience, enriching and diminishing experiences. A fun example that you use is that Starbucks has an enriching experience offering free Wi-Fi, and yet the experience is diminished by small tables that make it more difficult to use the free Wi-Fi.

The goal becomes to design for the memory of experiences instead of the actual experiences. Why is the story or memory that we create around experiences more important than the actual experience?

FY: Well, they're obviously interrelated ideas. Taking from *Thinking Fast and Slow* by the behavioral economist Daniel Kahneman, it's because the remembering self—the one that has the memories—is the one that makes the decision the next time, and because we are trying to influence people's commercial decisions on an ongoing basis, that is the version of the experience that you want to have the most impact upon.

Now, the way people remember things is very specific. Bits tend to get dropped out very easily. Things you weren't expecting tend to be much more memorable than things you were expecting, and the beginnings and endings are hugely important. So, the story that people leave with based upon their experiences becomes both what drives the decision the next time and the thing they pass on and tell people.

The challenge to constantly supersede expectations is very difficult—people habituate very rapidly. As soon as you begin to expect a certain thing, it stops being that certain type of memorable piece. I also think that small defining brand gestures work really well. The example that I like is the DoubleTree Hotel because they give you a warm cookie when you check-in, which somehow overrides the experience of the hotel entirely.

DP: Speaking of brand gestures and experiences, you touched on this earlier— what does it mean to move beyond a model of advertising that is ad based?

FY: Well, it makes things more complicated. Previously, when there were only 4-5 units that you could create, it was hard to make great work, but the type of unit you created was clearly defined. For example, can you afford TV or not? If so, then you would make TV and go from there because those were the mass-market channels available that were efficient to use at scale.

The challenge now is that the decisions up front—the strategic process—get far more complicated because it's no longer about can I afford TV. It's trying to understand from a huge infinite gamut of things you could do what is the right thing to do. So, the decision is strategic up front—what type of solution will solve this best, most efficiently and most effectively?

Even in terms of content, there are no pre-determined restrictions. For example, because YouTube is infinite, 30 seconds or 30 hours of content could be appropriate, but so could music or pieces of software. There are equally appropriate things in digital spaces. The evolution that is required in some spaces at the strategic/function level is providing a solutions-architecture rather than just a set of insights that leads to a brief for advertising. It's also about trying to understand the business needs and the audience you're trying to help vs. jumping right into ad production.

DP: I talked with Robert Scoble about his latest book Age of Context, *and things like Google Glass, sensors, wearable technology, etc. I'm curious how do you see those things impacting advertising?*

FY: The Age of Context will be important. The hope would be that we can begin to glean from human behavior when advertising will be more useful; the fear is we use it to become more intrusive.

There is a tendency to fill any screen with as much advertising as possible. But I hope in looking at people's behavior in aggregate that we can understand in ways that were never possible. People in groups have emergent properties. Look at these massive groups with massive data sets and determine what types of solutions can we provide.

The challenge is to not do what everyone does and fill everyone's view with spam. People will have the ability to broker their own information. Right now, behavioral data is used to serve ads, but that behavioral data could be much more valuable. Perhaps there is going to be some way to auction that data, where brands could lobby for access via a software intermediary and get value.

DP: Kind of like a real-world contextual ad model

FY: Yes, where everyone has the rights to their own data, you have preferences set about who and what can access data, and that data would be anonymously brokered in exchange for additional value. I think people are comfortable with their data being shared and used. Kevin Kelly says the price of relevance is transparency—but I think the value is having it transferred back to the individual or the audience, so the value isn't just extracted by the industry. Instead, it is creating a more equitable transfer between the audience and brands.

DP: In my conversation with Frank Speiser of SocialFlow, he has this idea that data can make you sound more human because you can send the right message at the right time. How do you serve ads or send messages that are relevant without coming across as spam?

FY: That's the huge challenge of the contextual advertising model. So, for example you're driving past a pizza place, and you've eaten pizza there before, and so you get a push notification for a pizza. Bank of America had an example recently where people responding to their politics were being messaged with inquiries about how to assist with opening accounts.

Messaging to real people is hard to do at scale, and there is something valuable about access to real people. There is a desire in a social world where I should never be on hold again. The direction should be you reach out to me, rather than vice versa because I'm the customer. Software gets people to respond faster, but purely automating stuff can become dangerous.

DP: This has been really great, and in moving towards wrapping up why don't we end on a fun note. On your blog, Twitter, and LinkedIn profile, you say that you're in search of the awesome and the future belongs to the most awesome.

Tell me a little bit about how the future belongs to the most awesome.

FY: (laughs) I use the word awesome in its original or traditional sense—something that inspires or creates awe. I think human beings are fundamentally emotional beings and emotional resonance is the driver of communication. We want to share things that make us feel. So, in a world where there is an infinite body of content, there are algorithms that use people's engagement with content to optimize how it is shared and viewed.

The metaphor of the website has given way to the metaphor of the constantly flowing stream, so the algorithms that dictate what we end up seeing are dependent upon sharing. Now the things that are shared the most are the things that create the feeling of awe—the most shareable, spreadable emotion is awe, because it's inherently something that you want to show people.

Things that are awesome are massive in scale and change the way you think about reality. The Cro-Magnon man who experiences the Northern Lights for the first time experiences awe: "Wow, that's amazing. I need to go find someone and show them." Being awesome is that kind of shareable quality. So, the future belongs to the most awesome because if people aren't collectively sharing the things that brands create, then eventually nobody is going to see them.

Faris Yakob *is a strategist, writer, public speaker, creative director and the founder of GeniusSteals, a planning and innovation consultancy. Previously he was Chief Innovation Officer of MDC and founding partner of Spies&Assassins, the creative technology boutique. Before that he was Chief Digital Officer at McCann Erickson NYC, and Head of Digital Strategy at Naked Communications. He was named one of the most respected planners in the world by The Planning Survey, and one of 10 modern-day Madmen by Fast Company.*

He writes on technology, media, brands and creativity for a variety of publications including FastCompany and he wrote the first chapter of Digital State: How the Internet Changes Everything, *just published by Kogan Page. He is lucky enough to be invited to speak all over the world.*

You can find him online @faris and www.GeniusSteals.Co

WAVE BRANDING

Terry Young

Terry Young pioneered an approach to advertising and branding that leverages culture, identifies breaking trends and then rides them to a crest through a process he refers to as *Wave Branding*. This newsroom-style approach to content and activations is probably the most sophisticated example of what Brian Solis was referring to as digital convergence and Steve Rubel talked about in the context of the content imperative:

- How tools and technology empower a non-calendar-based approach to advertising
- Fast and slow culture, brand analysis, and prediction scoring of breaking trends
- Creating content buckets and third-party providers for a more robust strategy
- The broader implications of how companies can act at the speed of culture

Terry and the agency he founded sparks & honey are doing such incredibly innovative and cool stuff that the real value of their method and approach may not be fully realized or understood for a few years. It's almost as if they are reverse engineering in real time how to build a company and brand based on breaking trends. An absolute must read!

DP: You developed an incredibly innovative approach to creating content that you refer to as Wave Branding, *leveraging proprietary technologies and mapping trends into different Content Networks. This sounds really awesome—how does it work?*

TY: The idea behind Wave Branding is that as opposed to being tied to a calendar-based approach to building your brand—for example, saying I'm going to launch my brand on Thursday, or being tied to a traditional model of paid media—we now live in a world where we can map culture, and then use what's bubbling up in culture to amplify what we're putting into the market in order to build a brand in a different way.

The idea of Wave Branding is that if we have the right tools and the right technology to identify culture when it first emerges, then you can capture it early and ride it to its crest. That process of amplifying based on culture is much more effective in creating sharing and engagement opportunities across different audiences than the traditional calendar-based approach.

DP: sparks & honey takes a newsroom approach to advertising. A quote from FastCompany piqued my interest from one of your presentations:

"The pace of change in our economy and our culture is accelerating—fueled by global adoption of social, mobile and other new technologies—and our visibility about the future is declining."

You followed up by saying that commercial creativity only matters if the context is right. The problem is that context is a moving target, and as a result speed is a matter of survival. This speaks directly to the theme of this book—how to become a leader in an era when disruption is the new norm.

Why is speed and velocity of creating content so important now?

TY: We believe that things are expanding exponentially. We live in a world of hyper or rapid change, and this does not hold true only for technology. Because technology is a great enabler, exponential change is happening everywhere. This increases the speed by which companies go from nothing to being completely explosive in the market—it has completely shortened that time horizon. Think of a company like Wikispeed, for example. They are crowdsourcing the complete development of an automobile and taking a process that traditionally took seven years down to seven days. It's pretty amazing when you start applying technology and collaboration to completely speed up a manufacturing process.

Now, all of those same tools are also shaping and shifting the way that brands are built. Because change is so rapid, it requires us to move at the speed of culture. In order to move at the speed of culture—to be part of conversations and create an authentic connection—you need to have a methodology and process. For example, you could look at a given brand in a 90-day period, and then map all of the missed opportunities to understand how much sharing and engagement these bursts threw off.

So many brands today have opportunities to connect in an authentic way with things in culture—things that their consumers share—but the reason they don't do that is twofold: (1) the traditional model of advertising isn't built around that system; and (2) they don't have a modern approach to do it, which is where the advertising newsroom comes in. What an advertising newsroom does is take the practices of a CNN—fast, lean, making decisions in real time—and treat opportunities that arise in culture like a responsible journalist covers stories. You can react and go into a market to build a story over time, and then the content gets more sophisticated as the story progresses.

This newsroom-style approach allows us to act at the speed of culture. You need not only the tools on the front end—the technology and ability to quantify what you're seeing—but also the ability to build out content in rapid form. The brands that aren't embracing how to leverage the sensibility of an advertising newsroom or really tap into the zeitgeist of culture are leaving opportunities to connect in truly hyper-relevant ways on the table.

DP: Do you think all of these developments will lead to the creation of new ROI models and ways of understanding the value of advertising?

TY: That's an interesting question. Why don't we back up and explain a bit more about how the process works and then tackle ROI. So, basically we ingest all different data sources: Twitter firehose, YouTube API, scraping Facebook, plus our cultural strategists that curate what they are seeing in real time. Everyone on the team has a different beat, like a reporter following science, technology, fashion or movies. Plus, we have an influencer network that is also aligned to those categories and then scouts that are global.

We take all of those data feeds into our cultural database and use our proprietary algorithms to score on two dimensions: (1) the energy level, or how big something is in the here-and-now; and (2) a prediction score on how long we think it is going to last. Next, we take these phenomena and connect them to one of our 96 Content Networks. This allows us to understand the oscillation between fast and slow culture. Fast culture is something that we see bursting in the here-and-now, whereas slow culture is something that we think will impact brands in the next 36-48 months.

What we're doing is trying to translate the noise in the world into signals that we can quantify, understand and cluster in order to determine if there are real opportunities for brands. So, we're taking things going on in the world and translating them into untapped opportunities—content, new innovation ideas—bringing the future into the present. This can even be applied to manufacturing, where you look at inspiration in culture and do just-in-time commerce to put something into market. So, it plays out in advertising content, but it can be applied to speed in innovation, product development and even real-time selling of products inspired by culture.

Now we can get back to the question of ROI. Today, what we measure are metrics associated with culture: things like energy, prediction, sentiment, engagement, the way people talk about things and the language that they use, plus harder ROI calculations like sales conversions. Traditional metrics are mostly used because what we're doing is bringing people into a new world—*if you build your brand this way, social, digital, advertising, etc.*— and presenting them with a set of KPIs they are used to.

What we do is add culture to it—and if you get culture right in a timely fashion, then it will outperform traditional KPIs. Are there new KPIs needed? Probably. As we progress with the model, we are experimenting with new ways of measuring impact in real-time marketing, based on cultural identification and culture mapping.

DP: What happens when you find that a brand is out of synch with culture? How do you approach concepts of brand identity, and if everything is changing so fast, how can brands develop a consistent identity that does more than just hold up a mirror to culture?

TY: I think what you stand for as a brand, what you do as a brand, your higher purpose and values need to be constant; they are your North Star. As you watch what goes on in culture, you need to make choices based on those cultural shifts, but you can't veer from your North Star. Culture informs the stories that we tell based on what we stand for—what you might call your higher purpose.

Whether you are building a brand from scratch or have an established brand image, you can use the Wave Branding approach because culture allows you to know when to tell the right stories to create relevance around what your brand actually is.

DP: You've identified what you refer to as a "seismic shift in traditional values to what is now the new normal"—things like gender fluidity, non-religious affiliations and a new spirituality, family by design, co-working, LGBT, etc. My first book Red Bull to Buddha *is about these same types of shifts in a larger global context, and I spent a decade in academia studying these shifts as a scholar of religion and culture.*

I'm curious how they relate to advertising. In particular, how do you find the right balance between traditional and modern, and how to position brands at the cusp of what is next without appearing too far ahead into the future? If people are consuming less and sharing more, how does this change in buying behavior impact the way that we market and sell products?

TY: Those are some really big topics. We watch closely all of the topics that you mentioned—the modern family, a shift in family configurations, how fast that is happening, the doubling pattern and exponential shift that applies to same-sex marriage, for example. Just as we've talked about exponential change in technology, it is happening in social shifts. So, if I'm looking at a particular brand and they want to do a deep dive of 65+, mobile natives or Millennial parents, then I'll take a different view and lens to translate culture in a different way.

The way one thing translates into different age groups or demographics can vary significantly. We watch these big macro-trends—sharing economy, Collaborative Economy, task economy, the modern family, social shifts and the new normal to identify how brands have an opportunity to be on the same journey with consumers. Take same-sex marriage for example. They have been on a journey from very little acceptance to higher, or extraordinarily higher acceptance to people under 30.

As a brand, understanding that you want to be in the middle of the conversation and then embracing it 100% is key. General Mills did this by saying, "We believe in same love." They had an interracial couple Cheerios ad and that's a great example of a company saying, "We believe this in our DNA. Not everyone might agree with this, but as a brand we're going to lean into it because it's the right thing."

In the past, we used to stay away from politics, sex and social movements, but today in the world of hyper-transparency, the walls brands built that made them seem inhuman are crumbling. Brands are now taking on a new role where other institutions are failing. They have an opportunity to step in and guide the conversation. Look at some of the things that Starbucks has done with Create Jobs For America, or Whole Foods or The Container Store. They are really pushing a consciousness agenda and trying to take on challenges and social issues that are much bigger than what brands typically participated in.

DP: Your team has folks with a traditional news background from CNN, advertising and creatives, programmers and hackers, and your office has eleven large screens with live data streams.

This all sounds futuristic and awesome! How do you strike the balance of human and technology? To what extent can you automate creation of trend reports and mapping culture, such as leveraging data and the social graph, and at what point does your team's expertise come in?

TY: The magic of what we do happens at the intersection of the tools and human analysis and synthesis. We built a proprietary platform that takes noise to signal and gives us something to work with. The tools narrow, quantify and cluster, but it's our team that translates it into opportunity. What is the real meaning behind it? What are the semiotics around it? What is the language? What does this truly mean as an opportunity?

We have people from CNN, trend-watching agencies, data scientists. The tools are extremely valuable because they allow us to harness and score data, but the magic happens when the team analyzes and turns it into valuable opportunities for brands.

DP: Imagine that I'm a client that wants to launch a new product in a campaign that might run over the next year. Where do we start, and how do all of the trend reports that you regularly create shape the strategy, content production, and execution?

Anytime we work with a client, there is a set-up period. We use over 25 different tools to monitor culture. We start by creating a cultural framework, by which we map brands to key categories in our Content Networks. We then begin the process of understanding what events on the near-term horizon can impact or shape culture in a way that can impact a particular audience. Next, we do a series of exercises to understand the DNA of a brand.

This is similar to what you do in traditional advertising. You want to go in and understand the values of a brand, but we do it from the perspective of the brand's voice as well as listening and seeing how consumers talk about a brand in culture. Then we try to connect those two components. So you have culture frameworks (a brand DNA) and then a risk assessment.

If we're producing content for a client, then we have to understand what the elasticity of the brand is from a brand standpoint and also a content standpoint. This means we have to talk about things like politics and sex, humor and stances on certain issues and how far you are willing to stretch. In the cultural conversations of a given person that we're trying to reach, there are lots of things that consume their daily lives that are beyond that brand. So, we want to understand what is going to be authentic based on your brand DNA, and what is off limits based on your higher purpose and risk tolerance.

Then we use our proprietary tools and algorithms to conduct deep dives on patterns to understand what trends have been percolating in the last 90 days—what promotions have been in the market, what events and partnerships have created bursts and map all of that activity to understand how they behaved in the past. Past behavior or historical behavior is one input in predicting how things will unfold in the future.

This analysis allows us to build out culture clusters: areas within culture that are coalescing, plus the topics within those clusters that we can build content against. All of this then informs a more robust content strategy that includes both calendar and event-driven content, but more importantly culture-based content.

Once we've done all of that, we go back every 30 days and review everything that we're doing from a strategic point, we refresh the content, and it becomes like a newsroom machine at that point, with teams watching what happens every day—what is percolating, pulling content out of our arsenal, producing new content, and modifying as we go.

DP: That sounds really awesome! Content marketing is becoming huge, and there are a lot of different approaches, from a traditional PR and advertising agency model to companies like Percolate or Contently. How does what you do relate to these larger trends in content marketing, and what possible opportunities do you see for partnership and collaboration in the future?

TY: Basically, I walked you through our process. Now, when we're creating content we bucket into three areas: (1) unexpected creation of content–very rapid development like a breaking newsroom; (2) pre-planned content that we've built out portions of the content, and can modify in real-time; (3) curated content that comes from partners.

We might do any of the following: go to Contently and activate bloggers across different topics, use NewsCred to curate content, Film Buff to map our cultural topics against, or to Big Think for the video archive. There are many content creators with portions of content that we activate.

You have to be open minded in how you collaborate and partner with content creators because the reality is that when you're moving fast and trying to stay in sync with culture, you are not always going to be able to build highly sophisticated content on the fly. You need great technology and content partners that you can leverage in order to get the best production quality.

DP: You have 96 different Content Networks, including persona-types such as the "Power Woman" and "Kidults," as well as trends like "Oneness" and "Hackdesign." Can you tell us a bit more about how you create a Content Network, and at what point does an outlier start to migrate towards the center of culture?

TY: We do daily briefings in our office that are open to guests. I would encourage people reading this interview to come in and see exactly how it works. Each briefing is curated by two strategists: one for fast culture, and a second that follows slow culture.

Today, we saw an interesting discussion about how doctors are now taking on group patients, where you can sign-up and go in groups of 5. It's a form of the sharing economy coming to the doctor's office, and a term called "public practice." As we hear those terms, we write them on post-its on this huge board. For example, we are tracking the push-and-pull between incognito, which is trying to detox from digital versus life logging and being totally immersed 24/7.

As we get enough connections in one particular area, we will then birth a new Content Network. Something fringe 2-3 months ago can become huge very fast. Think for example of the Collaborative Economy. You see all of these different manifestations like sharing, Kickstarter, Lyft, and then eventually we'll coin a phrase and a new Content Network will be created.

DP: Is this similar to what Malcolm Gladwell famously referred to as a "tipping point"?

TY: It's a little like the tipping point, except that its when something really takes off and moves the needle. We have 96 content networks that we refer to as a Table of Cultural Elements. A lot of things are fringe and haven't taken off yet. For example, certain things may cluster in art, or the scientific community, and yet they have enough momentum that we believe they constitute a Content Network worth tracking. So, there is enough of a tipping point in a particular area to name and cluster it, but not necessarily to a point where they are spilling out across multiple industries and segments the way Malcolm Gladwell talks about.

DP: It sounds like you're expanding in a number of different directions. What is your vision for the future, and do you see the methods that you're pioneering as the future of advertising, or are you even going beyond that in terms of product development and other things?

TY: Even though we track the future, I don't know 100%. I do believe that this is the future of advertising. At a very base level, this is a disruption to the advertising industry. These methods will be adopted by many brands and advertising agencies in the next 3-5 years. We're at the very front end, pioneering side, even within the advertising newsroom space. This is probably the way that you're going to do advertising in the future.

I've come to think that what we're doing with sparks & honey—curating knowledge, breaking down the walls of collaboration and reaching out into the world in real time—is almost a new model that can be applied beyond advertising back into the institution for the way innovation is driven. We had John Seely Brown (JSB) in recently, who runs the Deloitte Center for the Edge, and he said, "You don't even know what you have in the model, because this is not just about advertising. It's about a completely different approach to doing what is next." I don't know what to do about that, except to think about what to do next.

DP: That's the great thing about innovation—thinking about things you've never thought about before, and then trying to figure out what to do next.

TY: Yes, exactly.

....

Terry Young *is CEO and Founder of sparks & honey. Terry launched his first digital startup in 1995 at IPG and built it into a top 50 digital agency at the age of 27. He then joined McKinsey & Co. in Greater China to work with the Fortune 500 C-suite and incubate new startups and Internet companies in Asia. In his next move, he took his strategy and digital experience to the top CRM firms at Omnicom (Targetbase and RAPP) and ultimately Epsilon. His deep understanding of digital and CRM experiences, technology platforms and consumer behavior allowed him to architect sparks & honey and a next generation marketing approach called Wave Branding.*

Terry also spent 27 months volunteering in Uralsk, Kazakhstan, supporting microcredit financing initiatives, incubating new businesses and launching programs for the local orphanage. Terry says that each experience has given him a different lens for viewing life and more importantly understanding people and culture. This perspective has helped to shape the vision of sparks & honey.

....

C3 METRICS AND ATTRIBUTION

Mark Hughes

Mark Hughes led one of the most successful viral marketing stunts in history—the renaming of a town, Halfway, Oregon, to Half.com—and literally wrote the book on *Buzzmarketing*, which became an international bestseller. He is now a pioneer in attribution, which has the potential to disrupt how online ads are trafficked and sold:

- The three factors of disruption—convenience, price and style
- How word-of-mouth is a philosophy and way of life
- Pursuing a two-fold strategy of disruption, industry leaders and bottom-up
- The disruptive potential of attribution and the challenges of changing behavior

Mark Hughes is also one of my favorite people in the world: an innovative marketer, bestselling author, CEO and co-founder of C3 Metrics, and just an all around great guy that I look up to and admire. His story of renaming a town is an absolute must-read, but the real lessons are in his approach to innovation and his latest work on attribution.

DP: You led one of the most successful and disruptive launches in history. Half.com was sold for $300m within six months of being launched. Tell us a bit about how what you learned and how it relates to disruption?

MH: Disruption happens when you have one of three things come to the surface and done really well: convenience, price, or style. When it came to Half.com, we were basically saying, "Hey, listen, rather than auction off your book, TV, or video game on eBay, why wait 5 or 7 days? Just sell it like you would in a retail store."

You could buy it conveniently like you would on Amazon versus having the more cumbersome option. eBay didn't have that functionality then. So Half.com hit on convenience and price. Items were half price or less, sometimes a bit more, but about half price. I don't know that it really hit on any kind of style, but Half.com was stylistically easier than eBay. Half.com hit on convenience and price.

In general, when you talk about disruption, it's usually about these three things. You've got to have much greater convenience, a much greater price advantage, or much better style. Stylistically, from a design standpoint, it was much better than what eBay had at the time (remember it didn't own PayPal at the time). So we had two out of three of those from a product standpoint. Then you have consumers. Are they regular consumers, for example, a woman who lives in Iowa who plunks down her credit card on something? Or is your consumer more of a B2B consumer? It differs depending on the end user of the product or service. For us, it was Mrs. Smith the American consumer.

We knew we had a disruptive product. In fact, we had offers to sell the company before we launched. It was also a crazy era. Anything with dot-com at the end of a word automatically got you a valuation. So the question was how do you get into the minds of the media and consumers and have them engage with and evangelize about a disruptive product?

A lot of products out there are disruptive. The tactics definitely vary. The motivations definitely vary depending on who the end consumer is. The barriers to entry were very low. "5 bucks for a book? Okay I'll put my credit card down and try that. It's cheaper than buying the book full price at 14 bucks." So the barriers to entry were pretty low and we had to maximize the opportunity. The overnight success of a company or product does not usually happen in one night. It's usually a result of either a lot of money behind it, or a lot of money plus a lot of hours behind it.

DP: You came up with what marketers consider one of the best marketing ideas ever in terms of launching a product.

MH: We changed the name of a town to Half.com, Oregon.

DP: Can you explain how you came up with that idea? It would still be considered revolutionary now. That type of marketing wasn't really done back, so in terms of walking towards the fear and really kind of doing something big, can you just walk us through the story of how that happened?

MH: It was at a time where venture money was very easy to get because there was a lot of it available, but everyone was doing the same thing and taking their venture money to Madison Avenue ad agencies.

My boss Josh Kopelman said, "People are just putting their money on a train and sending it to New York. We can't do that. It's not going to work. If you do the same thing that everyone else is doing, it's not going to work. We need to do something spectacular. We need to do something that's going to capture the attention of as many consumers and as many media outlets as possible."

He gave me a spreadsheet of pure math: here's our year one plan for how we're going to get customers with the line items of radio, TV, print, PR, word-of-mouth, etc.. Looking at those line items, the assumption was that for TV it would cost 100 dollars to acquire a customer. Print was 60 dollars. But word-of-mouth was basically 5 bucks to acquire a customer.

So we focused on word-of-mouth; did a ton of research trying to understand consumers better: where they might live and what they might do. We discovered that they were outdoorsy. We know that they index really high for mountain biking. We needed to do something monumental. So combine the consumer habits of e-commerce purchasers of the stuff that we're selling. Combine outdoorsy with something monumental.

We thought, hey, what about monuments: The Boulder Dam, The Grand Canyon, The Statue of Liberty, etc. We started throwing out ideas. "What if we shot this banner across the Grand Canyon, 007 style, and the banner said, 'Damn high prices! Go to Half.com!'" Yeah it made people giggle a little bit. We were starting to roll with it. We thought, "What if we took the Statue of Liberty and had helicopters approach it one night and put this massive T-Shirt on the Statue of Liberty where the T-Shirt said, "Raise your hand if you want to pay half?'" So we came up with those types of crazy ideas.

Then it came to me as my mind was scanning a virtual map of the United States. I was thinking maps. I was thinking towns and states. There must be some town that had the name half in it. What if we could get them to rename their town to Half.com? That way we would literally put our name on the map. We looked up all the towns with half in the name and there were like twenty or thirty. We chose the smallest one because we wanted to pay the cheapest price. There it was: population 350 Halfway, Oregon.

So I got on the phone and called the city manager. "Is the mayor there?" "No, the mayor's out." "This is Mark Hughes from Half.com. I want to discuss business opportunities." A day goes by. I hadn't gotten a call back. I call again. "Did you give the message to the mayor?" "Oh yeah, I gave the message to the mayor." "And? And?" "Well, the mayor doesn't really keep hours."

I was going out to San Francisco for another meeting and so I said, "Tell you what. I'm going to San Francisco from Philadelphia. Why don't I swing by Oregon?" "Swing by?" "Yeah. I'll be in that general neighborhood." "All right. You got to fly to Boise and then you've got to rent a rig, and make sure it has four-wheel drive because it's icy and watch out for the deer."

DP: *Sounds like it was out of* Northern Exposure!

MH: It was definitely right out of *Northern Exposure*. I had nothing to lose. I was out in San Francisco meeting with our traditional agency. At the end of the meeting, they said, "Where are you going now?" "I'm actually going to Halfway, Oregon trying to get them to rename their town to Half.com Oregon." The head of the agency drove me to the airport snickering at my story, but three weeks later, we're on the cover of USAToday.com and *Good Morning America* was telling our story on TV.

I went out there and said, "I can't really say what Half.com is because we're in stealth mode, but I can say we're a brand backed by this venture capitalist, and we're looking for towns. We're considering a few other towns, but I need to know if you guys are interested because I don't want to waste my time here." "Oh, we can get back to you really quickly."

Somehow the message got garbled. People started to check us out. They called up *The Philadelphia Inquirer* and said, "Are these guys for real?" So *The Philadelphia Inquirer* said, "Why do you want to know? Who are you? Why are you asking?" They said, "They're trying to rename our town." "What?" "Yeah, they're trying to rename our town." The story kind of got garbled as if we did rename the town already.

The thing is we wanted the press the moment when we launched the website—not then. So when they called for comments we asked, "Can you sit on it? We'll give you an exclusive." That just made them realize they had something really good. So *The Philadelphia Inquirer* published the story much to our timing dismay. To make sure we got our story out correctly, we sent out a press release on Saturday, the worst day for that in the world.

Monday morning, my boss Josh Kopelman calls me on my cell phone. I thought, "Oh crap. Here we go..." "Mark, we're on the cover of USAToday. com!" "Watch *Good Morning, America*. They did a segment." This is Monday morning. We sent out a press release on Saturday. And all of a sudden these guys are picking it up. I would imagine there was a certain amount of divine intervention. The stars aligned. But it involved method, invention, and hard work, too.

We all worked really hard, and our idea for literally putting our brand on the map was pretty innovative. It was just one of those things where everything worked. There was an element of secrecy. Now many companies stay in stealth mode, but back then, not a lot of folks were launching in stealth mode. So everyone was asking, "What is Half.com? What the heck are they doing? Selling half price babies?"

There was this element of intrigue plus an element of controversy because of course the news crews sent people to the odd little town of 350 in the middle of nowhere interviewing people on the street. It was very easy to find people who said, "Screw those guys! They aren't going to name my town! Screw off!" This made it even better because controversy in the media is opportunity. The controversy just fueled the fire.

Then there's the actual act of trying to rename the town, which required hard work, as well as shaking hands, having coffee with townfolk, meeting the bank manager and the guy who makes fly fishing rods, answering the same questions again and again and again, and, quite frankly, taking a lot of punches. But it's 15 rounds. You have to compete until it's all done.

Slowly but surely, we humanized the brand. So instead of being another one of these dot-coms trying to get rich shooting gerbils out of a cannon, the townfolk actually came to know me as a person. They said, "Well, I don't know about Half.com, but that guy Mark Hughes, he seems OK." We brought more people, Clint Schmidt, Matt Jesson, Mark Harrington, and even Josh. The townspeople said, "These guys aren't so bad. They're just like you and me." So we humanized the brand, and we gave people an opportunity to like us.

A lot of people say marketing has to be very logical. You have to demonstrate the benefits, all that traditional marketing stuff I learned at my Ivy League business school. But what you don't learn in business school is that a lot of decisions related to consumer purchases are based on emotion and personal relationships.

DP: Can you tell me a little bit about how the experience with Half.com helped you shape some of the core ideas in your book Buzzmarketing, *which ended up becoming an international best seller?*

MH: Fear can be a motivator and a shaper...there's negative and positive fear. Think about a baby being born. The baby might say, "Look, I'd much rather stay in this womb where it's nice and cozy and warm. I don't want to come out. Why would I want to come out?" Coming out of the womb, the transition, is actually the hardest part. That's a big concept in yoga. I started yoga about three and a half years ago. It's transformed my life along with faith.

There are many parallels to business and life in yoga. Once you're in a certain position, whether it's a yoga position or a business position or role, you're there. You're good. "Got it. Mastered this." Then you transition to another position that's maybe harder. Getting there from the position you were in, that's the transition. That is the part that's hard. You've got to focus, execute, visualize. You've got to believe that you can do it. Transitions are the hardest in business, in life, and in yoga.

So, Buzzmarketing is a philosophy of transition and change, of going straight to your fears, and doing things people are not doing. It's sometimes having to be mocked and criticized but sticking to it. Not everything is going to work out. It's a marathon. It's a full-on change, not a short-term diet.

DP: With C3 Metrics, you went from being a well-known marketer to be-
ing a founder and CEO. Can you tell us why you started C3 Metrics? What
is attribution and how is that disruptive in relationship to all these larger
changes?

MH: The way everyone tracks online advertising is based on systems developed in the mid 1990s. After the first dot-com bubble burst and the crash,
everyone stopped investing in Internet technology. A lot of VCs lost a lot
of money. "Why on earth would you ever invest in Internet infrastructure,
especially tracking? Has anyone looked at the Internet advertising market?
It sucks!"

In the early 2000s people started putting more ad dollars toward the Internet. Targeting got more sophisticated, but the tracking systems gave credit
to the very last ad clicked or the very last ad viewed. The Internet was simple in the 1990s—no social sharing, no blogs, no YouTube videos, not much
display, and only the early glimmer of paid search. But now you might see
an ad 8-10 times across different channels before finally deciding to click
on it or go to the site in a different tab. The idea behind attribution is to at-
tribute credit to all of those past experiences leading up to the conversion of
e-commerce transactions, recognizing that it takes a team of players.

Only 3% of the time, on average, is there one paid media source involved.
The thing is that ad servers are meant to serve ads. They weren't meant to
contain everything. Ad servers weren't originally built to contain search.
Ad servers don't typically contain affiliate. Ad servers don't typically contain earned social. And who knows what'll be coming down the pipe? So
we made our C3 Metrics platform independent, so that whatever ad server
you're using you don't have to switch, you don't have to take everything out
of Commission Junction or Linkshare or whatever and put it into something
else. We can just piggyback on your existing channels to make it really easy.

DP: You started to recognize that advertising and conversions are a team ef-
fort around the same time as advertisers started to think about social media
and engaging communities, brand building, and focusing on building teams
around their brands, which is pretty interesting.

MH: Yeah. It was about the same time. We also reduced it to one metric,
ROAS, to make it simple. What we'd seen from our competitors were reams

of data that would take weeks to clean and prepare, so we said, "You don't understand how the media world works. This is how the media world works: The CFO walks into the CMO's office and says, 'Hey, Bob, you know how I gave you that 6 million dollars this quarter to spend?' 'Yeah.' 'And you know how it's two months into the quarter already and we've got one month left?' 'Yeah.' 'Well, I need X million of that back or I need X hundred thousand of that back because earnings kind of tanked. I need a plan on my desk by tomorrow at 2 p.m.

You don't have time to prepare spreadsheets for two weeks before you can even analyze it. Or the flipside is he'll walk into Bob's office and say, 'Hey, listen, I need you to spend more money, but don't spend it inefficiently, spend it wisely. And oh, by the way, I need a plan on my desk by 2 p.m. tomorrow.' That's how the media world works." We had to design so that it was convenient and robust enough that people could make decisions in about an hour.

We developed it at a time when media forms were blossoming, and we developed it so early that we bought all of the domain names like AttributionModel.com, AttributionModeling.com, TVAttribution.com, ViewableImpressions.com and about 50 more from GoDaddy for 8 bucks a year. We had first mover advantage on those category-level attribution domains.

DP: No one was thinking about them.

MH: Yeah. When it comes to disruption, I use the toilet as an example. The toilet was invented in the 1700s, but toilet paper wasn't invented until 70 years later. Why is that? It doesn't make any sense.

The same principle applies. Once you have attribution solutions out there, people don't adopt them. The understanding of last click attribution and tracking systems, which most of us online advertisers are still using, is low. "What? Are you telling me that what I've been doing for the past ten years is wrong? See my spreadsheet? It says this in black and white." You need to break through the behavioral habits of weekly reports, monthly reports, quarterly reports, which have been done again and again and again—using an incorrect method of tracking and success determination.

"No, I'm sorry, you have been doing it wrong, and you've been doing it wrong for a long time." Convincing online advertisers and their agencies is not an easy thing to do quickly. But with the consumer, you can. She says, "Hey, five bucks, and I can buy a half-priced DVD tomorrow? What is the risk?" B2C is different. The cost associated with a change in B2B is far greater and multidimensional.

The first dimension is that someone has to fess up to the fact that you've been doing it wrong, and there is a lot of fear associated with that in a corporate environment. Of course, advertisers want more ROI, but when you have that accountability discussion, you open yourself up to the possibility of getting fired. Online advertising has been going up steadily since 2004. So, where is the problem as a growing category masks the sins of a flawed tracking method?

Behavior is a hard thing to change. When you're talking about a brand-new behavior, it's a clean slate. Look at the tablet. No one has ever experienced a tablet before. It's kind of easy. But when you're trying to change a behavior, you have to go back to that word in yoga: transition. Transition is the hardest part. Now that you are comfortable in one position and then you get to the next position and you're comfortable there. You made it. The hard part is transitioning.

We were super early in attribution, and against the grain for VPs and marketers. I don't know how fast attribution will take off—Gartner pegs it at 1-5% adoption today. Are people just going to ignore it and keep on measuring stuff the way they have for half a decade? Odds are, they probably are. Even though it doesn't make any sense and they are losing tens of millions of dollars in some cases. Behavior is a very tough thing to change. And change is not something that is enjoyable. Change is something that is painful.

DP: When the recession hit, there was a need to really demonstrate ROI. Do you think that that may have accelerated adoption and interest in things like attribution?

MH: Yes, but only for the right players. For example, we spoke to a luxury car company, and they told us outright, "We don't care about attribution. All we care about is that our banner ad and our online activity are in the right places. Elite. We're the company of the elite. ROI is not what we're concerned about."

At the end of the day, you are not talking to a company. You are talking to a person, and that person is going to make a decision based on the health and welfare of their name and their professional reputation. That also relates to B2B sales. Do you trust the person in front of you? Do you have a good relationship? You want to know that person is going to be there for you.

Some of our success has come from a category perspective where more and more people are talking and writing about attribution. We don't do a lot of PR anymore because the PR is being done for us. Why would I write another article about attribution when three people are writing articles on attribution this week, even if they aren't the articles I would have written? I'm going to let other people do my marketing for me in this period. So part of the success is a function of the category growing.

But it also gets back to the old Half.com "Hey, listen, you and I have a brand and it's not just C3 Metrics. We are Mark Hughes, my co-founder Jeff Greenfield, and Frank Guzzardo." It's the people behind those relationships that get developed over time. At the end of the day, people just make decisions because they like you more than other people, assuming the technologies are roughly the same—and they know you've got their back. We're trying to humanize the brand like we did with Half.com.

DP: You also do that by walking them through the data so that you humanize the technology. The thing about attribution is that it is such a simple, commonsense idea: in such an interconnected world, where ads and content are trafficked everywhere, why on earth would you only give credit to the last click?

MH: Yeah, to give you some numbers behind that, we have one client for whom the average number of media touch points in their consumer funnels is 31. So if you're giving 100% credit to the last media touch point and ignoring those 30, then why spend money on them in the first place? It's a flawed last ad system, because those originated, and partially accelerated to consumer to conversion—without planting seeds, there can be no crop. Any American farmer knows this—advertisers have to understand the farming cycle of conversion.

It's kind of cool to show them the data and see that "a-ha" moment occur, "I can't believe I was buying media in that antiquated way." What's interesting is that the people who are using our products voraciously are mostly brands you've never heard of and you probably never will. They spend like $20-40k/month, which is small in relationship to larger brands. Small to mid-sized companies care about ROI and don't have the legacy concerns about change.

It's those little clients that get really upset because every dollar counts for them and it's also a matter of pride. The more they can make their dollar work, the more they might get noticed. The more value they bring, the more security and longevity they bring to their company. The attribution market could also be disrupted by a couple big media companies. If a large advertising conglomerate said: "From this day and time forward, we are never going to measure online advertising unless it's with attribution." The attribution and online ad measurement market could change from either bottom-up with small business, or top-down if a few 800-pound gorillas make a shift.

We're pursuing a dual-prong strategy: high and low at C3 Metrics. We don't know which will take off faster—that's part of any new technology, especially when you're doing something innovative and disruptive. But your clients actually help you a lot because they see the value and want you to succeed. They point out things. You discover things together. Sometimes it's like "Wow, C3 Metrics should be paying you!" So it's a fascinating slow-rolling process. It strikes a chord when I read the phrase, "It was a 10-year overnight success."

We offer more convenience and a better price, but just because you have a more convenient product and can save clients a lot of money doesn't really mean that you are going to disrupt the marketplace with rapid adoption. That's got to happen with other means. It's the transition of how you get from a great product with the three key elements of disruption to the actual adoption.

DP: I guess maybe to wrap things up, you've been a successful marketer, written a bestselling book, and now you've successfully founded a company as an entrepreneur, what advice would you give to someone who's aspiring to do that, who's maybe coming out of college or maybe thinking about a career change?

MH: You've got to be flexible. When something is not working, the worst thing you could do is continue down that path. The best thing you could do is make the call and say, "It's not working." You've got to change something. That's hard to do. It's hard to see because you are so optimistic as a young entrepreneur or marketer. The whole nature of being an entrepreneur is to be an optimist. Look at Larry Ellison or Steve Jobs. Everyone who was working for Ellison and Jobs in the early days said, "We have the worst product! We have nothing! We have the worst thing in Silicon Valley. It's not even good!"

Yet Larry Ellison and Steve Jobs were selling it like it was the best thing since sliced bread. To be a successful entrepreneur, you have to be an optimist. But at the same time, to be a successful entrepreneur, you have to recognize when things aren't working. You have to be flexible and shift fast. It's a skill set of opposites. You've got to recognize that optimism is a great trait, but it has a time and a place.

You also have to be able to change and shift quickly. Be prepared for a lot of pain. The most common thing of all entrepreneurs is not enough revenue, and not enough cash. When someone calls you asking for advice or wanting to have breakfast, in that stage whatever it is, you can predict one of these two things: I don't have enough revenue, or I don't have cash. It's going to be one of the two.

One of the best pieces of advice is it's never as bad as it seems, and it's never as good as it seems, either. I tell my wife after getting back from a really killer meeting with so-and-so, and I think, "Gosh, you know this happened, and, gosh, this is great," and then my wife will say, "I'm not getting on this roller coaster with you." She knows that I'm up, and then when that deal doesn't come through, I'm down. You wonder, "Holy smokes, what is it all for? It's never going to work."

You have to develop a stomach for uncertainty and pain, and there's a certain individual who has that. Immigrants with a bad family situation. People who grew up in war zones in the Middle East. My Dad grew up on World War II with the Germans bombing his neighborhood, and he had to sleep in a bomb shelter most nights at a young age. These people who have experienced real hardship probably have a better chance of entrepreneurial success than someone who grew up in a middle-class family—someone who never experienced pain or never lost anything. If you've lost things, then you have weathered the storm. People who experience loss before have a better chance at success in a startup.

My advice is not to go out and live in a war zone, but you need thick skin. At the end of the day, it's time, it's money, and there are lessons. I think you also have to be prepared as an entrepreneur to walk away, to say, "Hey. That didn't work. There's something better for me. There's a better plan. This plan wasn't the one that ultimately was for me." The same thing with careers. The job that you're in may not be the one that's right for you. It may just be the road, the path, the lesson that gets you to the right one. You have to view it as, "OK these are not all my eggs." Even though it may feel like they're all your eggs.

It takes a bunch of stamina and recognition of when to change if things aren't working out and a willingness to walk away. Not necessarily quit but a willingness to accept that this is not the way it's supposed to be. I'd say that is probably the best advice. The other advice I'd give is to try and meet with people that you think never in a million years would take your meeting. Steve Jobs called Bill Packard on the phone when he was 13 years old and said, "Hey, listen, I'm building some computer stuff and I wonder if you have any parts that I could have." And of course, it's Hewlett-Packard. Of course he had parts. He was bold enough and crazy enough to call.

Most people would have been like, "There's no way, I'm not going to call that guy!" or rename a town. That's crazy! And everyone will laugh at you. When C3 Metrics started, I got the former CEO of Nielsen as one of my advisors. I thought, "Who is the biggest baddest name in the media measurement business that I can find?" Of course, with Nielsen, I couldn't get the current CEO, but I could probably get the former CEO.

He turned me down *three* times. He said, "No, no, no, no," but then I finally convinced him to listen. "You have to do this. You can't let advertisers waste their money like this. It's a crime." I said, "You can't in good conscience let this happen. Join me." So the last piece of advice would be try to get someone with real star power on your team. Why not? What do you have to lose?

DP: It's like they say: Your rejection rate is always 100% if you don't ask. I took that same philosophy with this book. I put together a list of the best possible people in the world in each area of innovation, and said they have to give me an interview. I need you in this book because you are the best.

MH: Yeah, exactly. Get someone with incredible star power in your particular niche, industry, etc. associated with you in some shape or form. Be bold.

Mark Hughes *grew eBay's Half.com from zero to 8 million online customers as its VP of Marketing in less than three years. Half.com was sold to eBay for over $300 million six months after launch.*

He has spent $100 million online ad dollars, planting the seeds for C3 Metrics' advertising effectiveness SaaS platform—helping Advertisers DSPs and Networks discover previously ignored revenue drivers and increase ROI with: attribution, patent pending viewable impressions technology in cross-domain iFrames, Viewable Conversions, and Upper Funnel Conversions. Hughes brings a wealth of creative and quantitative experience in consumer marketing from PepsiCo's Pizza Hut Division; Pep Boys, the automotive aftermarket retailer; and American Mobile Satellite.

Hughes is the son of a Pulitzer Prize winning journalist, and Hughes' own book, Buzzmarketing, *is published in 15 languages. In its first year of release it was heralded by* Fast Company *as one of the Ten Best Business Reads of the Year and named by* The Financial Times *of London as one of the Best Business Books of the Year along with* Freakonomics.

Mr. Hughes holds his MBA from Columbia Business School in Marketing and International Business.

USING TECH TO SOUND HUMAN

Frank Speiser

Frank Speiser is a brilliant technologist and co-founder of SocialFlow doing pioneering work at the intersection of big data and social media. We sat down to talk about how social media is a broadcast platform that builds upon things we have always done. This simple approach makes it easy to understand the future of media and technology:

- How social media can exponentially create more value
- What it takes to forge partnerships with Facebook and Twitter
- Why big data can allow conversations to sound more human
- What a company is for founders, investors, and employees

Frank is one of the smartest and most well rounded people that I know. We were fortunate to be colleagues together at Heavy, and have remained friends for years. Our incredibly geeky and wide-ranging conversations helped shape the concept of this book, and Frank deserves special thanks for being a guinea pig as my first interview.

DP: A lot of people complain about how social media is making us dumb and reducing the world down to lowest common denominators, and yet its promise is to be this incredible platform to share and communicate ideas faster and more efficiently, which includes using tools like SocialFlow. Tell us a bit about your motivations for founding SocialFlow and what you do.

FS: There are so many people doing so many great things that really the world is not dumbed down. It's just that you see the dumb stuff as much as you look for it. It almost becomes this self-fulfilling prophecy, where if you go looking for dumb stuff on the Internet, I guarantee you you're going to find it. And obviously, if you find it once, you're probably going to find it a lot more. But it depends on what you're looking for.

One of the reasons why we started SocialFlow was to make sure that the right messaging got to the right people at the right time, so you could make the most use of it. Now, if you want to click on stories about Kim Kardashian, that's great, but it doesn't marginally improve your life that much to where I could notice it. However, if you start discovering news or ideas and then acting on them faster, then the world gets better the more that happens. By getting people paying attention to things with a lot of utility and seeing each other doing better because of it, the world starts to re-align around value exponentially faster instead of around perceived value or gratification.

So, if you switch from the model based on gratification towards one of lasting value—happening to as many nodes in the network as possible—then you start to get a better self-ordered world instead of feeling dumb, lost and disconnected. Seeing other people benefit from making smart choices, and sharing useful ideas, is going to make the best advertisement for sharing the good stuff you come across.

DP: You take this idea of lasting value a step further by trying to use data to help someone sound more human. Can you explain how data helps us to have meaningful conversations at scale?

FS: It's not any different from what we have always done. When you come across something useful and pick up the phone to call someone, you are exchanging data, just on a peer-to-peer model, right?

Everybody talks about how social has changed everything, but really, social is just the next iteration in broadcast media. It's not a conversational medium for the most part. It's like we all have independently-owned TV stations. I broadcast, but then I can get feedback to change things. Data lets you know whether or not you are connecting with people, and it lets you assess what the appetite is for what you want to share.

If you have something important, data can help you overcome your selection-bias and avoid missing your audience. I think that is probably the most important role for it, because by nature it is our tendency to think what you're going to say is the most important—if you count, in a set of one, it's definitely the most important thing.

As you start expanding the possible reach of your message, the odds of your being right drop dramatically. You go from being sure it's the most important thing, but then, even in the example of your calling on the phone–now you're only half as sure. When you open it up to a set of a thousand followers on Facebook or Twitter, your odds are pretty low that you are going to hit the best time to deliver your message if you are only polling yourself. Data on what people are topically connecting with allows you to model-out how to get the right messaging in front of the right people at the right time.

DP: This type of modeling out communications using data is also related to what people refer to as an interest graph. Can you explain the concept of an interest graph?

FS: An interest graph is the landscape of what people are talking about, but it also has a temporal component to it as well. It's not just a demographic assessment of what we've been connected with; it's a map that shows how interesting something is to me at one given time.

There could be a thousand possible things that I could talk about, but it's all a function of the context that I'm currently engaged. So when you look at the interest graph—all of the participants that you could potentially assess— it's a field guide to what those people are willing to talk about at a given moment. A good analogy would be an electrical circuit; what would conduct across that interest graph? Then imagine that circuit board rewiring itself every few minutes.

It's like mapping of nodes with the context of the topicality in play, and the estimated shelf life across each of those topics.

DP: You founded SocialFlow in 2009 when a lot of stuff was going on in the economy. Why start a business at that moment, and why did you choose Twitter?

FS: Mike Perrone and I started SocialFlow to solve our own problem. Mike and I had just left companies because they had been sold. I just had a kid and was taking some time off. When you sit around talking to an eight-month old kid, and it is impossible to overstate how amazing that is in its own right, there is not a lot of stimulating adult conversation. So we decided to do something interesting and started a podcast.

The problem was that we couldn't get anybody to listen to it. We sent out an email with a link in it where we could track the 300 people who got that email, and nobody clicked the link. After six hours, we said, "We can't take this." I think a normal person would have just quit and moved on, but Mike and I are both pretty stubborn and we were like, "Let's make this work." So we started sharing the link to people who had used the topics we had tagged to our podcasts our podcast in their Tweets or status updates for Facebook.

The "a-ha" moment came pretty quickly when we realized that you have a greater than one-to-one conversion rate: For every message you share, more than one person would click the link or interact with the message. Mike had a direct marketing background and he was going through the stats the day after we started doing this and he realized, if you can connect with people when they want you to connect with you, then you get this great distribution and there's huge upside.

We started comparing it with traditional, existing forms of media and we realized it's way cheaper to distribute things this way because the platforms carry the cost of the messaging for you. You don't have to pay to tweet or pay to post to Facebook at least to some part of your audience. The problem of, "What's worth paying to go over and above that?" came later, but we still figured that out pretty early on as well.

As far as starting during the recession, I think we never really thought it was a recession. I mean, recession for whom? Tech people never really went out of work and there was no slowdown in technical advancement; Twitter was ramping pretty quickly, Facebook was growing like crazy. This was an opportune time to start a company like ours, so we went full speed ahead. It is also important to understand what a recession is: a slow-down in spending. During these times, entities move to save instead of spend, which means if you have a good idea, the deeper you get into a recession, the more cash is out there to deploy against those good ideas. If you have a good idea, it's a good idea: do something with it.

DP: Do you think the economic crash may have actually accelerated the adoption of social within larger companies because of better ROI and better ways to track engagement more cost-effectively?

FS: Yes, because the companies had to do something. Their profit margins were shrinking, because if you have an economy that's based on access to capital and credit, and it starts to become harder to access capital, you have three choices: (1) You find new capital, which is not that easy in a situation like that; (2) You can die off, which is not a viable option when you have a vested interest in your high-paying job still being there a year from now; or (3) You can trim costs.

Things get kind of real once money gets tight. It forces people to start looking at ways to get the same, for less. Technology shortens a certain amount of time and labor to accomplish something—it's this same mechanism over and over throughout human history that has gotten us to where we are now.

DP: Social media has been very disruptive to traditional publishing. Thousands of leading news and magazines went out of business in the last few years. Many of your clients are larger enterprise, traditional publishers that managed to survive disruption and continue to remain market leaders.

How does a company like SocialFlow help enterprise publishers to engage and build their audiences?

FS: You start by thinking what business you are in. Are you in the business of reporting the news or are you in the business of selling the media when the news comes up? I don't think that anyone would sit down and argue that physical media newspapers are the wave of the future. I don't even go to the end of my driveway to pick up my newspaper—I get kind of mad when people throw a trial newspaper in my driveway because I have to walk all the way out there and pick it up, and it's yesterday's news. Meanwhile, I have today's news right in my pocket on my phone.

A lot of our customers realized that business on the Internet is the next frontier. Some look at it on its own P&L. Some have a subscription and/or ad-supported business and they can figure out how much they put into it vs. how much they're getting out. They also realize they're not in the business of deploying messages or deploying physical media to get the news out. They are in the news or the content business and the way they get return on investment is by driving people to their site.

We help them do that without having to put a lot of labor into it. They don't have to prepare or format the content—our platform takes care of all that for them—which allows them to do what they do best, which is create great content. So they focus on content, and we help them get the content where it needs to be, when it is most likely to pull people into their content experience.

DP: SocialFlow is one of the select few Certified Partners for Twitter and you have also developed a great relationship with Facebook, including winning a Facebook Innovation Award. How does a company go from being a startup to negotiating a partnership with a market leading company like Facebook or Twitter?

FS: You have got to hustle, that's the first thing. It starts there and you have really got to try hard. The second thing is, you've got to do something different. So you can't start off by saying, "We want to be like them."

We came at it from the perspective of, "How can we make this better for the users of these products?" SocialFlow is valuable to Facebook and Twitter because people get better results from using both platforms by using our product. Anytime you're developing a product, you should think, "How do I make this work for the person who's paying for it?" "How do I make their life better by doing this?"

Being an entrepreneur is actually a great line of work because you get paid to, A) discover the truth, and B) make someone's life better. Then you go to the platforms and say, "This is how we want to work with you. This is the opportunity. Look at the problems that we solve and how we're making things better."

So, there's a mechanical piece where you put the work in and get in front of them whenever you can, but the real reason why they want to do business with you is because they can see that you are out there making the lives of the users on their platforms better, and the experience of using their platform better.

DP: That brings up a larger theme related to this book. A lot of people use the term "disruption" all the time in tech. People tend to say, "we're disrupting this market" as if they want to ruin or attack legacy businesses. The way you've described what you're doing could be considered disruptive, but it is disruptive in the sense that you are offering a better and more unique solution.

FS: Yes, that's the only kind of disruption that works. Disruption advocates on behalf of the people who are usually penalized. That's the best part of the technical revolution. If there wasn't disruption—say, in the information industry—instead of having Google, what you'd have is a really awesome-looking card catalog at the library, and some really powerful telephone-operators union that connects people. But that doesn't exist and is way more expensive than just searching on Google and distributing things that way. People's lives are better for that and they don't miss the old days.

Everyone is worried about shipping jobs overseas and all these other problems, but it only impacts the people whose jobs got shipped and whose jobs were dependent on that. The people who buy the things they're producing are not complaining—they're getting things at a better price, faster. So it's not just a loss. There's an upside to it because people can go out and get what they want cheaper, which is what disruption does.

It's a good thing; it's progress. It's something to look forward to, not to fear. It is easy for us to say that on the edge of the technical revolution, and learning new skills amidst the uncertainty is scary—but it is heroic in the sense that each person who chooses to take up this challenge is moving humanity forward. When you can use technology to harness this momentum, things change pretty quickly. It's an amazing trait of humanity, especially this generation.

DP: Looking back on the last few years, what assumptions did you have when you started that turned out to be right or wrong? For example, did you think Facebook or Twitter would become as big as they are now?

FS: By 2009, I was sure they were going to get pretty big because all signs pointed to people preferring to communicate in that manner. I was a little surprised that text messaging didn't improve as a response against Twitter. I thought that there would have been some other industry that made text messaging awesome, so I'm surprised that didn't happen. On the flip side, it's a little surprising to see how big Facebook and Twitter got in such a short time.

Facebook also brought in a lot of the edge cases much faster than I thought. For example, now I can see my father, aunts and uncles on Facebook. It seems completely normal that people co-exist—it's kind of like our generation's TV or radio. Every generation in the past 120 years has had a massive leap forward in terms of how well and how quickly they communicate, and this was ours. I think Facebook cemented that and Twitter changed the way you distribute information.

DP: Related specifically to Twitter, there's a great example on the SocialFlow blog of when Keith Urban broke the Osama bin Laden tweet. You tracked how it spread exponentially over time across all of these different nodes and networks.

Can you walk me through how a message starts propagating and growing, the point where it breaks on Twitter, and how a platform like SocialFlow helps to track and manage its spread?

FS: Those kinds of things aren't necessarily managing as much as you're strapped to the bullet and ride when it starts to take off. Everything to a lesser degree is an example of that. What matters is when you enter the conversation. In the case of Keith Urban, that was a breaking news example and it showed you the power of pre-existing trust. Urban didn't have much of a network to speak of when he sent that tweet, only about 900+ followers. What made his tweet important was that people knew and trusted him. So, in order to succeed, you need to have context, predictability and utility. Urban had all three.

Urban's tweet was picked up by Brian Stelter, who has a pretty big network— not a huge one, but at the time it was big enough—and he broadcast it out there. Then all of a sudden, it was *the* tweet that got out there. The people who connected on that one were trusted enough to be verified and their opinions were valued, and the resistance to sharing it decreased, the further out it got. This is the opposite of what a normal message looks like that doesn't have a lot of utility. When you get a message that has a lot of usefulness behind it and people can see information being used the right way, then they tend to share it. This is also kind of why believable hoaxes get so much traction so quickly.

DP: The promise of the Internet is that it helps to bring people together. At the same time, communities tend to form around likeminded ideas that can often become polarized differences. How do we find a balance between these common aspirations versus being an echo-chamber for self-centered opinions?

FS: I've been thinking about this question a lot. I was just having a casual conversation with some of our partner managers over at Facebook, and I was making the observation that the Hegelian dialectic doesn't seem to exist. I've never really seen where a group of people that believes very strongly in something is exposed to a competing ideal and then synthesizes that to some sort of common ground.

Instead, what seems to happen is people's ideals become more entrenched and re-trenched, and what they start doing is finding ways to differentiate what they are talking about, and maybe strip away the things they don't believe as strongly. But that core actually gets harder, not softer.

I think it's not a matter of the ideals you currently hold, but it's never going to get softer until people can visibly see their lives getting better by the process in which they engage in discourse. It has to be one of those things where it has to be cool to discuss things the right way, instead of slapping fives and scoring points for telling someone off.

There has to be almost a societal revolution that values respect in discourse. People need to get better at knowing that they do not know and then get better at filling the gaps. It can happen because now, everybody can see it happen. On social, you can reorient the rules by choosing who you associate with, who will allow that discourse to happen. This goes back to what we talked about in the beginning of the interview and the reasons behind why we started SocialFlow—social media and community engagement has the possibility to create discourse and dialogue.

DP: Related to that, with a lot of platforms like Facebook and Twitter now at mass adoption, how do you see the way we're sharing information evolving in the future? What does the next 5-10 years of the Internet look like to you?

FS: I think the sharing problem is on its way to being solved and in terms of destroying the boundaries of how information flows, it's going to keep crumbling from now onward. I think a lot of people have answered this question—it's about curation and discovery and things like that. That ship is already sailing.

Connecting the usefulness of those things to applied outcomes in the real world is still very much foreign—we could still mess that one up. I think since so many things are flowing around information-wise, and the permutations of what you can do are increasing exponentially, we're going to need easy, frictionless ways to take what we know and apply it to the things in our lives. And that stuff is not even close to being built yet—that's the future of the Internet in the next 5-10 years. With so many uses for things, in so many different contexts, the concept of pricing itself needs to change more quickly. That has a ways to go before it is done right.

DP: Kids today are like the first generation growing up with technology from day one. You're a father of two boys with a passion for teaching and philosophy. Is there a good way to teach kids to use technology?

FS: Yes, there is. The first rule is: don't mess them up. A lot of what we grew up with was our ability to memorize and repeat, and people who knew facts and had good recall were considered smart. What I've done with my kids is put a conscious effort into valuing pattern-recognition and the application of things, as quickly as they can. For example, if I teach them something, I try to teach them how to apply it. So if I show them math: 2+2=4, I'll say to them, "There are two people in this room and there are two people in that room. How many people are there in this house? There are four."

This way they can start to see how one thing bridges into another. If you get them to do that, humans retain their rightful place, I think, in terms of the process-chain where we're valued for our ability to derive novel outcomes. Humans are not going to win the game of discreet computations. Subject evaluations and applying those things keeps us within the domain of what we should be doing.

When you can know an outcome and there is a pre-established way of getting to that outcome, why rebuild the pathway it took to get there? You should constantly question that and not always take things as fact. When you know you're going towards an outcome, one of the most valuable lessons is to not rebuild things that get you the pieces that you're building with. So you can teach kids how to use what they're learning quickly. Language is good for that, so teaching them multiple languages is good, as is showing them how the thing that they're learning is working. They need to see you doing it too.

DP: The last time we met, you made some comments around your management style that I found interesting. You said that you expect two hours a day of brilliant code from your developers. The idea of expecting two hours of productivity from full-time employees might seem a little strange to a general audience. How do these coordinated moments of brilliance make SocialFlow stand out, and how did you develop this management style?

FS: SocialFlow is not solving pre-established problems. It's not a manufacturing-pipeline way of thinking. We are paying people to come up with novel solutions to problems that a lot of people didn't even know existed. We are trying to get people oriented toward overcoming problems that you can't turn to someone else and ask for help.

In that regard, if you take chess as an analogy, you and I could probably play 50 games of five-minute, speed chess, but none of them are really going to be our best game. We may have flashes of brilliance in those games, but if we're just going for volume, at some point, it becomes a law of diminishing returns.

Here, we have deadlines and things that we are aiming for, but within the confines of the circadian rhythms of life. We want to let people think about the really important stuff as long as they can, need or want. When you want to solve a problem in a finite amount of time, the only thing you have is each person's mind at that time. So if you don't foster the conditions to let them do that, then what you get is a bunch of average code that does average things that yields, at best, slightly-differentiated results.

At SocialFlow our stuff works in orders of magnitude, or at least we try for standards of deviation above what you put it up against. We've sat down and thought about what it needs to do, why that works the way it does, how to apply that in a way that makes sense to the users and that does not take a whole lot of effort to do it with. Taking those problems and making them elegantly usable is an art form. At some point, the way you deploy technology becomes an aesthetic choice.

You don't get the results that we need by rushing things through a pipeline. I don't want eight hours of common results; I want two hours of brilliant results. It's up to you what you want to do with the rest of your time. To be honest, most people have a couple of days where they exceed that window; some people never get there inside of a day.

DP: Related to management style, you told me once that every company is three things: it's one thing for its customers, one thing for its investors and another thing for its employees. Can you elaborate on how that applies, especially for an aspiring entrepreneur?

FS: If you are an aspiring entrepreneur, you have to remember first and foremost that in order to succeed commercially, you need to make the experience awesome for the users—to be better, more helpful, and create lots of value. Next, the valuation of your company improves to the people who may invest in you—that's your second customer of business, your investors—in relationship to how much better you are at making the usefulness of your products awesome.

The third and most important thing is that you really have to think about how you make the time that your employees spend at the company irreplaceable. When they get to be 80 years old and look back on their life, you want to make it so they don't think, "Oh, I wish I had done something else." You owe it to them to make the work something they wouldn't want to trade in. The time you and the people spend against your company is the most important "product" you'll ever build, and you only get one shot at building that piece.

So the three aspects of any business are the experience for the users, the value for the investors and the time for the people. If you do it right, then as the entrepreneur you are always all three of those things.

DP: Technology entrepreneurs pioneered a lot of best practices such as the lean startup method, customer-centric selling and growth hacking. What best practices have you seen come out of the startup world that could impact a lot of big businesses?

FS: Obviously, a focus on the customer and customer-centric development is the way to go. Once you have a platform out there, it's the concept of minimal viable product. What is the minimum thing I can offer you that is going to differentiate us?

Get users based upon what differentiates and then pay attention to the people using it because they have a real opportunity cost. If they don't use it, what could they have used? The people paying attention are also the best people to solicit feedback from. Customer development is about getting feedback and building the things they want. It is also about knowing what's a one-off request vs. what's a scalable request, because you can only build a business based upon what scales.

That being said, I think the lean startup method can be a mistake. We did it and I wouldn't do it the same way again. I think once you know the right thing to do—once you know what is the right thing to scale—you should get there as fast as you can. The lean startup method penalized us a bit because once we knew what was going to provide the value and we had verification, we should have ramped up right away, rather than going slowly.

In the beginning, when there are two or three folks doing things, that method makes sense. I think the concept of going slow is to get feedback, build on it, and iterate fast until you demonstrate traction and need. But you reach a point where it is off to the races and you need to stop being lean. That is also why you raise money—to invest in talent and infrastructure to scale as fast as you can. So the best practice is to pay attention to the customer and once you know the right thing to do, just go.

DP: Any final words for the aspiring entrepreneur?

FS: If you don't do it, it's likely no one is going to do it. Even worse, if you don't do it, some schmuck is going to do it and fuck it up. So when you're sitting around thinking, "Should I do this or shouldn't I?" be sure that's what you want to do, and then don't complain if someone comes along and does a much-worse version of it. That's the reality of the situation. You can say, "Oh, I had that idea five years ago!" Guess what: you didn't do it, or you didn't do it well enough.

Once you want to go do something, the only time you're ever going to be in a position to act on it is right then. If you don't act on it within a reasonable time frame, somebody else is out there working on the same idea and they're probably not doing it as well as you would like it done. In this world, the downside of not doing things you believe are better, or leaving them as-is, should be obvious.

Frank Speiser *is the Co-Founder and Chief Product Officer of SocialFlow. He's a huge proponent of non-coercive, voluntary interactions. For the past several years, he's been active in advising startups in the NYC area and he's spoken frequently on the ethics of technology and technology's impact on journalism and the news. Frank has been programming since age 8, and doesn't ever plan to stop. He has also dropped out of five different universities, and is really bad at doing what he is told. Frank lives in Connecticut with his wife and two great kids.*

POSTSCRIPT

STRATEGIES FOR DAILY LIFE

SOCIAL MEDIA FOR JOB SEEKERS

Joshua Waldman

Joshua Waldman carved out a brilliant niche as an expert in how to leverage social media for networking and job seeking. The idea of a career path is now being replaced by the reality of gigs and temporary jobs, where we can reinvent ourselves online and must take control of our own reputations. Joshua provides essential advice for us all, including:

- How social media changed recruiting and the way we search for jobs
- Why personal positioning is essential to networking and reputation management
- Making decisions creates momentum that pushes your career forward
- How social proof relates to risk mitigation and reinforces your personal brand

Joshua literally wrote the book on the subject—the international bestseller *Job Searching with Social Media For Dummies*. Whether you are CEO of your own company, or looking for your first job, there are practical, straightforward tips that can be quickly integrated into your professional development.

DP: How has social media changed the way people look for a job and how has it changed recruiting?

JW: I knew this question would come up and I was thinking about *Downton Abbey*, which I'm a huge fan of. What's cool about this show is that they introduce technologies that we really take for granted. The first series starts off by introducing electricity. It's such a big deal, sort of like voodoo magic to the characters, particularly those who are less educated.

There's the question of, "In which rooms will we put electricity?" Towards the second season, the question becomes, "In which rooms will we put the telephone?" Eventually, they introduce the toaster oven and when a character first toasts bread, it burns and people come rushing in with buckets of water because they don't know what's going to happen. There is a lot of fear around innovation, which is very interesting to see in the context of a period piece. Eventually, they take the technology for granted and turn on switches and start using the telephone casually, and it doesn't take long for this to happen.

If you think about it, that's what's happening with social media. It started off as this thing that people pay attention to, but now, it's more about online reputation and less about what the tool is, what it does, and who owns it. At the end of the day, it doesn't really matter. When someone Googles you and your latest tweet shows up or your LinkedIn profile shows up or a blog post shows up—at the end of the day, it's someone looking you up, whether to recruit you or to decide to buy from you.

Therefore, I think it's less about social media and a lot more about reputation management. I think what will happen is we will start to zoom out. In the early days, 2008, it was about the tool. It was about a low-cost alternative to job boards. Recruiters and hiring managers had to find talent and they didn't have budgets or training to be recruiters. They just needed someone to fill a role, so they turned to their network. Then LinkedIn started to get used and professionals picked up on that.

It all starts upstream. It all starts with the recruiter changing how they're using the tool and how they're sourcing. People pick up on the fact that, "Oh, my buddy had his profile reviewed by a LinkedIn recruiter and got hired from that. Maybe I should do that too." And it trickles down from there.

DP: Do you think that the recession may have accelerated the adoption of social media from a recruitment perspective?

JW: I think that was a big part of it. It's cheaper, it's better, and it's faster. For example, Coca-Cola reported saving around $8 million in recruitment fees over the last four years by using social media. The process worked better, and the people who come from those social referrals last longer and are higher quality. It is a teaching agent, there's no doubt about that, but is also a better medium for posting openings and recruiting talent.

The whole concept of the job board comes from two outdated modalities: (1) a bulletin board and (2) a job posting in the classifieds section. What a job board tried to do was to take a global community pin board from a cafe and combine that with an online newspaper—just deliver classified ads virtually. That made sense in an anonymous Internet, but with social media, we are no longer in an anonymous Internet. Now, the Internet is very personal. This is also partly the reason for the shift.

DP: How do you go about crafting a personal social brand if everything today seems to be about reputation management? How do you manage your online reputation?

JW: I think there are three key elements to doing this that most people ignore. The first one is to realize that these social networks do not have your best interest in mind. They could care less if you look good or bad online. All they care about is making their investors happy by having large membership numbers. That's it: "My membership number is bigger than yours." And then they drill down: "My membership numbers stay on my website longer than yours." It's a dogfight and they'll do whatever it takes to keep you there.

For example, the psychology that goes into how Facebook and LinkedIn deliver news and customized experiences is to get people to stay on longer. It's all in their own best interest, not yours. It's very easy to sign-up and fill in profiles and that's what most people do. The secret sauce is really this: The individual needs to—before they fill out the profile—know what their message is.

So the first step I call "personal positioning," because we get first impressions very quickly, in a matter of milliseconds. We look at somebody, we hear the sound of their voice, we hear the vocabulary they use. And then above that, we hear what they have to say, whatever it is. It's not quite an elevator pitch, but the answer to the question will be due. If they don't answer the question, it's a muddled personal brand and you're just wasting my time. I don't have time to figure out what you do.

So whether or not you're an active jobseeker or a sales professional, you need to make it easy for people to learn about you. The easier you make it, the better off you'll be. That's personal positioning.

Step two, once someone has figured out what their message is—that one thing you want people to remember about you emotionally—then it's time to get all geeky with your profiles. This is where most people get stuck. You have to get those messages delivered and polished. TheLadders did a study and found that recruiters only spend about six seconds on a LinkedIn profile. They only look at three things in those six seconds: your picture, your headline, and your most recent position. One of those three things better intrigue them or else you're toast.

This is the funny thing with technology: we say it's going to make our life easier and we'll do less work, but actually the expectations of how much we can get done go way up. For example, recruiters, maybe 20 years ago, had to only fill 10 positions per month. Now, social media makes it easier to fill positions, so they have to do 20-40 positions per month so they're really stretched for time. Despite how easy social media is, the expectations of how much they get done have correspondingly gone up. That's why having your profile polished and concise is important.

Step three is reaching out. I get this a lot. I sell a LinkedIn profile-writing service, which is important because sometimes it's hard to write about yourself. I always give away an action guide: Twenty things you can do with your profile so that you're not just sitting around waiting for something to happen. Even though I give away all this great information about what you can do proactively to advance your career, someone invariably comes back and says, "I uploaded my new profile and nothing happened."

That's nice, but did you reach out to anyone? What new people did you meet? What groups were you involved with? Did you share any valuable information with your network? This is the part I call publishing, where you actually use your profile as a platform to engage with other individuals. That's where anonymity goes out the window.

Traditionally, we never had to use our real names when we signed up for platforms. These days, you *are* your name. Because of that there is not an anonymous Internet anymore. We're in a very intimate and personal one. This is where people need to make their transition to being your authentic self with other people online in an engaged way.

DP: How can someone who's entering the job market demonstrate expertise and competency, and do things that might make up for their lack of experience? How can they leverage social media?

JW: I think it's less about what they can do on social media and more about what they can do to build a compelling online reputation. It just so happens that social media is the highest leverage tool today, but I think it's too easy to get focused on the tool. It's a mistake for career counselors to offer LinkedIn classes when they really should be offering modern job-search tactics that happen to include LinkedIn. It's like teaching someone how to build a house by having a hammer class, instead of teaching them how to read a blueprint.

DP: If you give out a 20-point list on LinkedIn, for example, what are some of the main things job-seekers should be doing?

JW: I think the photo is very underused. If someone is serious about building an online reputation, they need to put serious thought into their photograph. Stop cropping photos out of vacation shots. Everything is very subtle because there is so little space. The background color, the youth or maturity of the style of clothes worn, the expression on the face—all of these things go into making a very subtle impression that colors the interaction going forward. This seems like a very small thing, but remember, you only have on average six seconds and the first thing a recruiter sees is the picture. Very small changes to your photo can have very drastic effects in the real world.

Social proof is another thing that is underused. In the old days, you would write your own recommendation letter, print it on company letterhead, and get your boss to sign it. If you did that these days, then all of your recommendations would look the same. Also, they don't need to be as long as they used to be. With any length of profile, you can have the face of the person writing the recommendation right under the job you worked at. When you hover over that face, the role of that person comes up, so you can see if it's a direct manager who's recommending someone. There's no way to forge that because it goes through the system.

Social proof is also risk mitigation. Ultimately, the job of anyone online is risk mitigation, whatever kind of purpose you have. If you're looking for a job, customers, marketing a product or building a business, it's all about risk mitigation. How do I reduce the perceived risk of working with me?

You do that with a friendly face and you also do that by showing that other people like and trust you. This is not just with LinkedIn. I'm applying this principle to LinkedIn, but it would also apply to tweets getting re-tweeted, conversations you're having, comments on blog posts—all of these things are social proof.

The final point would be that as search becomes more social, social becomes more important for one's reputation. Bing is a very social-media oriented search engine. Google is becoming a lot more social-media oriented, and is very good at customizing displayed search results for the individual. Some people will cringe at this, but size matters a lot, particularly around certain hubs of your network.

I think we have to be a little more sophisticated about our network now. Your network is not just people you know or friends. There are hubs, con-nectors, influencers, coaches, motivators. There are categories of people who have certain functions in our lives and in a lot of ways. For example, if you are a jobseeker, then a recruiter is a hub because they have companies in their network that you might want to work for; they have other recruiters in their network who might want to look for you, and so on. Therefore, the size of your network, particularly around hubs or connectors, matters a lot.

DP: If reputation is so important and someone has a bad story about them that goes viral or they are tagged in messy Facebook photos, how do you mitigate the risk of that and what advice do you give in terms of managing those types of things?

JW: I went to this very interesting seminar that was organized by a company called Pinkerton Government Services. They're the oldest security compa-ny in the country. They used to be the Secret Service at the time of Lincoln. They own Securitas and they do a lot of insurance fraud, research inves-tigation through social media. One of their chief social-media researchers came to do a talk and he was showing us some of his tools. Someone in the audience raised his hand and said, "You know, all these things that violate my privacy that you're showing us, are the reasons why I haven't signed into any social media for the last five years. So I'm safe,"

So the instructor says, "Really? You're safe, are you? What's your name?" So he puts the guy's name into one of these freely available reputation sites to look-up people like Spokeo and the guy comes right up. There's a picture of his house, his zip code, and based on his zip code, we know what his average income and his political point-of-view might be. The guy turns bright red, "How did you know this about me?"

The instructor says, "Because you are not in control of your reputation, you let these software applications do it for you." The idea is really to jump into the lion's mouth. If the lion is going to bite you, stick your hand down its throat. If you're afraid of what's out there on the Internet, put more of yourself out there on the Internet. It's the only answer.

DP: What is the biggest misperception that college kids have about careers and job search?

JW: They are always shocked by how can you expect someone who is 21 years old to know what they want to do with their life? I'm still trying to figure it out. They have five things they're interested in and I tell them, "Pick one," and they say, "What about these other things?" It doesn't matter. Pick one, because it is the momentum that matters.

There is this huge fear around committing to doing something. Just like an entrepreneur has a hard time finding a niche, these students are afraid that they are going to make the wrong choice in their life. They have this sense—which I think they get from the Baby-Boomers who are coaching them—that you have to follow your passion. They have read too much Joseph Campbell, they're idealists. Their grandparents worked because they had to work and they hated their jobs until the day they retired. So the Boomers, who grew up in the 1960s in the age of idealism, refused to do that and they followed their passion, and then they wanted their children to follow their passion. (I'm totally on a soapbox here, and have no evidence for this, but this is what I think.)

So these Boomers tell their children, Gen-X'ers and Gen-Y, "Follow your passion." Then there is this very elevated stress around, "I better follow my passion or my life is going to be wasted." So they are very freaked out about picking something, even if it might be the right thing. I think that what happens when they pick one—maybe they have three different interests—is they'll get small wins. Because now, all of a sudden, their message is clear and this clarity helps build momentum, the momentum builds confidence, and with the confidence comes the knowledge of what they don't like to do and what they do like to do. And that feeds upon the decision-making process. It can be very iterative.

Now, the student might become a hairstylist and a year later, they hate it. They know that they hate it, but there are elements of talking to people that they like. So maybe they decide to go back to school to become a therapist. They wouldn't have gotten to that conclusion if they hadn't had that experience first. They can totally re-brand themselves and that's something most people aren't used to, which is, say you're a hairstylist today; the next week you go back on LinkedIn, change your headline, and now you're a therapist tomorrow. You can re-create yourself in a millisecond.

DP: What advice would you give to someone who's an aspiring expert or teacher or public speaker?

JW: Before committing your livelihood to building a business around your expertise, get in front of people who you help and speak to them. Because you'll learn very quickly, speaking is a mirror. If nobody shows up to the talk, you don't have a market. If people show up to the talk and you don't know what to say, you don't have enough expertise. You need both, so start speaking. Even if you don't want a revenue source from speaking, it forces you to do something a little bit scary, which can build your confidence.

The other thing is to blog a lot. If you start blogging and you run out of ideas of articles to write, this is not what you should be doing. For example, I've been writing about social media and job-search for four years and I have a huge list of around a hundred article ideas that I just can't wait to write. I could probably write every day for an hour this whole month, and do a new blog post every day without much effort. If you can't do that for your field of expertise, then you're not in the right place.

And if you're not a writer, that's fine. Even just talking, having something to say—you've got to find your voice. If you can't find it, then maybe you shouldn't be billing yourself as an expert.

DP: If you were to write one of those blog posts and it was on the three biggest opportunities to disrupt the job market in terms of recruiting and platforms, what might you say? Are there any up-and-coming platforms that you think are particularly interesting?

JW: There is one actually, called Apploi, that I think is going to disrupt the resume experience, particularly around the retail and hospitality market. First of all, retail or hospitality is very location-specific. Guess what else is location-specific? Your phone. So this application says, "I know you're sitting in Departures restaurant waiting for a happy-hour cocktail. Would you like to apply here?" Apploi will then pass on basic info such as your education history and your work experience.

This eliminated the trouble of paper applications and resumes. You put it on a piece of paper, the store manager looks at it, there are no opportunities; they put it in a filing cabinet and 30 days later, they throw it away because they don't have storage for all the papers. So they're losing a big candidate pool and you're losing out on a potential, future opportunity because of inefficiencies.

Apploi allows companies to store as much information as they want, plus, they get to ask really cool, specific questions that the candidate can answer through multimedia. You can speak or record videos for answers or you can type them on your mobile device. They can be very specific to that store's location, or the company. So it makes hiring more engaging, customized, and fun.

I think this kind of a thing is really disruptive. Everyone's talking mobile, but no one's really defining properly what that means. Apploi is the first company that's doing that. You're seeing some companies that are using mobile job applications, but who goes around applying for jobs on a mobile phone? You're applying for jobs on a mobile phone if you're in a location that's hiring, not because you like to type out your work history on a small screen. So I think, fundamentally, Apploi has gotten it right.

DP: What do you think the job market will look like in five to 10 years?

JW: I think job boards will be less centralized and more specialized. I think LinkedIn is going to grow in importance. Some people are predicting LinkedIn is just going to turn into another job board or just another thing that recruiters can tap into, which I hope is not the case because it will become less relevant if that happens. I think that with graph search and the power of referral, Facebook can easily be in the position—if they figure it out—of becoming the number one job-search resource. This is based on the sheer number of users and the fact that referrals happen between trusted people. There are more trusted people in your Facebook network than your LinkedIn network right now. I guarantee it.

....

Joshua Waldman *is the author of the bestselling book,* Job Searching with Social Media For Dummies, *which has sold over 10,000 copies in the US and abroad. He is frequently quoted by* Forbes, Mashable *and* International Business *Times for advice on using social media to find jobs.*

When he is not writing articles or books, Joshua enjoys presenting to students on finding a job online and training their career counselors on winning strategies so they always feel ahead of the curve. He has given over 100 talks and trainings to organizations such as University of Southern California, American Chemical Society, Texas Christian University, DeVry and many many more.

....

BUILDING YOUR PERSONAL BRAND

Srinivas Rao

Srini ironically has a successful career after rebranding himself as a corporate misfit who is allergic to cubicles. In this interview, he shares insights and best practices on personal brand building drawn from his experience interviewing hundreds of bloggers, entrepreneurs and innovators as host and co-founder of BlogcastFM. Highlights include:

- How to build a small army by focusing on just 150 connections
- Why we all need to be unreasonably confident and remarkable
- How vanity metrics and best practices actually undermine your success
- In an era where everyone is loud, it is great to pursue an intimacy strategy

Srini is now capitalizing on the emerging trend of podcasting and personal brand building, which he has been doing for over four years, and plans to disrupt the live events and conferences space with his next project The Instigator Experience. This is a great read, and I strongly encourage you to check out his show, BlogcastFM.

DP: You co-founded and host BlogcastFM, one of the leading podcasts and media brands featuring interviews with engaging bloggers, innovative leaders, and visionary entrepreneurs.

What drew you to doing this type of work, and how has it evolved over the years?

SR: It's funny, the irony of my work in social media is that it was designed to get me a day job, and now I have branded myself as a corporate misfit. What's interesting about the evolution is that I discovered a talent that I didn't know I had, and that I created far more value for people outside of an organization than I did in the context of a day job. I worked for about 10-12 years, and only really created value in the last year.

I jokingly say that you could add up all of the value from 10-12 years of working and put it into one week. I didn't really do anything besides crunch numbers. The unfortunate tragedy is that we look at a job description, alter our resume, and if the bullet points match then you get a phone call, so your whole focus is on making the bullet points fit. What you're really doing is altering yourself by putting a square peg through a round hole. They don't say, "You suck at this, let's get you back to average and mediocre." So, the goal is to "suck less" and as a result you will never be extraordinary.

We've entered an era where you can ask a much bigger question, "What can I accomplish in this lifetime?" The gap between creativity and technology is narrowing, and there are all of these tools that enable us to create more than ever before. I've interviewed hundreds of entrepreneurs, built an audience of thousands of people around the world, and effectively created a job for myself, which is nice because nobody really would want to hire the "real me," as cliche as that might sound, because the real me is a corporate misfit allergic to cubicles. I've created demand for myself by doing this, so it's evolved from a strategy to get into the corporate world into being an instigator of experiences.

DP: I love that you describe yourself as a corporate misfit. You're also a passionate surfer. When I hear you talk or write about surfing, I get excited because I feel a connection to you, even though I'm not a surfer. It makes you personal and real, and that sense of intimacy and emotion makes the rest of your content more meaningful.

How does surfing and your outside interests inform your work, and what can you recommend to people in terms of integrating all aspects of their life to create a unique voice and personality that is distinct and remarkable?

SR: Well, you could write a book on that one question, and many people ᵛe tried. Surfing has been this really transformative and informative experience in my life—it's everything, the driving force behind my life—and I would never have expected that because I'm Indian. We're not predisposed to star athleticism. I was the worst player on my basketball team growing up. What I realized was a sense of peace was missing in my life and this ability to be present. I never really understood what it meant to be present until I surfed, because when you surf you can't think about anything else but surfing.

To create something, you need to be really present. You have to learn how to shut off the noise, and the only way to do that is to get to this place of presence. What's strange is when you're in the water, you don't think about anything else but being in the water. Yet your mind works in the background and ideas bubble to the surface. Everyone needs to find something unrelated to what they are trying to accomplish.

There is a direct connection between surfing and creativity in the sense that I can say surfing made me a better online marketer. I think that is where we get trapped—we try to operate through this lens of rational and logical thinking. We basically look at the past and everything created before, and the best thing we can do is a better version of history, so we end up cutting off the possibility of arriving somewhere new. So in surfing like in life, everything is an unknown and a blank page, and as a result it brings out an innovative and creative side of you.

If we keep looking to other experts and don't trust this sense of intuition, then it becomes very difficult to arrive somewhere new that is remarkable.

DP: I've never surfed, but I snowboard and skateboarded for years. There is a way in which you get comfortable with a sense of uncertainty, it forces you to live in the moment, and that is one of the keys to being remarkable.

One of the things that I love is your recommendation to be unreasonably confident, become an instigator, and just be extraordinary. You say, "The world doesn't need more copycats. It needs you to be you." Increases in blog traffic and results are side benefits. Can you tell us a bit more about this?

SR: A lot of this is a byproduct of observation and what I see in the online world after years of interviewing and meeting hundreds of interesting and successful people. I get a unique view into the web because of how I built my platform. It goes back to that conversation about matching bullet points on your resume to a job description, and as a result you just become a pale imitation of other people. Things change once you kind of let go of all that and just say, "I'm going to tell my story."

I'll give you an example. The other day I was looking at my page for Blog-castFM and it hadn't been updated in a really long time. And the copy was a list of my accolades—I did this and this and this—and it was written in the third-person. This isn't my story. There is nothing real or authentic about this. I'm done telling this story, and basically I opened the About page and rewrote it: I'm an instigator and corporate misfit who is allergic to cubicles and office buildings, and I told a story about how I'd been fired from almost every job.

What I realized was that people relate to that much more than this pedestal. I'm not a guru or thought leader or expert. I'm just a guy who likes creating things. And I think for me, when you get to that place of being—to use a very overly used word—authentic, you become a lot more relatable to people, and strangely we avoid that because to be so vulnerable to admit failure doesn't seem unreasonably confident. But at the same time, you do have to be unreasonably confident and assume that they will lead you to better places. Maybe this is career suicide, but at this point who cares? It takes a level of confidence to do that.

I think a lot of us have bold ideas, but we resist our bigger ideas because our immediate sort of reaction when we think of something really audacious is, "How the f*@k is that going to happen?" But what's interesting is once you take the first step. To be unreasonably confident is not the same as being fearless. Being unreasonably confident is saying, "I'm not going to die and I'm not going to go bankrupt if this doesn't work." Once you develop that type of filter, it's really interesting what kind of work you do, and you find yourself doing things that most people say that's audacious, and that's remarkable.

The thing is, it's not about taking these huge leaps. There is this mantra per-petuated by the blogosphere to quit your day job and travel the world. People hear that and think of un-packaging something from wrapping paper and discovering the world. But if you've traveled the world, it's not as per-   ` as the pictures make it out to be. Traveling is tough.

The real question is how to be yourself. A large part is doing something and sticking with it for a long time when there might not be external rewards. Scott Belsky says that our external rewards system conditions us to do things quickly and expect rewards quickly. As a result, we avoid audacious goals. Big dreams don't come at bargain basement prices.

DP: You said that you failed at building a massive audience, but succeeded at building a loyal one—a small army of people who love you and are interested in everything that you create and do.

One of the core ideas in the opening of your book The Small Army Strategy *is what you refer to as the paradox of success. Basically, every time you try to replicate something, it fails because you end up trying too hard, or there is a lack of authenticity. Best practices might actually hurt you.*

Can you tell us a bit about how to find a balance between following techniques that are proven to be successful vs. being so formulaic that you end up just falling flat?

SR: This is one of my favorite subjects to talk about. There are always things that you bring from one project to the next, and those are best practices. There is also this paradox of popularity. Look at Hollywood, for example. *Godfather One*, amazing movie, *Godfather Two,* pretty good, *Godfather 3*, total piece of shit. You try to squeeze blood from a stone because you become dependent upon what works in the past.

It's only when we explore the unknown and the things that might not work, that we arrive at places we never arrived at before. I'll give you an example. I'm teaching myself how to draw. Now, I'm not terrible, but I'm no Picasso. What's interesting is that all of these dots connect in my head, and then I had a major breakthrough for a product idea. It's similar to surfing—teaching myself how to draw has nothing to do with interviewing people or my podcast. Exploring that unknown place led to a lot of other things.

There is room for creative chaos. I think you should build chaos or creative anarchy into your process. The problem is most people judge things while they are creating them, because you are constantly backspacing, editing and deleting before you are done creating, and I think you should let the anarchy be there during the creative process. You need a bit of structure, but your day-to-day process doesn't have to be linear. I just go to work and have the end in mind, but chances are that I'll put it together like puzzle pieces.

People have been taught their whole life to do things in a linear fashion—this is the order you are supposed to go through in life. When you are willing to play in a non-linear space and explore the unknown without any concern for what the result will be, then the benefits will eventually come.

DP: There is so much written about social media best practices that it can seem daunting to a beginner. You basically ask—what's your intimacy strategy? In an age where everyone is shouting so loud into the same crowd imitating and competing with each other, and we're all drinking from the firehose, why is intimacy with your audience so important?

SR: We are inundated with inputs and drinking from the firehose, like you said, so people are constantly bombarded with thousands of emails, tweets, status updates, etc. You can either try to compete within the noise, or be intimate with a handful of people. This is why I'm not allowing more than 60 people to be at my first event, which I joke sometimes makes it like trying to build a religion and plan a wedding at the same time.

Intimacy is highly underrated in a world where there is this much noise, so you stand out when you are intimate. I'll give you an example. If you send someone something in the mail, they always remember it. Now one of the best ways to create a deep connection is to send something in the mail.

DP: Lots of readers of this book will come from a media background. Some metrics such as traffic, likes, follows, and comments you describe as dangerous, while others such as email subscribers, open and conversion rates, and revenue are what matter. Most marketers and media folks seem most interested in the former "dangerous" metrics. Why are they a distraction from the latter that are most important?

SR: So many metrics in my experience did very little besides inflate my ego. I've had lots of posts go viral, and they did nothing. If 60-80k people hit a site, how long are they really going to stick around? People don't intentionally arrive at these places with a goal of looking at that one thing, whereas if you have a loyal audience they are specifically there for you. Conversations open in things like an email newsletter.

For a long time, I thought the measures of success were all of the conventional metrics we've talked about, and as a result my real success has been limited. You can buy vanity metrics, but intimacy, trust and loyalty has to be earned.

DP: You recommend that people create their own manifesto and give it away for free. In the opening of your Extraordinary Manifesto, *you quote* Making Ideas Happen *by Scott Belsky, "Even more powerful than the obstacles around us, however, are the obstacles within us. The most potent forces that kill off new ideas are our own limitations."*

How do we break free of our limitations, and how do we even be honest with ourselves to recognize and acknowledge them in the first place?

SR: The last part is the starting point—to recognize and acknowledge them in the first place. When we don't recognize and acknowledge, then we resist them. What we resist persists. Now, some people say that I'm a good writer. I've blogged for years and have written several books and eBooks. But I make a lot of grammar mistakes, and do a lot of things that would make many writers cringe. As a result, I get critiques all the time.

The interesting thing though is that critics that can never do what you do are more than happy to offer advice, but if you put them in your role, they can never replicate. A big part of overcoming limitations is seeing that they are there, and going forward anyways. It's pretty audacious to go from a business like I have, to pulling off a conference that will change the industry forever. That's pretty audacious. I went from writing a book that costs $2.99 to an industry-defining event. It's a huge leap.

I always go back to something that Seth Godin said when I interviewed him, which is "Anytime I start a project, I say to myself, this might not work." Personally, I ask if I'll go to jail, die or go bankrupt? Probably not. Once you eliminate these extremes, you develop a filter and can then start to take steps forward. Things start to reveal themselves, and you keep going.

DP: One of the things that really struck me in your manifesto was that if you are in constant anticipation of hitting benchmarks for success, you will forget to enjoy the journey and never arrive.

Even though goals can be limiting, they're also hugely important to provide focus. In my own life, I create what I refer to as my own internal rewards program. For example, if I finish a draft of a chapter by Friday, then I can go out dancing or to a rock show on Friday night. If I finish preparing for an interview early, then I can enjoy a nice dinner and movie. This has the added bonus of providing structure to my week, which can be challenging when working independently.

You blog and also podcast, and have what I would consider some of the most consistently good and unique quality content on the Web. Can you tell us a bit about how you put together your own content strategy? How did you define your own best practices? Do you have a daily and weekly routine, and how do you plan ahead and set goals?

SR: It comes down to managing your energy more than it does your time. It took a long time for me to understand when my most creative times are. Through trial and error, I've come to see that my most creative times are in the morning. Now, much of the quality is also a result of experience doing this for a long time. You can compromise your integrity by following a formula—The Best 10 X, The Top 10 best practices, etc.—but those things put you into a box.

I see myself as an artist first, and an entrepreneur second. When I pick my guests for a show, I always think, "Who is going to be better as a result of this?" I've ended up scrapping interviews because of this. You can't compromise integrity. The impact filter is the most powerful—that is the starting point. What is your motive? Why are you doing this? Are you aiming for vanity metrics, and is this a vanity project?

There is this misconception that because everything is online, people can't understand your real intentions. But they can. On a daily basis, I have structure and routine. Now, what you don't know is that 80% of what I produce is crap. 20% is going to be what actually results in quality that I put out. You have to be willing to go through the 80% that is awful in order to get to the 20%. I wake up in the morning and I block Facebook for 2 hours. I use an app to block it because Facebook is a minefield of distractions. I don't stop until there is nothing else to write.

Now, sometimes that might not lead to anything. It's about showing up and doing the work, even when you don't feel like it. You have to grind it out.

Most people only see the end result, but what goes into it is in all honesty not that glamorous. We glamorize the lives of creatives because what we see is the end product. TV shows like *Mad Men*. Oh, this is the life of the creative. As an author, you can probably understand this—there is a grind component, and most people don't want to do the grind.

DP: You've been podcasting for several years now, and have one of the top shows and a dedicated loyal audience. Can you give us a few tips on podcasting, where to start, how to define your voice, and how do I use this as a platform to really start building out my tribe?

SR: The first thing is: Do you have something to say that is relevant to other people?

One of the things that is very overlooked is that as a podcaster, you are an entertainer just as much as you are a marketer. What I do is a show more than just a podcast. I don't listen to other podcasts because I don't have the attention span for them. This goes back to our conversation about art: look at what is successful in mainstream media—John Stewart, The Colbert Report—what keeps them coming back again? What are they doing? You don't have their resources, but you also don't have any constraints either— you can say or do whatever you want.

Then, it comes to grinding it out. You'll try a lot of things. I'm the beneficiary of a trend that became popular four years later. Ultimately, it's about creating value for your listeners. One of the criticisms that I got in the past is that I didn't really listen to my guests. Once you realize that this is always about creating value for the listener and not just a platform for you, things change.

Now, you have this bond with your listeners. The key is intimacy. For example, recently I mentioned one of my friends in a podcast, and he almost got into a car accident because he got so excited when he heard his name. This goes back to the bullet-point, step-and-repeat stuff we talked about before: if you try to imitate what you're told, then you end up in this cookie cutter problem.

DP: You wrote a post called "150 followers is all you need" that was shared over 1,000 times. 150 doesn't seem like that many people, but a few simple strategies applied consistently had an exponential growth. Can you explain to us what you mean, and also how this relates to Malcolm Gladwell's now famous concept of the "tipping point"?

SR: This is one of the core elements of how I have grown BlogcastFM and my personal brand. As I read *The Tipping Point*, it became clear to me that I'm one of the connectors. Looking at an entire group of friends, lots of them know each other because of me. So I called a friend and said, "Am I a self-absorbed asshole, or am I someone that connects everyone together?" and he said, "Actually, you're both."

150 is the maximum number of social relationships that anyone can effectively manage. Now, if you have a million followers on Twitter, how many are you actually going to talk to everyday? It's impossible to manage those relationships, even if you have no life and it's all that you do. When I understood the implications of the 150 relationships that we can manage, I decided to test it online on the Twitter platform.

So, anytime that anyone mentioned or started a conversation with me, I put them into what I called the inner circle. I focused all of my Twittering and all of my energy on those 150 people. The result was phenomenal. My connection with those people became meaningful. Over time, those people became my closest friends. Imagine if 150 followers that you're talking to on a regular basis shared or retweeted your posts. That's a very ideal scenario, but you can see how growth is exponential and it leads to all kinds of meaningful relationships.

DP: In a recent interview that you did with Tim Grahl, one of the leading masterminds behind book launches who has worked with hundreds of big authors such as Dan Pink, Pamela Slim, and the Heath Brothers, he said that often times email converts at a ratio of 10:1 compared to Twitter, Facebook, or other social channels.

I remember when I signed up for your email newsletter being blown away that you followed up with a personal email. Turns out that you do that with every subscriber. Can you tell us a bit about how you have used email to build a more direct relationship with your audience?

SR: Not everybody replies to me, but it allows me to get to know their story. That allows me to create content that appeals to my audience. Sometimes,

I'll go so far as to ask them what type of content can I create for you? When you solve a problem for a particular person, they get blown away. We have an opportunity to customize things for our audiences in ways that we never did before.

DP: While I love the recommendation of being extraordinary, ultimately a lot of people reading this will want to figure out how they can turn their passion into a source of income and leave the cubicle behind. What advice would you give to people that want to make a living being extraordinary, either through blogging, podcasting, online courses and trainings, or how do you map your version of "being extraordinary" to generating sources of income?

SR: I would suggest abandon a map and use a compass, because you don't know how it will turn out. I did probably 6-7 failed blogs before arriving at a success. Most people are too scared to fail to try, when the reality is that you probably won't be very good at it your first try. It doesn't really matter because the goal is to learn and get slightly better at something over time. If you end up hating it, then move on.

If you start to view your life as a laboratory where you are constantly experimenting, then you get to do lots of interesting stuff. Figure out what you like and don't like. You need to be careful creating a different version of the hell that you have been trying to escape, and that is what will happen if you use a map instead of a compass. If you use a compass, then you can arrive at a place where nobody has been before.

....

Srinivas Rao *is a connector, instigator and corporate misfit who is allergic to cubicles and office buildings. He's the guy you'll hear shouting "let's shift gears" in every episode of BlogcastFM. In other words, he is the host of the show. He's been fired from almost every real job he's ever had.*

In April 2009, he graduated from business school, was completely broke, and realized that he was unemployable. His world basically fell apart. So he did what anybody in that situation would do: he moved back to his parents' house and started a blog. That was just the beginning of taking the scenic route through life which has resulted in his #1 bestselling book The Art of Being Unmistakable: A Collection of Essays About Making a Dent in the Universe.

....

TECHNOLOGY AND MINDFULNESS

Vincent Horn

Vincent Horn and Buddhist Geeks in my opinion are doing some of the most interesting and important work at the intersection of technology, media and culture. I feel quite strongly that as innovation continues to disrupt our lives, mindfulness will gain widespread acceptance out of necessity to find balance. This interview is intended to serve as an introduction, and makes a great conclusion to the book:

- How meditation cultivates awareness of technology
- How mindfulness can inform leadership, design, and products
- The "Middle Way" and holding extremes in balance
- The co-evolution of online communities and conceptions of enlightenment

The Buddhist Geeks conferences, podcast, online communities, etc. are laying the foundation for best practices and mindful approaches to technology. Vincent was kind enough to have me on his show to talk about my first book *Red Bull to Buddha: Innovation and the Search for Wisdom*, and I look forward to many more conversations like this with him in the future that are totally Buddhist, and totally geeky.

DP: Let's start with a pretty broad, open question. How do Buddhism and technology fit together?

VH: They fit together in the way that everything fits with technology. It's hard to escape. It's a fact. What I've noticed is that most first-generation American and Western Buddhist teachers, especially in the 1970s—they were the big first generation—had a relationship with technology where they mostly rejected it as being antithetical to the aims of Buddhist contemplative practice.

Buddhist Geeks in some ways is a response to that—a different relationship between technology and Buddhism. We could actually see technology as potentially helpful in terms of putting dharma online and also utilizing some of these emerging technologies to completely change the way that we practice together and even think about those practices, change the way that we discourse, and change the way that we form communities—in short, basically changing most aspects of how Buddhism is practiced.

That is a different kind of narrative we're trying to explore. It has its own dangers, especially the idealistic dangers of not seeing the downsides of how technology can change things. For example, my wife and I just recently started playing with unplugging from the Internet one day a week. I've unplugged a ton in the past, like during meditation retreats, but it's different to unplug in the context of one's daily life.

Part of what I've seen from just that short experiment is when we're so immersed within technological frameworks, it's really hard to see the ways in which they're negatively impacting things. So that's the other part of it. Yes, we can have a narrative that's not anti-technology, but that doesn't mean there's not going to be huge downsides to how we do things that can only be seen once you step outside of it.

DP: In my own life, I have found that meditation slows down a reactionary form of behavior that allows me to make more informed decisions. Its benefits radiate out like spokes from a wheel. In the fast-paced, constantly changing landscape of technology, the practice seems to help me differentiate between what is a real trend in innovation vs. a passing fad.

How does having an ongoing meditation practice impact the way that you use technology?

VH: The main thing my meditation practice has done is given me a more sensitive awareness to the way my mind and body respond to the technologies I'm using. That seems to be the most important impact, as that real-time feedback gives me something to work with in regards to how I use technology.

I've found that with a mind that's more sensitively tuned in to the moment that it's possible to see if a particular technology makes me sleepy, energized, clear, distracted, calm, contracted, expanded, or something else. Once I have this information, I can begin to engage differently, or even disengage, with whatever technology I'm using. If technology acts as an extension of our senses and cognition, it makes sense that we'd want to develop are awareness of those extended capabilities and who they interact with human body 1.0.

DP: Many people have this perception of Buddhism in terms of non-attachment and separate from the world, but in recent years there is a new movement of teachers like yourself embracing what has been termed pragmatic Buddhism. Can you tell us a bit about that?

VH: Some of my earliest meditation teachers were Gen-X rebels, who, just like the Boomer generation before them, went to places like Burma and Malaysia, did the same kinds of meditation practices, and were exposed to the same maps, models, and texts, but they had a decidedly different interpretation.

DP: Like Daniel Ingram?

VH: Yeah, exactly like Daniel Ingram and Kenneth Folk.

DP: Daniel Ingram's Mastering the Core Teachings of the Buddha *is one of my favorite books, and I discovered it listening to him on one of your podcasts.*

VH: Daniel was actually one of my first guests. I found his e-book through one of his ex-college roommates. We knew each other. When I opened that book, and I said, "OK, this is what enlightenment is, this is how you get there, and this is how you know you're moving in the right direction. I shouldn't have to float through psychological fluffy New Age type stuff to see results."

That kind of dead-simple, cookbook-style approach just made a lot of sense to me—it was pragmatic dharma, a straightforward, pragmatic method to attain enlightenment. In other ways, it also fit with my shadow side and blind spots—the hyper-ambitious, driven, goal-oriented personality. Now that being said, I believe it's possible for people to experience real awakenings and enlightenments in the context of being goal-driven and ambitious. I know because I've gone through those experiences, and that was how I approached it.

The pragmatic part has always been to ask the question in terms of practice, "What works?" Daniel Ingram's book was an example of him answering that question: "What worked for him?" The next level of pragmatism is asking the question, "What works for what?" It's actually stepping back a level of abstraction and saying, "What is it that I'm actually aiming for and what is it that's driving me? What are the questions I'm trying to answer on this path?"

Once I can actually answer those questions, then I can orient toward finding something that works to support me in going deeper in that direction. The pragmatic dharma movement continues to evolve in the direction of asking very pragmatic questions. It strips away the mysticism of the mystical path, if you will, by making it a very straightforward and practical way of being in the world.

DP: That's a great lead in to another question I wanted to ask around the pragmatic use of technology. Technology connects early adopters and encourages innovation. I remember in listening to your podcast over the years, I felt a sense of connection to a community of people I don't know and have never met. This encouraged me to continue and grow my meditation practice because I felt part of something greater than myself, this idea that there were Buddhist geeks like me basically everywhere.

VH: Totally!

DP: How did technology help you to foster dialogue and bring people together to really build a movement around mindfulness, technology, and Buddhist practice?

VH: Technological shifts in the mid-2000s, in particular things like blogging and podcasting, opened up the ability for pretty much anyone with a computer and access to the Internet to become a publisher.

When I started Buddhist Geeks, my partner and I were in our early twenties with no recognition within the Buddhist establishment or within any other establishment. Podcasting allowed us to start having conversations with different kinds of people who maybe didn't get airtime on more traditional media. We immediately attracted a small following of people for whom the way we were approaching things resonated. Podcasting enabled that sort of one-to-many connection for people who didn't have a lot of resources and who were just inspired and driven. That was a big shift, and we were part of it.

Physical events are nothing new, but they are one of the oldest ways we have of switching from the many-to-many interacting with each other, so we utilized them. I wouldn't necessarily call them a technology. They do form a technology, but not a new technology. From there, part of what we realized was that we have this invisible network of Buddhist Geeks. Like you were saying, you felt like you were somehow connected with these other folks even though you may not know who they are. There is this sense of finding a group that has a shared mindset. So we realized after the first couple of conferences how clearly we needed to continue to work to make that invisible network visible to itself.

Now there are some technologies emerging that are really exciting, particularly things like Google+ and their Hangouts system—real-time video that's finally gotten to the point where it actually works reliably. We utilize these new tools pretty heavily to build a sort of cloud-based Buddhist Geeks community. It's a shift from the asynchronous text-based forum technologies that I think everyone was using for a long time toward a more synchronous real-time audiovisual-based community. Now we can actually meet up, hang out, and talk together whether or not we live in the same place. These technologies have the capability to change how we organize and experience being connected. It's pretty amazing.

DP: From my perspective, The Buddha can be considered one of the greatest innovators in world history. Basically, through years of trial-and-error he quite literally discovered and mapped out a sophisticated method for mastering the interrelationship between the mind and body that has been practiced and taught for nearly 2500 years. Would you consider meditation and Buddhism a form of innovation? And how have Westerners innovated on Buddhism since it started to come over and spread?

VH: Definitely to me it's an innovation. No question. And it's interesting, too, because The Buddha was also innovating on top of all kinds of other earlier innovations with the Hindu tradition, particularly with the ability to traverse different strata of consciousness. He was sitting atop of all of that restless struggling at the cutting edge of where things were at the time, and then he had his own kind of breakthroughs contributing to the broader stream of inner contemplative practice.

DP: Which is why Buddhism is considered the middle path between the extremism on the one hand of the rituals of the Vedas, and on the other hand the asceticism of the mystics of the time.

VH: Yeah, he was running into these paradoxes and tensions. The practice of the middle way, as I understand it, is to hold two extremes simultaneously and to see what emerges from holding them. It seems like he did that with certain tensions and paradoxes of his time, and that led to these middle way breakthroughs. I think that has continued from his time onward clearly in that there were huge innovations in the Buddhist tradition with Nagarjuna, the whole Mahayana Movement, the innovations Zen and Dzogchen offered, and definitely Tibet, which was like this little isolated laboratory of innovation for a thousand years. The amount of innovation across all of these non-dualistic traditions that emerged after The Buddha is incredible.

The innovations I've seen happening since Buddhism hit the global world are all related to taking wisdom in other disciplines and seeing how they might apply to Buddhism and vice versa. Obviously, psychology was really big for the Boomer Buddhists. They worked a lot on integrating Western psychological notions of Eastern psychological notions, and they reframed Buddhism as a kind of psychology, which eventually led to things like mindfulness based stress reduction that is now taught in places like Harvard Medical School. Even the term enlightenment comes from a crushing together of ideas from the Western Enlightenment and rationality, and Eastern ideas of awakening.

DP: Buddhist Geeks has also evolved from being totally Buddhist and totally geeky to encompassing a range of overlapping interests with technology and global culture. You've also since been featured in a number of leading publications like Wired, The Guardian, Fast Company, *and* The Atlantic. *So can you tell me a little more about how Buddhist Geeks has evolved and what your vision for it is in the future?*

VH: Like you said, in the beginning, the emphasis was mostly on being Buddhist and geeky, but the more I've personally gotten into Buddhism—and I've seen this with a lot of other people—the more the question comes up:

How is this relevant to the rest of my life? What is the meaning of this? How do I make sense of this?

This happens the more you get into different approaches, traditions, and maps, and working with people who are doing it themselves. This goes back to the earlier conversation about pragmatic Buddhism. It's not like we're Buddhist monks, in a fixed context. We're practitioners who exist in many contexts all in one day: we're in relationships, we're entrepreneurs, we're academics, we're parents, and so on, and we have all these hobbies and side interests. We have all these things that we're interested in, and then we throw Buddhism or meditation into the mix. So we ask, "What *is* this? How does it work?"

Those questions were huge for me, especially as I looked to the Boomers, and I saw so many things that seemed to be generational assumptions on their part. I saw all the ways they were interpreting Buddhism as a liberal political ideology. They took liberal political ideologies and mashed them up with Buddhism in a way that was unacknowledged. They said, "This is Buddhism."

What they were really saying was "This is our understanding of Buddhism mashed up with all the other things that are important to us." Our approach has been to acknowledge this tendency, instead of trying to have Buddhism be this pure thing that has this authority of tradition because it's unchanged or because The Buddha said so. Why not own the fact that we're changing it? Why not try to acknowledge the ways that we're trying to innovate, and that not all our attempts at innovation are successful?

We take things we're learning from different disciplines. For example, in business and technology things like user-centered design methodologies, lean startup methods, and agile software development. Let's take the stuff we think is brilliant and see if there are really obvious ways that that could inform the conversation about what Buddhism is, what it means in a global context, and how we do it. So, our conversations are moving more in the direction of a mash-up or convergence of different perspectives.

I think the path we've been trying to take is the same path The Buddha describes: the middle way, holding the tension between various perspectives—conserving and adapting without assuming one is going to dominate the other or win out, but rather that they may have something fundamentally different to offer each other that would completely change our under-standing of both. That has become the inquiry or koan that we're holding and that is guiding what we choose to do, which is how this convergence of Buddhism, which has been around for 2500 years and has evolved and changed in all these different contexts and is just now converging in on it-self, too. There is this increasingly global culture, which has been global for hundreds and hundreds of years with this crazy, out of control, evolving technology, this runaway, exponential burst of technology and innovation.

Having a question or a koan as a vision is different from having an idea where we're going. That's one thing we've struggled with. It fits in with some of the core principles of Buddhist practice anyway. The way we hold the question is in some ways more important than our vision for where we're going because we start from there.

DP: We're also entering an era where we're living in a constant state of un-certainty, right?

VH: That's right. Having a long-term vision, like the waterfall approach of software development, where you come up with this fixed idea of what it's going to look like when you're done and you just spend the rest of the time getting there, ignoring reality, and not changing, is not a responsible way to build things anymore. That's the way to build something that's destined to be irrelevant by the time it's released. That's something I definitely noticed from other industries and we try to incorporate that into how we do things with Buddhist Geeks.

DP: That's a great lead in to another question I have. Disruptive innovations can allow us to see the world from a newfound place of openness, which in Buddhism is often referred to as a beginner's mind, whereas innovations can also be a source of stress, leaving us trying to constantly keep up. How can we use innovations that we're seeing in the tech world to open us up instead of closing us down?

VH: First, I would say carefully. Second, bringing a sense of care to the proc-ess of testing to see how does this technology changes what we're doing.

I'll give you a practical example. In the Buddhist Geeks community, we are playing a lot with spaces in which we sit (meditate) together in real time through the Google Hangout system. Had I not had the experience of sitting together with people in a room for a long time, I don't think I would have the ability to really know how that works in terms of past experiences and what it has that's completely novel and new. Like Marshall McLuhan would say, "Every new technology brings something back from the past, but then it also makes something irrelevant." Sometimes it does things that are actually important. It's like, "Oh, well actually there is a sense of being part of a group and sitting together."

You get some of the same benefits that you get when you're sitting in a room with other people. They can see you. They can hear you. There's a sort of social pressure. You can't just get up and leave, which you could have done with a telephone, actually. And at the same time, it's very weird. There are some things already I can tell are missing and are weird. One is that you're hearing sounds from multiple places at once. There isn't a sense that you're in a shared environment. It's actually a sense that your environments are mashing up together in one environment.

I don't know what that does to the meditation process at all, but it definitely changes the ambient environment. It's also really difficult with the current technology. In a normal meditation session, after you're done, you get to hangout and chat with people. It's very hard to do that with our current technologies. You can't just hang out and talk afterward because you're all forced to be in this one space. You can't break off into multiple spaces. You can't turn one space into multiple spaces yet. There are all sorts of things that are downsides in terms of how communities are normally cultivated and relationships are created in a community space.

So for us, the approach we've taken is to try things out and then assess how they're working. The other way to harness innovation is to use user-centered design processes in creating things so that you're actually testing your design assumptions with the people you're creating it for as you go because that puts into question a lot of the assumptions that are driving the creative process and helps more quickly hone in on something that might be workable. The Lean UX started out with a user-centered design and service design.

All of those things seemed brilliantly poised to be utilized to come up with innovations in terms of contemplative technology or to see how to use technology for contemplative ends.

DP: Meditation is in many ways being commodified and secularized. This allows us to innovate in the teaching of meditation. You can bring it into the workplace, sports, healthcare, and education, for example, yet, as a result of that, I often hear people say things like, "I would love to meditate, but I can't afford to take classes." The idea is that you can only learn something in this particular setting.

How has productivity and business impacted meditation, and how do we find a balance between that and these sort of deeper original intentions of the practice?

VH: That's a really tough one. On the one hand, like you're saying, the fact that meditation has entered into the commodities sector and the market, and is now playing by the current market's rules, enables it to be spread, be relevant, and become integrated into the culture in a new way that might not otherwise have been possible.

For example, look at the monastic model of Theravada Buddhism. It's been a complete and utter failure as a model to adapt to the West. If it were up to the conservative Thai forest monks, there would be no Buddhism in the West. There would be maybe 10 people doing it. It would be the people doing Theravada monastic Buddhism next to the 1700s Kentucky Flint Rifle enthusiasts, hanging out next to each other, preserving this ancient form of tradition.

Now, with the pragmatic Buddhism movement, and my own teaching and Buddhist Geeks, I haven't been that concerned about charging money. There's a huge taboo against that still in Western Buddhism, charging for the "dharma" based on the idea that money and Buddhism can't or shouldn't mix. On the one hand, it's based on some historical misunderstandings.

There's one project that I thought would be fun to do, which is to take the Business Model Canvas that breaks down the business into different elements, try to apply that to traditional Buddhism, like the monastic model, and describe the monastic situation as a business model because the fact is it was a model of financial sustainability involving monks and the community. We do have to find new models that work and sustain contemplative practices and teachings. They are some of humanity's greatest assets.

On the other hand, changing the model changes the thing itself. You can't change a financial model without changing the thing you're trying to sustain.

One thing that I've noticed that's very challenging in a consumer situation is for people to form longstanding deep relationships with another. There's a certain kind of relationship that just can't be transactionally based. The most important relationships I've had with teachers have been those that weren't based on transactions.

Maybe in the beginning, they started that way paying to attend classes, but it became more of an intimate relationship. I really don't think you can charge for that. You can charge to be a meditation teacher or a therapist. You can have that kind of model where it's like, "I'm serving you." But the kind of relationships I've found most profound, more transformative, are the ones that even went beyond that, where there was a shared sense of humanity, a bilateral flow of information. And it wasn't just about me. So I think there are some things we've got to be really aware of as meditation shifts into and becomes adopted in these markets.

DP: Building upon what you just said, what do you think Buddhism might have to offer in terms of leadership within organizations, which they're currently not doing? I think you started to just touch on that with the relationship to teachers.

VH: What I see happening—and I think it's across disciplines, not just in Buddhism—is people shifting away from a certain kind of top-down model of leadership: "I'm the leader. I embody all the qualities in the vision of what I'm trying to do. I get people to rally around my vision, and we then enact the vision. We bring it into fruition. We bring it to life. As the leader, I'm at the front of that movement, and I'm harnessing resources and energy. I'm the CEO. Or I'm the great guru-teacher."

The shift that I've been noticing that I think is really profound is the leaders who are more interested in creating conditions for things to happen. This ties into what we were talking about before. Instead of taking an idea of what should happen and imposing it on reality, they are having a sense of something that is wanting to emerge, and then they create conditions for it to happen, knowing that they're not the ones making it happen.

Instead of inspiring and encouraging, they design the environment in such a way that something can emerge from it that's unexpected. First, there is the deep sense of not knowing, the deep sense of getting in touch with the reality that we actually don't know what's going to arise next. On a first-person subjective level, *we don't know*. Also, in terms of the collective-social level we don't know.

That mindset of not knowing, but simultaneously not giving up or not getting fixed on some idea of what's emerging, is actually the right mindset to bring to our current situation of uncertain, constant, disruptive innovation because we can actually open to what's happening and relate to it directly instead of relating to our fixed ideas about it, which always seem to be wrong.

DP: You're embracing a sense of uncertainty that's just the nature of our existence, to some extent.

VH: Yes, Jack Kornfield calls it the wisdom of uncertainty. I think there's something on a first-person level that when people are able to step into that not-knowing space—and you were talking about this earlier—it puts them in a position where they can respond to things differently. It's a kind of dynamism. That not-knowing comes out of the Zen tradition. Zen is all about dynamic, spontaneous responding to the moment-*ness*.

DP: This has been really great. For some readers this interview might be their first encounter with the possibility of integrating Buddhism and technology into life and potentially leadership. Where should such a person start? What should he or she do?

VH: I think the first thing is to acknowledge if you're in the business realm or any other corporate system like that, then you've probably been focusing on external things—cash flow, building businesses, and all these third-person objective systems. That perspective is obviously extremely profound, and it works, but the thing it doesn't acknowledge is what Buddhism has so brilliantly to offer: The internal, subjective, first-person experience is also simultaneously wrapped into the stuff we do, all the businesses, and all the projects. It's all happening *within* us as well.

If we only have tools and models to address the outside vs. the tools and models to address the inside, then trying to be an innovator really leaves us impoverished without the resources that we need and without an inherent, deep, personal meaning. What is the purpose of innovation aside from just putting something out into the world? Isn't it also a personal journey of some sort? Isn't there a transformative process that we're going through as part of that?

I think the first thing is to recognize a need for those inner resources and tools to draw upon because they are an integral part of the process that we're going through as innovators. We can't ignore them. We can meditate and try to cope, but that's different from fully utilizing the inner world as part of the process. Buddhism is one of many ways of approaching that. It has a lot to offer a culture that is still in reaction to its own religious heritage in the sense that it's not so displeasing. That alone might be reason enough to check out Buddhist approaches. I think that's where I would start.

DP: Going back to what I said earlier, what is our actual deeper motivation for why we are innovators? What is the thing that's driving us?

VH: If we don't have ways of examining these types of questions, through contemplative practice or even psychological practices, then a lot of what is motivating our projects could be these completely unexamined and imma-ture things within us. That's really painful—to be driving projects with those motivations. I think there's something in finding tools that you can use to help you look at what's driving you to begin with so that as you go you're not being driven by these invisible forces that you have no conscious awareness of. I think it's impossible to avoid completely, but Buddhist practice offers lots of tools for doing that.

Vincent Horn *is a Buddhist Geek and digital innovator. In addition to being an ex-perienced meditation practitioner and teacher, Vincent co-founded the popular media company Buddhist Geeks where he currently serves as Chief Geek. His work focuses on the fusion of nascent technology and contemplative wisdom, and has been featured on the pages of* Wired, Fast Company, Tricycle, *and the* Los Angeles Times. *Along with his wife Emily, he makes his home in Boulder, Colorado—that is until the distinction between atoms and bits dissolves completely.*

Made in the USA
San Bernardino, CA
17 December 2013